Reading Scripture to Hear God

Reading Scripture to Hear God

Kevin Vanhoozer and Henri de Lubac
on God's Use of Scripture in the
Economy of Redemption

KEVIN STORER

PICKWICK *Publications* · Eugene, Oregon

READING SCRIPTURE TO HEAR GOD
Kevin Vanhoozer and Henri de Lubac on God's Use of Scripture in the Economy of Redemption

Copyright © 2014 Kevin Storer. All rights reserved. Except for brief quotations in critical publications or reviews, no part of this book may be reproduced in any manner without prior written permission from the publisher. Write: Permissions, Wipf and Stock Publishers, 199 W. 8th Ave., Suite 3, Eugene, OR 97401.

Pickwick Publications
An Imprint of Wipf and Stock Publishers
199 W. 8th Ave., Suite 3
Eugene, OR 97401

www.wipfandstock.com

isbn 13: 978-1-62564-543-2

Cataloging-in-Publication data:

Storer, Kevin

Reading scripture to hear God : Kevin Vanhoozer and Henri de Lubac on God's use of scripture in the economy of redemption / Kevin Storer.

p. ; cm. — Includes bibliographical references.

isbn 13: 978-1-62564-543-2

1. Vanhoozer, Kevin J.—Contributions in Hermeneutics. 2. Lubac, Henri de, 1896–1991—Contributions in Hermeneutics. 3. Bible—Criticism, interpretation, etc.—History—20th century. 4. Bible—Criticism, interpretation, etc.—History—21st century. I. Title.

BS476 S65 2014

Manufactured in the U.S.A.   09/29/2014

Contents

INTRODUCTION | vii
Theological Interpretation of Scripture and the Opportunity for Evangelical and Catholic Dialogue

> Kevin Vanhoozer: God's Speech-Acts
> Beyond Postliberals and Revisionists | x

> Henri de Lubac: Ressourcement
> Beyond Modernism and Neo-Thomism | xvi

> Description of the Project | xxii

CHAPTER 1 | 1
God's Use of Scripture for Self-Communication: Divine Speaking in the Literal and Spiritual Sense

> Introduction: Vanhoozer and de Lubac and the Literal and Spiritual Senses | 1

> Kevin Vanhoozer: God's Authorship of Scripture and the Sufficiency of the Literal Sense | 2

> Henri de Lubac: Christ's Presence in Scripture and the Necessity of the Spiritual Sense | 26

> Conclusion: Persistent Challenges and Dialogue | 50

CHAPTER 2 | 54

Vanhoozer's Covenantal Ontology and de Lubac's Sacramental Ontology: Different Models of Christ's Self-Mediation in the Economy of Redemption

Introduction | 54

Vanhoozer's Communicative/Covenantal Ontology
and God's Use of Scripture | 56

De Lubac's Sacramental Ontology and God's Use of Scripture | 73

Convergence: Trans-Figural Reading and the Spiritual Sense of
Scripture | 90

CHAPTER 3 | 103

God's Use of Scripture and Church in the Economy of Redemption

Introduction: Vanhoozer's Covenant Ecclesiology and
de Lubac's Sacramental Ecclesiology | 103

Vanhoozer's Covenant Ecclesiology | 106

De Lubac's Sacramental Ecclesiology | 116

Convergence: Development of Doctrine as Extending Canonical
Meaning Potential or Reading as the Totus Christus? | 133

Conclusion | 151

Bibliography | 155

Introduction

Theological Interpretation of Scripture and the Opportunity for Evangelical and Catholic Dialogue

In the past several decades, the theological interpretation of Scripture has emerged as an identifiable discipline within systematic theology.[1] The theological interpretation of Scripture emerged as an attempt to bridge the ugly ditch between biblical studies and systematic theology which has been dug since the Enlightenment. In response to this modernist divorce between theological disciplines, the theological interpretation of Scripture attempts to explain how Scripture functions as the "soul of sacred theology," by articulating how Scripture operates as a locus of God's ongoing self-communicative action, and why scriptural reading must be primarily an activity performed by the church and for the church.[2] As the field of theological interpretation exists at the intersection of philosophical hermeneutics and contemporary theologies of revelation, it generates insights in dialogue with many of the great theological debates and trajectories of the twentieth century.

As new discussions about scriptural reading have developed, so has new dialogue between evangelicals and Catholics. Recently Dan Treier has written that evangelicals and Catholics stand in a unique position to

---

1. For an overview of what is involved in the theological interpretation of Scripture, see Treier, *Introducing Theological Interpretation*; Vanhoozer, *Dictionary for Theological Interpretation of the Bible*; and Moberly, "What is Theological Interpretation."

2. "Dei Verbum."

advance the project of theological interpretation of Scripture together.³ Recently, a number of evangelicals, such as Hans Boersma, have taken an interest specifically in the so-called *Nouvelle theologie* movement, which influenced the Vatican II council.⁴ In it, they have found a theological method defined by a return to Scripture and the centrality of Christ. Yet they have also found that this "new theology" is a particularly Catholic method which places great emphasis on the church as the locus of Christ's self-mediation and develops a sacramental understanding of Scripture. Naturally, then, evangelicals find themselves both drawn to the movement and wary of its appropriation.

This book will place a leading representative of evangelicalism, Kevin Vanhoozer, in dialogue with a leading representative of the Catholic Ressourcement movement, Henri de Lubac, regarding the role of Scripture in the economy of redemption. These authors have been chosen for several reasons. First, both are leading representatives in their respective traditions on the theological interpretation of Scripture. De Lubac was involved in the writing of *Dei Verbum* at the Vatican II council, and Vanhoozer has been a leader in the evangelical resurgence of theological interpretation of Scripture.⁵ As a result, both have taken leading roles in developing the theological interpretation of Scripture within their respective traditions, and conversation between them could open new possibilities for convergence between Protestants and Catholics.

Second, both insist that God's use of Scripture for self-mediation to the church is the central theological presupposition from which all methodological considerations for reading must proceed. Both understand Scripture as the locus of God's continuing communication, and both develop their projects to show how God communicates by means of Scripture. Consequently, both emphasize that any theology of Scripture must be developed within the context of Scripture's role in the economy of redemption. This shared starting-point opens new questions about how to best describe God's present self-communicative activity to the church, and how the church participates in this communication. It is this shared starting-point which enables focused comparison between

---

3. See Treier, *Introducing Theological Interpretation*, 21–32.

4. See Boersma, *Nouvelle Theologie* and *Heavenly Participation*.

5. For a good discussion of the influence of de Lubac on *Dei Verbum*, see Bertoldi, "Henri de Lubac on Dei Verbum." For Vanhoozer's influence on the theological interpretation of Scripture, see Vanhoozer, *Dictionary for Theological Interpretation of the Bible*, 19–26.

Vanhoozer's covenantal ontology and de Lubac's sacramental ontology, and between Vanhoozer's *sola Scriptura* and de Lubac's insistence on the normative role of tradition and authority of the Magisterium. Attention to the specific ways in which Christ uses Scripture and church for self-mediation in the economy of redemption, then, provides a lens through which to view a number of important theological differences.

Third, it is specifically the focus of each author on the role of Scripture in the economy of redemption that has allowed each to move beyond substantial hermeneutical impasse in dominant theological trajectories.[6] Vanhoozer emerged as a student of the revisionist/postliberal debates during a time when deconstructionism was making its way into the field of biblical interpretation. Vanhoozer's chief concern was to ground Scripture's authority in God's speaking action rather than in some mode of human experience, reader response theory, or philosophical model of church tradition. Vanhoozer found in speech-act theory useful conceptual tools for articulating God's past and present speaking action in Scripture. As this project expanded to a communicative ontology, Vanhoozer was able to explore the way in which God's use of Scripture grounds its authority. A generation earlier, Henri de Lubac began his academic career during the latter part of Catholicism's anti-modernist movement, as Catholic systematic theology was dominated by the neo-Thomists and Catholic biblical studies were dominated by scholars wishing to fully incorporate higher critical method into their scholarship. De Lubac's chief concern was the preservation of Scripture's central role of mediating Christ to the church in a context where neo-Thomists tended to reduce scriptural meaning to a set of proof-texts and biblical scholars tended to reduce Scriptural meaning to its historical backgrounds. De Lubac found in the exegesis of the church fathers and in Maurice Blondel's Christian philosophy useful conceptual tools for articulating God's continual self-mediation through Scripture. As Blondel's philosophy is combined with

---

6. The "economy of redemption" refers to the ordering of the various parts of God's action in salvation history toward God's final plan for creation. See here O'Keefe and Reno, *Sanctified Vision*, 37, who explain the ordering of the economy in Scripture as a "careful sequencing of events in historical narratives," a well-plotted story, and an outline of a text, in which Christ was the interpretive principle by which all Scripture was read. Furthermore, the term "economy" also refers to the understanding that God has established various realities to mediate the mystery of Christ to human beings for salvation and the organization of these various parts of God's redemptive action among human beings. It is in this sense that the term "economy" is used throughout this work.

insights from the church fathers, de Lubac develops a sacramental ontology which articulates God's use of Scripture and church alike for present communication. What is common to both projects is a central focus on God's use of Scripture in the economy of redemption as the means by which new options can emerge which advance discussions of scriptural reading beyond contemporary theological impasses.

For these reasons, I believe that a comparison of Vanhoozer and de Lubac will provide important conceptual resources for Protestants and Catholics who wish to engage theological interpretation of Scripture together. As Vanhoozer and de Lubac have each realized that greater analysis of God's use of Scripture in the economy of redemption could advance discussions beyond present impasses in their own respective traditions, I believe that comparing their work will yield insights which will help to advance the discussion beyond current impasses in the dialogue between Catholics and Protestants. This introduction will provide a short overview of the way in which each has advanced the dialogue within his own respective tradition, in order to make their respective projects more intelligible and allow them to be compared with each other in chapters to come.

KEVIN VANHOOZER: GOD'S SPEECH-ACTS BEYOND POSTLIBERALS AND REVISIONISTS

The revisionist and postliberal impasse: In the closing decades of the twentieth century, theological dialogues in the United States were marked by a prominent debate between revisionists and postliberals, both of whom were attempting a theological interpretation of Scripture which would free scriptural interpretation from its captivity to higher critical scholarship. Revisionist theology is a trajectory of theology committed to reforming Christian belief and practice in dialogue with contemporary culture and philosophy.[7] One of the distinguishing emphases of this movement is a commitment to the public accessibility of theological discourse, which tends to assume a general mode of human understanding by which

---

7. See Placher, "Revisionist and Postliberal Theologies," 392. Placher claims that Revisionist theology should probably be considered the most dominant theological trajectory in the United States in the last fifty years, and notes such names (besides Tracy) as "Catholics like . . . Leslie Dewart, Gregory Baum, and Michael Novak, and Protestants like Langdon Gilkey . . . Edward Farley . . . Schubert Ogden . . . Gordon Kaufman . . . [and] John Cobb."

specific religious claims can be related to human reason.⁸ Among revisionist theologians, a group of narrative theologians has recently arisen, who have used phenomenological hermeneutics as the starting point for critical correlation.⁹ The Chicago school begins their reading of Scripture from a general hermeneutics, even though they admit that the very referent of Scripture is so reorienting that it stretches the general hermeneutic beyond the explanatory power of general rules. Perhaps the most definitive characteristic of the revisionist project is the insistence to employ some criterion of correlation between orthodox Christian thought and contemporary modern society. Revisionist theology could be understood as a critical response to modernity which seeks to place Christian faith in mutually critical dialogue with postmodern philosophical thought. As revisionists think that the very understanding of God, Christ and human beings revealed in Christian faith requires critical engagement with the world, revisionists are interested in keeping theology in the public sphere in mutual dialogue with secular fields of thought.

Postliberal theology is a recent trajectory of theology which arose in response to revisionist theology and is grounded in the work of Hans Frei and George Lindbeck.¹⁰ Postliberals attempt to understand Christian reality primarily through a straight-forward reading of the Gospel narratives.¹¹ Consequently, postliberals propose that theology must be

---

8. Placher (ibid., 397) argues that revisionist theologians "seem to presuppose a universal human something-or-other which various religions, in their various ways, express." Yet Tracy is insistent that he and other revisionists have incorporated a hermeneutical turn into their theology (See Tracy, "Lindbeck's New Program for Theology").

9. See Comstock ("Two Types of Narrative Theology") who notes that this group includes Paul Ricoeur, David Tracy, and Sallie McFague, all of whom are "revisionist, hermeneutical, Gadamerian-inspired correlationists." This group is often associated with the university of Chicago, and is often called the "Chicago school."

10. See Frei, *The Eclipse of Biblical Narrative* and *The Identity of Jesus Christ*; as well as Kelsey, *The Uses of Scripture in Recent Theology*. James Buckley ("Revisionists and Liberals," 229) names influential representatives as Stanley Hauerwas, Romald Thiemann, James Buckley, Joseph DiNoia, Garrett Green, George Hunsinger, William Werpehowski, Bruce Marshall, William Placher, Katheryn Greene-McCreight, Serene Jones, Joseph Mangia, Eugene Rogers, and Katheryn Tanner. The movement of "postliberal theology" became visible after the publication of George Lindbeck's influential 1984 book, *The Nature of Doctrine*.

11. Lindbeck, "Toward a Postliberal Theology," 95. As Lindbeck puts it, "The narrative does this, not through accounts of what God is in and of himself, but through accounts of the interaction of his deeds and purposes with those of creatures in their ever-changing circumstances. These accounts reach their climax in what the gospels

developed through "intratextual" reflection rather than by critical correlation. Furthermore, postliberals emphasize that apologetics must be undertaken in an *ad hoc* fashion in order to prevent a particular method or philosophical description from overrunning the self-description of the church and its beliefs and practices.[12] Postliberals insist that "religion is more like a cultural system that one linguistically inhabits, and within which one is shaped into a form of life, so that becoming religious is something like learning a language."[13]

The distinctive characteristics of these different trajectories have been seen most clearly in the debates between David Tracy and Hans Frei, and it is in the context of these debates that Kevin Vanhoozer entered the academic discussion. Frei's chief complaint about Tracy's theology is Tracy's employment of a systematic correlation between Christian tradition and human experience, which Frei feels grants authority to human experience over text and tradition. Frei sees Tracy's systematic correlation as leading to the prioritizing of a general philosophical scheme over specific Christian claims (most importantly, the particularity of Christ), and the prioritizing of apologetics over the internal structure of the Christian faith.[14] Tracy's concern about Frei's theology, on the other hand, is that Frei's exclusive focus on realistic narrative of Scripture and the self-description of the church will prohibit the church from developing a truly public engagement with the world.[15] Tracy sees Frei's refusal to develop a correlational criteria as leading to the church's failure to make its message relevant to modern culture, the church's failure to incorporate

---

say about the risen, ascended, and ever-present Jesus Christ whose identity as the divine-human agent is unsubstitutably enacted in the stories of Jesus of Nazareth. The climax, however, is logically inseparable from what precedes it."

12. Fodor, "Postliberal Theology," 231. Fodor defines the term *ad hoc* as when "the occasion arises, in connection with a particular issue, relative to a specific context, with respect to particular interlocutors."

13. Hunsinger, "Postliberal Theology," 54. This movement has led to a general tendency in some postliberals (such as Lindbeck) to understand "truth" as a matter of internal coherence, as doctrine is interpreted "in 'cultural-linguistic' or 'regulative' terms . . . as communally authoritative rules of discourse, attitude, and action." Placher ("Revisionist and Postliberal Theologies," 397) also suggests that Lindbeck sees doctrinal "truths" as more a matter of internal coherence to the Christian system than "truths" based on some general form of logic (see also Lindbeck, *The Nature of Doctrine*, 18).

14. See Higton, "Hans Frei and David Tracy," esp. 577–86.

15. For a summary of mutual criticisms, see Tracy, "On Reading the Scriptures Theologically"; Frei, *Types of Christian Theology*, 60–65.

truth found outside itself into its own identity; and the church's stifling of the necessary pluralism within the church rooted in Scripture itself.[16]

Vanhoozer's contribution: Throughout his career, Kevin Vanhoozer has specifically attempted to move beyond this impasse between Frei and Tracy.[17] In his doctoral dissertation, Vanhoozer provides a fair and thorough analysis of the discussions between Tracy and Frei. Vanhoozer appreciates Frei's insistence on reading Scripture in such a way that the particularity of Christ is proclaimed without incorporating some predetermined criteria of meaningfulness.[18] Vanhoozer's greatest complaint against Frei concerns Frei's later decision to invest authority in the community rather than in the text itself,[19] and Vanhoozer notes that the later Frei seems to propose a "certain optimism with regard to the believing community. Interpretive might makes right."[20] On the other hand, Vanhoozer appreciates Ricoeur and Tracy's emphasis on the importance of the "plurality of biblical genres" (form) to communicate the text's message (content), as well as Ricoeur's explanation of how the biblical text, as a text, is disclosive of transformative truth.[21] Yet Vanhoozer complains that Ricoeur and Tracy's method for biblical hermeneutics ultimately collapses into general hermeneutics, and therefore cannot account for the particularity of revelation.[22]

---

16. For these criticisms, see Tracy, *The Analogical Imagination*, 113; *Dialogue with the Other*, 114; and "On Reading the Scriptures Theologically," 43–57, respectively.

17. Vanhoozer's doctoral dissertation is a study of Paul Ricoeur's hermeneutics, and it devotes a chapter to the debate between Tracy and Frei (see Vanhoozer, *Biblical Narrative*, 148–89). Vanhoozer's first articles make suggestions about how to move past the impasse between the two (see Vanhoozer, "The Spirit of Understanding, 207–35).

18. Vanhoozer, *Biblical Narrative*, 154. Vanhoozer appreciates that Frei is not a "pure narrativist. . . . Rather, Frei is an Anselmian theologian who is seeking to understand the Christian faith, particularly its central narrative expression, on its own terms" (178). Vanhoozer likewise appreciates the early Frei's category of "realistic narrative," yet insists that ostensive reference should not be dismissed as unnecessary to establishing meaning (225).

19. Vanhoozer ("The Spirit of Understanding," 219) complains that Frei has "exchanged his hermeneutical birthright for a mess of pottage, or rather Fish-stew? It is the community, ultimately, that enjoys interpretive authority."

20. Ibid.

21. See ibid., 216–18, and Vanhoozer, *Remythologizing Theology*, xv.

22. Vanhoozer (*Biblical Narrative*, 225). Vanhoozer claims, "Ricoeur has not shown us that theological hermeneutics is significantly different from his philosophical hermeneutics, only that his philosophical hermeneutics receives its most fruitful development when applied to the Biblical texts" (155). Vanhoozer further suggests

Vanhoozer's two major later works are substantial responses to postliberal theology (*Drama of Doctrine*) and revisionist theology (*Remythologizing Theology*).²³ In these more mature works Vanhoozer recognizes that one way beyond both revisionist and postliberal difficulties is to understand the unique and authoritative role of Scripture in God's Trinitarian self-communicative action. As its title implies, Vanhoozer's book, *The Drama of Doctrine: A Canonical-Linguistic Approach to Christian Theology*, offers a critical appropriation of George Lindbeck's *The Nature of Doctrine: Religion and Theology in a Postliberal Age* for evangelical readers.²⁴ In it, Vanhoozer argues that postliberals have obscured the nature of doctrine by shifting authority from canon to community.²⁵ In response to the postliberal project, Vanhoozer puts forth "*a postconservative, canonical-linguistic theology and a directive theory of doctrine that roots theology more firmly in Scripture while preserving Lindbeck's emphasis on practice.*"²⁶ The book goes on to describe the church in terms of its mission to further God's speaking action which has been encoded in the canonical Scriptures. Thus Vanhoozer's answer to the postmodern shift of authority to the church is to reinvest authority in Scripture as God's speaking action.

Vanhoozer's latest book, *Remythologizing Theology*, rejects revisionist theology on the grounds that it does not sufficiently attend to God's

---

that Tracy's analogy between religious classics and art cause "[t]he claims to truth in both art and religion" to "stand or fall together" (158).

23. Vanhoozer, *The Drama of Doctrine*.

24. As the title of Vanhoozer's book suggests, Lindbeck's "nature" of doctrine will be changed to a description of doctrine as "drama," and the determining factor of "culture" is replaced by "canon" as the constituting feature of the church (see here especially ibid., 133–41). Vanhoozer suggests that doctrine is strangely absent in the church today for several reasons: "sound doctrine is suffering from confusion about its nature, from disagreement concerning the locus of its authority, and above all from its captivity to a debilitating dichotomy between theory and practice" (3). As the book progresses, it becomes quickly apparent that the first problem (confusion about doctrine's nature) finds its roots in the second (disagreement about doctrine's authority). Vanhoozer suggests that the church will continue to be confused about the nature of doctrine until it understands that its authority comes from the scriptural canon, not the church.

25. Vanhoozer (ibid., 10) notes, "Though Lindbeck's postliberal proposal initially appears to swing the pendulum of authority back to the biblical text, a closer inspection shows that he relocates authority in the church, that singular 'culture' within which, and only within which, the Bible is used to shape Christian identity."

26. Ibid., xiii (emphasis Vanhoozer's—Vanhoozer italicizes many points in his books, and all italicized quotes in this chapter are his).

self-communication (primarily revealed in Scripture) in its attempt to make revelation relevant to contemporary human beings. Vanhoozer suggests that theologians should be divided between "those who seek to speak of God on the basis of nature (including human nature) and those who believe that speaking well of God is ultimately possible only on the basis of God's own communication."[27] Hence "remythologizing theology" is intended to provide as sweeping and radical a challenge to contemporary systematic theological method as Frei's "great reversal" provided to post-enlightenment Christology.[28] Vanhoozer emphasizes that the Scriptures are first God's self-communicative action to which doctrine is a human response, and the prioritizing of the self-communication of God in the economy of redemption, Vanhoozer feels, will reestablish Scripture as the authoritative foundation for the church's life and practice.[29]

Vanhoozer understands that the debate between Tracy and Frei has narrowed the discussion about scriptural interpretation to the relationship between text and reader, thus preventing theological reflection on the way in which the triune God uses Scripture in the economy of redemption. This refocusing of the discussion specifically to the economy of redemption allows Vanhoozer to make a substantive contribution to scriptural hermeneutics which will move beyond the debate between Frei and Tracy. God is now described as pure, triune self-communicative act who extends communication to human beings uniquely through Christ and Scripture. With Vanhoozer's later work, the doctrine of God emerges as the central hermeneutical norm, and reflection on the nature of God's communicative action specifies the roles that Scripture and the church play in the divine economy. With this new starting-point, Vanhoozer is able to develop a much richer method for the theological interpretation of Scripture which seeks to respond to God's self-communication.

---

27. Vanhoozer, *Remythologizing Theology*, 182.

28. Vanhoozer (ibid., 29, thesis 5), argues that to "remythologize theology is to reverse what Hans Frei called the 'great reversal.'"

29. For example, Vanhoozer (ibid., 272) argues, "Whereas Christian doctrines are for Schleiermacher descriptions of *human passions* (e.g., the feeling of absolute dependence)—'*accounts of the Chrisitan religious affections set forth in speech*'—the remythologizer conceives doctrine as the conceptual elaboration of *divine action*. Better: doctrines are *accounts of triune communicative action set forth in speech.*"

Henri de Lubac: Ressourcement Beyond Modernism and Neo-Thomism

The Modernist and Neo-Thomist Impasse: In the first half of the twentieth century, the Catholic Church was engaged in a significant controversy between modernism and neo-Thomism about the place of history as a theological source for Christianity. At the base of this controversy was the very important concern by the Catholic Church that serious engagement with the development of Christianity would result in doctrinal relativism.[30] For some time Protestants had been employing the historical critical method to both Scripture and the history of doctrine and they seemed to have convincingly shown that the scriptural texts and all subsequent doctrines were in some way determined by, and must be understood within, the historical contexts in which they arose. At the same time, philosophers such as Kant and Hume had produced powerful arguments demonstrating the inadequacy of human reason to prove the existence of God or understand the nature of God. In the wake of these philosophers and the normative use of the higher critical method, many modernist theologians were looking for, as Hans Boersma puts it, a more credible "approach to religion that took its starting-point in the natural, subjective, immanent, and moral needs of human beings" rather than in "supernatural, objective, external, and propositional revelation."[31] In response, neo-Thomists insisted on maintaining the plain, propositional nature of revealed truth and the unique role of the Magisterium to define revelation.

For some time the neo-Thomists had perceived the modernist movement to be a formidable foe to the Catholic faith, since the modernists were skeptical about the ability to know propositional truths about God. Modernists could be characterized by a strong emphasis on the autonomy of historical study in isolation from theology.[32] Consequently, the modernists tended to separate the truth of religion from the historical character or experience of religion, and more closely associated revelation with religious experience than with dogma.[33] Modernists understood Christian faith to have developed within the normal progress of history, so that neither the Scriptures nor subsequent dogmas held

---

30. See Wood, *Spiritual Exegesis and the Church*, 16–17.

31. Boersma, *Nouvelle Théologie*, 36.

32. Boersma (ibid., 19) notes especially Loisy's "insistence on the radical autonomy of history and of critical exegesis" in his debate with Adolph Harnack.

33. Ibid., 20.

inherent authority over modern Christians. De Lubac suggests that this emphasis leads to a historical immanentism, in which Scripture, church, and the development of dogma were studied almost exclusively as natural historical processes. Whatever content of Christian faith could not be demonstrated through the scientific methods of secular history was regarded suspiciously, since it was not able to be defended by historical evidence. The logical result of immanentism was that Christian faith was viewed as only a historical or social reality, without any relationship to a transcendent reality. Eschatology was reduced to the more observable and predictable category of human progress, and God was often reduced to the ideal image of humanity.[34] Although modernism was officially condemned, de Lubac was wary that some of its underlying presuppositions, such as naturalism and relativism, were often alive and well in the practice of scientific exegesis of Scripture.[35] Especially after the Second Vatican Council, de Lubac began to see immanentism as the primary danger confronting the church, as he perceived a growing tendency in the church to dismiss the eschatological dimension in order to focus on what he perceived as one-sided emphasis on the visible, this-worldly church.[36] Much of de Lubac's later writing centered on the danger of immanentism in the church.

Neo-Thomism arose as a response to the modernist controversy, and attempted to re-establish confidence in objective human knowledge of revelation and the supernatural.[37] Neo-Thomism was characterized

---

34. See Blondel, *The Letter on Apologetics*, 237–38. Blondel claims further that when secular history replaces real history, "The historical facts will be given the role of reality itself; and an ontology, purely phenomenological in character, will be extracted from a methodology and a phenomenology" (240).

35. Boersma (*Nouvelle Theologie*, 18) notes that modernism was officially denounced in 1907, when Pope Pius XVI condemned sixty-five modernist premises in in his decree *Lamentabili sane exitu*, again condemned the "agnosticism, immanentism and relativism" of modernism in his encyclical *Pascendi dominici gregis*, and imposed the "anti-modernist oath" upon all clergy from 1910 until 1966.

36. De Lubac's stand against immanentism is seen in *The Church*, 122–23, where de Lubac provides a list of qualities that will characterize the person of holiness for the future church. Most of these qualities center on a resistance to immanentism: "They will not . . . be ideologists. . . . If they bring something truly new to the world . . . it will not be by means of worldly generalities on the necessity to create and invent . . . tradition will be a source of strength, not a millstone round their necks. . . . They will not confuse the openness of life with the dissolution and disintegration of death, nor the idolatry of man with brotherly charity."

37. Boersma, *Nouvelle Theologie*, 40, claims that Pope Leo XIII's 1879 encyclical,

by a desire to preserve an Aristotelian epistemology which undergirded St. Thomas's arguments for the existence of God, as well as the desire to establish a strong distinction between nature and the supernatural.[38] The epistemological framework of neo-Thomism supplied the major theological force behind much of Vatican I's optimism toward the ability of human beings to know God based on natural reason alone, as well as its emphasis on miracles as rational proof of the truth of Christian faith.[39] As Boersma puts it, "For neo-Thomism, the task of fundamental (or apologetic) theology was . . . a positive one: to prove the fact of divine revelation by means of signs and miracles."[40] The neo-Thomists tended to resist the employment of critical scholarship in the study of Scripture, and tended to be interested in the historical record of Scripture primarily for its apologetic value.[41] Practically, the use of Scripture was

---

Aeterni Patris, gave official approval to Thomism as the normative theological expression of the Christian faith. While this is implicit to the document itself, the document certainly emphasizes the ability to know God from natural reason (see "Aeterni Patris").

38. This separation between nature and the supernatural was the hallmark of leading neo-Thomist theologians such as Reginald Garrigou-Lagrange and Charles Boyer. Garrigou-Lagrange wrote a key article accusing Blondel, etc. of modernism, coining the term *Nouvelle theologie* and defining, as he saw it, the errors of the movement (see Reginald Garrigou-lagrange, "La Nouvelle Theologie ou va-t-elle?" 126–45). Garrigou-Lagrange (ibid., 133), claims that de Lubac was "totally uninterested in the *pronunciata maiora* of the philosophical doctrine of St. Thomas." Charles Boyer was also a leading neo-Thomist opponent of de Lubac (see Boyer, "Sur un article des Recherches," 152–54). See also Boersma (*Nouvelle Theologie*, 219–23) for the debate on the development of doctrine. Pope Pius XII's encyclical *Humani generis* (1950) raised concerns about "compromising the gratuity of the supernatural order," and many understood it to refer to de Lubac (see "Humani Generis"). De Lubac, for his part, insists that *Humani Generis* did not refer to him, instead "borrows a sentence from me to express the true doctrine" (see de Lubac, *de Lubac*, 4). However, de Lubac was asked to stop teaching following the encyclical until 1954, and several of his books were banned (see Nichols, *From Newman to Congar*, 15).

39. See Boersma, *Nouvelle Theologie*, 40. See, for example, the Vatican I pronouncement *Dei Filius* §2, which argued that "The same Holy Mother Church holds and teaches that God, the beginning and end of all things, can be known with certitude by the natural light of human reason from created things" and *Dei Filius* 3, which emphasized "divine facts, especially miracles and prophecies which, because they clearly show forth the omnipotence and infinite knowledge of God, are most certain signs of a divine revelation" ("Dei Filius").

40. Boersma, *Nouvelle Theologie*, 56.

41. Blondel, "History and Dogma," 230. At first, Blondel claims, the use of higher criticism in Scripture was tolerated, since it appeared the whole of the Scriptures remained a reliable historical testimony. Crisis occurred when criticism yielded so many

often reduced to little more than proof-texting. Typical in theological method at the time was what Voderholzer calls an "'instruction theory' of revelation," where Scripture was truncated to a set of propositions, a major proposition taken from revelation and a minor proposition taken from philosophy, and through deductive reasoning certain consequent propositions could be made about the content of Christian faith.[42] De Lubac suggests that this method, which relied on propositionalism and foundationalist apologetics, downplayed the importance of God's revelation in history and God's providence over salvation history, and hence disregarded the uniquely historical character of Christian revelation. Furthermore, it tended to reduce the Scriptures to a book of propositions from which principles of dogma could be gleaned and authorized through logical deduction.

De Lubac's contribution: For de Lubac, both errors were attempts to reduce the paradoxical nature of mystery to apprehension by human reason, neo-Thomist extrinsicism by reducing the historical character of revelation, and modernist immanentism by reducing the transcendence of God. De Lubac's *Ressourcement* project proposes a middle way between two false reductions of the paradox by which mystery is approached.[43] In formulating a response to these reductive alternatives, de Lubac relies heavily on Maurice Blondel. Blondel suggested that both extrinsicism and immanentism, though completely opposed to each other, were really two sides of the same coin. Both reduced the revelatory action of God in history; extrinsicism by limiting God's action to the 'proof' that can be adduced from it, and historicism by limiting God's action to what the secular historian can ascertain. Neither approach is useful for apprehending the reality of Christian faith, as both have disconnected spiritual reality from historical event.[44] De Lubac's *ressourcement* (return to the

difficulties that the authority of Scripture as a whole was questioned, since when the dogmatic credibility of Scripture was understood to be grounded on the proofs yielded by historical facts, historical criticism was seen to be able to topple the credibility of the whole Christian faith.

42. Voderholzer, "Dogma and History," 649–50.

43. De Lubac's theological project is best located in the *Ressourcement* movement of French theology. Other theologians commonly classified in this movement are Jean Danielou, Yves Congar, and Marie-Cominique Chenu, Gaston Fessard, Henri Bouillard, and Pierre Tielhard de Chardin (for a description of the movement and its opponents, see Wood, *Spiritual Exegesis and the Church*, 6; Boersma, *Nouvelle Theologie*, 1–34; and D'Ambrosio, *Henri de Lubac and the Recovery*, 2–3; 20–21).

44. See Blondel, "History and Dogma," 244–64.

sources) of the Christian faith sought to recover both the transcendence of the Christian mystery, and the intrinsic relationship of that mystery to the human being. De Lubac argued that what is first received in revelation is the event, the "redemptive Action," the "gift that God makes us of himself in his Son." It is this event "which, at first undivided, forms the total Object" of revelation.[45] De Lubac calls this the "Whole of Dogma," and argues that it is unsurpassable. However, understanding about this "Whole of Dogma" necessarily increases, solidifies, and at times becomes normative expression for the Christian faith, as Christ uses the sacramental realities of Scripture, Eucharist, and church to mediate the mystery to human beings. Revelation, then, is both unsurpassable in its original gift, and yet is mediated to human beings in the matrix of history, as God uses Scripture, church, and history to lead the church to better understand the mystery.

De Lubac's attempt to move beyond the debate between neo-Thomists and modernists took shape in a holistic project in which he treated various topics in different books and essays. De Lubac's first book, *Catholicism*, emphasizes that the church acts as a sacrament of Christ to the world, and hence the church is the locus of God's redemption of all human beings. From this book emerge a number of specific themes that de Lubac will explore in subsequent books. One aspect of de Lubac's response is his development of a sacramental ontology, described in books like *Surnatural, The Discovery of God, The Mystery of the Supernatural,* and *A Short Catechesis on Nature and Grace*.[46] In these works, de Lubac denies the category of pure nature, insisting instead that human beings are created with a *natural desire* for God and hence have an intrinsic ordering toward their supernatural end. On de Lubac's account, the human being exists in a state of paradox, being both fully an animal creature and yet being a creature created in the image of God with a *natural desire* for God inscribed upon her. God is always already and inescapably implicitly known by the human being, as the "divine operation constitutes the very center of man."[47] De Lubac calls this the "mystery of the supernatural."[48]

---

45. De Lubac, "The Problem of the Development of Dogma," 273.

46. De Lubac, *Surnaturel, The Discovery of God, The Mystery of the Supernatural, A Brief Catechesis.*

47. De Lubac, *The Discovery of God*, 16.

48. See De Lubac, *The Mystery of the Supernatural*, esp. chapters on "The Christian Paradox of Man" (101–18), and "A Paradox Overcome in Faith" (167–84).

God is not obligated to give the gift of grace, yet human beings need this gift in order to be truly human.

De Lubac develops another aspect of his response to modernism and neo-Thomism in a series of works on the sacramental nature of the church. Works like *The Church, Paradox and Mystery*, *The Splendor of the Church*, *The Motherhood of the Church*, and *Corpus Mysticum*[49] further develop the central idea in *Catholicism* that the church operates as a sacramental mediator of Christ in the world, visibly embodying the gospel, inviting all human beings to share in their one true humanity in Christ, thus extending the mystical eschatological union between Christ and the church, called the *totus Christus*. De Lubac's early work, Catholicism, became programmatic for the Ressourcement movement, as it stressed the "social character of the church as the true universal community in embryo, rather than as a mere external machinery for the saving of individual souls."[50] The church, as the social reality established by God which participates integrally in the mystery of Christian faith, mediates that singular mystery through its sources, and these must continually be re-approached for the revitalization of the church.

A third strand of de Lubac's response deals with the spiritual interpretation of Scripture. In works like de Lubac's four volume *Medieval Exegesis*, as well as his treatment of Origen's exegesis in *History and Spirit*, de Lubac argues that the recognition of a spiritual sense of Scripture is indispensable to Christian reading since Christ uses Scripture for self-mediation to the church and hence communicates to the church through this spiritual sense.[51] De Lubac was decidedly favorable to the use of the historical critical method in biblical studies, as he understood the unique nature of Christian faith to be grounded in God's revelation in history. Yet de Lubac recognized that the method could only go so far in explaining the Scriptures. De Lubac suggests a "critique of criticism" established with two goals: the recognition of the limits of the historical critical method as a science and the inherent assumptions that this method held.[52] What de Lubac recognized is that Scripture and church are, at their foundation, spiritual realities which have been given sacramental roles by Christ in

---

49. De Lubac, *The Church*, *The Splendor of the Church*, *The Motherhood of the Church*, *Corpus Mysticum*.

50. Milbank, "Henri de Lubac," 77.

51. De Lubac, *Medieval Exegesis*. See especially vol. 2; and *History and Spirit*.

52. De Lubac, *Paradoxes of Faith*, 107. See also D'Ambrosio, *Traditional Hermeneutic*, 262.

mediating the mystery toward which all human beings find themselves drawn. Scripture and tradition, then, are much more than ancient texts and past traditions; they were "wellsprings of dynamic spiritual life."[53] As Marcellino D'Ambrosio puts it, "The events and words of Scripture, the doctrine of the Fathers, the Creeds and decrees of the councils, the rites of the liturgy—all of these are, for them, vehicles and, in an analogous sense, sacraments of the dynamic and living Mystery of Christ."[54] The way to move beyond the debate between the modernists and the neo-Thomists, then, is to better understand the way God uses creaturely realities such as Scripture and church for self-communication in the matrix of history.

DESCRIPTION OF THE PROJECT

What both authors understand with remarkable clarity is that the theological interpretation of Scripture is guided more by an adequate description of God's ordering of creaturely realities in the economy of redemption than by general hermeneutical method. Theological interpretation of Scripture, for both, is a thoroughly *theological* activity which seeks to understand both text and reader in light of God's triune communication and governance of the economy of redemption. While the two projects have arisen out of different theological debates and initially appear very different from one another, they share a very similar theological sensibility about the interpretation of Scripture about the priority of God's authority over Scripture and church and his consequent use of these realities for self-mediation. As each author has used this focus to overcome impasses within his own theological tradition, both will be compared to see how focus on God's use of Scripture could overcome traditional impasses in Protestant and Catholic dialogue. The goal of this project is to serve the work of theological interpretation of Scripture between Catholics and Protestants by highlighting similarities which can be advanced, as well as differences to which both sides must work to overcome.

In the first two chapters, I will describe Vanhoozer's and de Lubac's project for scriptural interpretation in light of their foundational assumption that Christ uses Scripture as a principle means of self-mediation in the economy of redemption. Vanhoozer locates Christ's self-mediation in Scripture in the determinate meaning of the literal, canonical sense of

---

53. D'Ambrosio, *Traditional Hermeneutic*, 9.
54. Ibid.

Scripture, which plainly mediates Christ to readers by means of the present speaking action of the Spirit. De Lubac locates Christ's self-mediation in Scripture in the infinite meaning of a threefold spiritual sense of Scripture that goes beyond the literal sense to mediate Christ to readers. As a result, each author develops a different interpretive method to hear God's speaking action. Using the philosophical tools of speech-act theory, Vanhoozer places greatest emphasis on Scripture's determinate meaning, while de Lubac, using a sacramental model, places greatest emphasis on God's present speaking action in Scripture. Still, both projects show great similarity in their insistence on God's present action in Scripture and in their development of a participatory hermeneutic through which readers are incorporated into the body of Christ. Each project has particular advantages and inherent tensions, and I will show how each could benefit the other.

In the second chapter, I will show how each author's ontology (the foundational theological and philosophical model for understanding the God/world relationship) impacts scriptural interpretation. Ontology and scriptural interpretation always have a reciprocal effect on one another, and it is here that the rationale for each author's exegetical decisions will become clear. Vanhoozer develops a communicative ontology in which God's revelatory action in the world is disambiguated by means of God's speaking action concentrated in Scripture, and he understands Scripture as a covenant document which invites readers to accept and extend God's communicative action. De Lubac develops a sacramental ontology in which the unified Christian mystery revealed in Jesus Christ is mediated by Christ through the sacramental realities of Scripture, Eucharist, and church. I will show that each author's ontology affects his understanding of meaning, and therefore also the method used for recognizing and engaging the meaning of Scripture.

In the third chapter, I will show how each author's construal of the relationship between Scripture and church impacts his project of scriptural interpretation. While the Scripture/church relationship has traditionally established a central divide between Protestants and Catholics, explicit focus on God's structuring of the economy of redemption reveals much similarity between the two projects, and opens new paths for dialogue. Vanhoozer strongly emphasizes the authority of Scripture over the church, giving the Scriptures an active role and the church a passive role in the economy of redemption. Yet Vanhoozer's communicative ontology also highlights the necessity of the church to extend God's communicative action, thus showing that Scripture is incomplete without the church. De Lubac avoids active/passive language between Scripture and church by stressing Christ's use of both as sacramental mediators of the mystery. Scripture and church are used by Christ to exercise a reciprocal causality on each other, and while the role of Scripture is to confront the church, the role of tradition is to safeguard the Scriptures. I will specifically analyze the topic of doctrinal development to show each conceive the church's authority in relation to Scripture, and will suggest that each author's model possesses resources that could help the other.

The book will conclude by suggesting that these two projects have much in common, establishing potential for further dialogue between Roman Catholics and evangelicals. Furthermore, it will suggest that Vanhoozer's covenantal model could be appropriated as a necessary critical moment within de Lubac's larger sacramental ontology. Vanhoozer's communicative ontology should be challenged by de Lubac's sacramental ontology to understand scriptural meaning as infinite mystery, and to appropriate God's use of other creaturely realities in the economy of redemption, especially Eucharist and the church. Yet at the same time, Vanhoozer's covenantal model should challenge de Lubac's sacramental approach to better articulate Scripture's determinate meaning in the literal sense and its role in confronting the church and calling it to repentance.

CHAPTER 1

God's Use of Scripture for Self-Communication

Divine Speaking in the Literal and Spiritual Sense

INTRODUCTION: VANHOOZER AND DE LUBAC AND THE LITERAL AND SPIRITUAL SENSES

On first read, Vanhoozer and de Lubac would seem a most unfit choice of dialogue partners of the topic of God's use of Scripture. Vanhoozer insists on the sufficiency of the literal sense, while de Lubac insists on the indispensability of the spiritual sense. Vanhoozer develops an elaborate proposal for God's authorship based on speech-act theory, while de Lubac largely ignores divine authorship and instead focuses attention on God's sacramental presence in Scripture. Vanhoozer focuses on Scripture's determinate meaning, while de Lubac focuses on Scripture's infinite meaning. Yet what the two have in common is their persistent emphasis on God's active use of Scripture for self-communication to the church. In this chapter I will compare Vanhoozer and de Lubac's understanding of God's use of Scripture in order to show that there is significant agreement between Vanhoozer's proposal for God's communication in the literal, canonical sense and de Lubac's proposal for Christ's communication in the spiritual sense. Furthermore, I will suggest that Vanhoozer's argument that the Spirit's present speaking is best described as the perlocutionary effect of Scripture and de Lubac's argument that the Spirit's present speaking is best described as the spiritual senses of Scripture lead to quite similar conclusions about the theological interpretations of Scripture. Finally, I will observe a persistent tension in the work of each, and will suggest that these could be overcome through mutual dialogue.

KEVIN VANHOOZER: GOD'S AUTHORSHIP OF SCRIPTURE AND THE SUFFICIENCY OF THE LITERAL SENSE

Vanhoozer's primary emphasis throughout his career is to show that the Scriptures, as the authoritative Word of God, are God's communication to the church, and consequently that readers must employ a method of interpretation which will allow them to understand and submit to the plain meaning of Scripture. Vanhoozer argues that because meaning is encoded in a text by an author to be *discovered* by the reader, the meaning of a text can only be grasped as readers seek to understand the speech act of the author. The Scriptures are understood, then, by readers who rightly perceive what the author communicated in the text. Yet while this argument remains central to Vanhoozer's work, Vanhoozer develops the argument in a considerably different way in his early career than he does in his later career. Vanhoozer's early work focuses primarily on discerning the meaning of the text as it has been communicated by the author.[1] This stage of Vanhoozer's career is marked by an almost exclusive focus on human authorial intent as basis for understanding the meaning of the text. While this early work employs the useful tools of speech-act theory and clarifies Vanhoozer's understanding of Scripture's determinate meaning which will remain throughout his career, Vanhoozer's later work exhibits a distinct shift in perspective. During the early 2000's, Vanhoozer began to recognize that his focus on the role of the author actually caused him to focus more on the human author than the divine author of Scripture.

---

1. These early works span from the 1989 publication of his dissertation on Ricoeur (*Biblical Narrative*) to the 1998 publication of his first major book on biblical hermeneutics (*Is There a Meaning in This Text?*).

More importantly, Vanhoozer began to recognize that his early project, by focusing so persistently on human speech-acts, had actually contributed to the very problem that he was attempting to overcome. Vanhoozer began to realize that the real problem causing impasse between revisionists and postliberals was a nearly exclusive focus on the relationship between text and reader which led to the neglect of theological description about God's use of Scripture in the economy of redemption. In his later work, then, Vanhoozer switches his focus from a consideration of human authorial intent to a more focused exploration of divine authorial intent, and seeks to explain Scripture's location within the economy of redemption as a unique and integral part of God's self-communicative action.[2] In dialogue with postliberal and revisionist theologians, Vanhoozer argues that Scripture is authoritative for the church because Scripture is a unique set of documents which can be identified as God's communicative action. Proper reading of Scripture, then, can only start with a right First Theology, a stance of faith that the Scripture is God's speaking action.[3] Viewing God as the primary author

---

2. These later works run from 2001 with the publication of *First Theology* to the present, and include the significant works *The Drama of Doctrine* and *Remythologizing Theology*.

3. Two factors seem to account for Vanhoozer's change of focus from defending the authority of Scripture in terms of secular literary theory to an explanation of the role of Scripture in the economy of redemption. First, many of the changes in Vanhoozer's writing can be traced to his social context. Vanhoozer's early work begins in discussion with secular literary theorists at the University of Edinburgh, where one of his primary concerns became the safeguarding of meaning in any text (see Vanhoozer, *Is There a Meaning in This Text?*, 2). In this early work, Vanhoozer sought to protect biblical interpretation from postmodern "undoers" of meaning, such as literary theorists as diverse as Jacques Derrida, Richard Rorty, and Stanley Fish. Vanhoozer's later work takes place in dialogue with fellow evangelicals at Trinity Evangelical Divinity School in Deerfield, Illinois, and subsequently in discussion with the North American postliberalism and various forms of revisionist theology. Thus while Vanhoozer's early work proposes a challenge to the current secular postmodern tendency to disregard the authority of any text, Vanhoozer's later work proposes a challenge to the Christian postmodern tendency to grant authority to experience or community over Scripture. Vanhoozer decides that the postmodern transfer of authority from Scripture to community is best challenged by reevaluating God's use of Scripture in the economy of redemption. Second, Vanhoozer's change of location in 1998 takes place at the same time as the publication of his first major work, *Is There a Meaning in This Text?* While the 2009 tenth anniversary edition testifies to the popularity of the book, the primary criticism of it has been its lack of attention to the uniqueness of Scripture and lack of focus on God's agency in precisely these texts. These criticisms have forced Vanhoozer to focus more on the uniqueness of Scripture as God's communicative action and

of Scripture, Vanhoozer works out the implications of God's self-communicative action within the economy of redemption, specifying how God speaks (God's being is described as triune self-communicative act), what Scripture is (Scripture is described as God's covenant document to the church), and where Scripture fits in the economy of redemption (Scripture is described as constituting the church).[4] Throughout his later work, then, Vanhoozer seeks to articulate the relationship between God, Scripture, and church in a way that establishes the communication of God, through Scripture, to the church in the economy of redemption.

Establishing a First Theology: From God as Ground of Communication to God as Pure Communicative Act

Vanhoozer's early work: listening to the author as an other: In his early work, Vanhoozer works to overcome what he perceives to be the growing problem of postmodern relativism by proposing a particular method for reading which will establish the authority of scriptural meaning. Vanhoozer's goal is to establish the determinate meaning of Scripture and to safeguard biblical meaning from postmodern "undoers" (esp. deconstructionists and reader response theorists) who reject the claim that the biblical texts (or any other texts) possess determinate meaning. In response to such "undoers," Vanhoozer suggests that because all human communication is a gift grounded in the communicative action of God, the act of reading is an inherently moral and theological activity. Vanhoozer proposes a "theological general hermeneutic" in which "the Bible should be read like any other book, and . . . every other book should be

---

to draw out the implications of God as triune communicative Being (see *Is There a Meaning in This Text?*). This change of focus presses Vanhoozer to develop a distinctly Christian approach to understanding the role of God as author and the place of Scripture in the divine economy.

4. It is important to note that Vanhoozer never rescinds his emphasis on the determinacy of meaning and the role of the human author in the communication of Scripture, and throughout his career he insists that readers respect the author of any text as a communicative agent. Vanhoozer still insists that a fixed meaning is encoded in a text for readers to discover and understand. Ten years after the publication of *Is There a Meaning in This Text?* Vanhoozer claims, "I still think the substance of the argument—a proposal about textual meaning—is essentially correct" (1).

read like the Bible."[5] This morality of reading obligates readers to respect the author of any text. Vanhoozer claims that "[a]ll texts . . . invoke a certain debt that readers owe authors,"[6] and thus responds to Barthes's declaration of the "death of the author" by suggesting that interpretive "understanding" leads to the "death of the reader."[7] In all texts, "The voice of the communicative agent confronts us with a moral demand: 'Heed me. Hear me. Understand. Do not bear false witness.'"[8]

Since the "undoing of interpretation," is based on the immoral treatment of the author, Vanhoozer claims that "Christian theology, not deconstruction, is the better response to the ethical challenge of the 'other.'"[9] Vanhoozer draws two theological analogies to emphasize the moral obligation to listen to authors, and thus to rehabilitate the quest for authorial intent. First, Vanhoozer suggests that the author is like a creator.[10] Drawing a parallel from God's creation *ex nihilo*, Vanhoozer

---

5. Vanhoozer ("The Spirit of Understanding," 208) follows Barth and Ricoeur, who have made suggestions that reading the Bible has implications for the reading of all texts.

6. Vanhoozer, *Is There a Meaning in This Text?*, 228–29.

7. Ibid., 405. Vanhoozer suggests that just as the essence of Christian discipleship is to understand the author of the biblical text and die to self, so all interpretive understanding seeks to respect the intentions of the author.

8. Ibid., 401. Vanhoozer's insistence on respecting the author as an "other" seeks to provide a postmodern response to a characteristically postmodern disregard of authorial intent. Francis Watson (Review of *Is There a Meaning in This Text?*, 745), observes that while in much postmodern literary theory "the text must be dragged before a tribunal and subjected to interrogation about its own ideological tendencies, its tacit support for an unjust status quo, its stereotyping of marginalized groups," Vanhoozer shows that this "inquisitorial practice" is "unethical because in dealing with texts we are dealing with persons whose communicative actions the texts embody."

9. Vanhoozer, *Is There a Meaning in This Text?*, 199.

10. Vanhoozer's argument for authorial intent centers on answering the question, "What is an author?" rather than the questions, "Who was the author?" or "What was the psychological intent of the author?" Vanhoozer (ibid., 5) is clear that he is not trying to rehabilitate a notion of authorial intent that depends on "conscious awareness." Instead, Vanhoozer claims that authorial intent is an "aspect of action. Specifically, authorial intention is a form of agential intention. . . . By authorial intention, then, I have in mind not what authors *wanted* to do (too psychological) but what they *did*." Because "to be human is to be always having to interpret what other people are doing" (no human can avoid such action), interpreters must interpret the speech acts of authors. This means interpreting what persons are saying by "counting their sentences *as* promises, questions, commands, assertions, and the like." Interpretation for authorial intent means understanding the correct illocutions inscribed by the locutions. Because this information is encoded in the text, the search for authorial intent is not a

asks, "Why is there something rather than nothing in texts? Because someone has said something about something to someone."[11] The author "is responsible both for the existence of the text (that it is) and for its specific nature (what it is)."[12] Hence the author "is the one whose action determines the meaning of the text—its subject matter, its literary form, and its communicative energy."[13] When the author is viewed as a creator, the intended literary creation of the author (meaning) must be respected in order to appreciate the author.[14] Second, Vanhoozer moves from the analogy of creation to a christological analogy to explain the author's creative work of codifying a determinate meaning (i.e., content) in a text in a particular manner (i.e., form). Vanhoozer suggests that because a "text is an extension of one's self into the world, through communicative action," the author's meaning in the text is the incarnation of the author's intent.[15] On this account of authorship, it becomes clear why readers must respect the meaning intended and inscribed by the author. God is the paradigmatic author because of God's paradigmatic communicative act of creation and incarnation. Since all human communicative acts are analogously modeled after the triune God's extension of the divine Word as a communicative act, as Christians respect God by attending to God's self-communicative act, they will likewise respect human authors by attending to the author's self-communicative acts.

Unfortunately, Vanhoozer's attempt to ground respect for the author a theological general hermeneutic comes at a high price, as it tends to truncate discussion of God's unique use of Scripture by reducing God's communicative action in Scripture to an *a priori* assertion which grounds human reading.[16] When Vanhoozer explains the role of the Trinity in in-

---

speculation about the consciousness of the author.

11. Vanhoozer, *Is There a Meaning in This Text?*, 218.

12. Ibid., 228. The "what it is" of a text includes the text's determinate meaning, codified by the configuration in a particular genre.

13. Ibid., 230.

14. Ibid., 228. Vanhoozer claims, "Any theory of interpretation that misunderstands what an author is cannot hope to understand what a text is and how it conveys . . . meaning."

15. Vanhoozer claims that analogous to the manner in which "[t]he divine author embodied his message in human flesh," the "text is . . . a kind of 'body' of the author. It is this body, this medium of authorial agency, that I have sought to resurrect" (ibid., 229). Vanhoozer claims to have gotten this analogy from Thistelton, *New Horizons in Hermeneutics*, 75.

16. See Bowald, *Rendering the Word*, 1–23. Bowald has argued that the

terpretation, he suggests that *"The Trinity thus serves the role of what Kant calls a 'transcendental condition': a necessary condition for the possibility of something humans experience but cannot otherwise explain, namely, the experience of meaningful communication."*[17] Suggesting that God is a "transcendental condition" of communication fails to show what the triune God actually does during scriptural reading.[18] In his later work, Vanhoozer admits that his early project did not adequately show that "God is involved in the production and reception of the Bible in a way that is so qualitatively different that it makes of biblical interpretation a special case."[19] In his later work, Vanhoozer begins with the assumption that God uniquely uses Scripture for self-communicative action in the economy of redemption, and works out the implications for scriptural reading.

Vanhoozer's Later Work: God as Pure Communicative Act: Vanhoozer's 2001 book, *First Theology*, marks a distinctly new trajectory in his hermeneutical approach, as Vanhoozer suggests that a prior theological decision about God's use of Scripture ought to be the starting point in developing interpretive method.[20] Vanhoozer summarizes his First Theology in this way:

> [T]he way Scripture functions authoritatively in theology is inseparable from a view of God, an inseparability that I call 'first theology'; [and] one's first theology invariably involves an 'imaginative construal,' a decision to take the Bible *as* something

---

post-Enlightenment tendency in biblical hermeneutics is to understand God's action in Scripture in much the same way Kant has defined a "notional judgment": a piece of knowledge we need to conduct investigations, but which does not affect the process of investigation. Hence while terms like "inspiration," "infallibility," "inerrancy" may be necessary backdrops for biblical studies, they do not affect the process of "operational judgments"—those that influence the process of reasoning. Vanhoozer appears here to use the communicative action of "Trinity" in the same way—it is a necessary backdrop for human communication, but it does not affect the process of humans communicating.

17. Vanhoozer, *Is There Meaning in This Text?*, 456 (emphasis his).

18. Bowald (*Rendering the Word*, 65) claims that with regard to Scripture, "There is still no clear indication for how the actual influence or participation of God's speech action occurs with human speech action."

19. Vanhoozer, *Is There a Meaning in This Text?*, 4.

20. Vanhoozer, *First Theology*. Vanhoozer's introduction to the book (pp. 15–44) is the most helpful in showing his new trajectory in thought, as the book is composed mostly of articles written in the 1990s, and therefore better represents Vanhoozer's early work.

or other based on our discernment of how God relates to the community of readers via Scripture.[21]

Vanhoozer's First Theology specifies that God is the primary author of Scripture and that God actively uses Scripture as a covenant document to address the church. God is no longer the "transcendental condition" for moral reading, but is now the active being who uses Scripture for active self-communication in the economy of redemption. Vanhoozer's recent work has focused on developing a communicative ontology that suggests that God, both in essence and in personal relations, exists as pure communicative act and governs the economy of redemption primarily through communicative action, particularly through God's use of Scripture as God's speaking action to the church.[22] In this communicative ontology, God is the communicator, communication, and communicatedness. The triune God is the agent, act, and effect of God's own self-communication. As voice, the Father is the speaking subject who initiates the process of communication. As Word, the Son is what the Father speaks, the content of the communicative act. As the Breath that accompanies and conveys the Father's Word, the Spirit is the channel or medium of the communicative act as well as its efficacy.[23]

Understanding God as pure communicative act allows Vanhoozer to show how God speaks through Scripture to the church, thus ordering realities in the economy of redemption. Vanhoozer suggests that his

---

21. Vanhoozer, "The Apostolic Discourse and its Development," 192. Vanhoozer has received his idea of a First Theology from David Kelsey, who claims that prior to the theologian's use of Scripture stands "a decision a theologian must make about the *point* of engaging in the activity of doing theology, a decision about what is the subject matter of theology. And that is determined . . . by the way in which he tries to catch up what Christianity is basically all about in a single, synoptic, imaginative judgment" (See Kelsey, *The Uses of Scripture in Recent Theology*, 159).

22. Vanhoozer ("Apostolic Discourse and its Developments," xv) defines "communicative ontology" as "a set of concepts with which to speak of God-in-communicative-action."

23. Ibid., 261. Vanhoozer has often made analogy between the Trinity and speech-act theory that allows him to relate persons of the Trinity to specific parts of a communicative act. If the divine Persons can be analogously associated with the parts of a speech act in this way, then, Vanhoozer claims, "[T]he Trinitarian language of 'procession' is apt: as the Spirit proceeds from the Father and the Son, so the literary act proceeds from the author, and so too does the perlocution (persuading, convincing) proceed from the illocution (claiming, asserting)" (ibid., 410). This same analogy is used in "The Spirit of Understanding," 227; *Is There a Meaning in This Text?*, 457, 429, etc.

project is "a way of viewing God, Scripture, and hermeneutics in terms of their mutual implications, all coordinated by the notion of communicative action: the triune God is the ultimate communicative agent of Scripture; Scripture is an element in the triune God's communicative action," and the church is responsive to Scripture.[24] Scripture, in this model, is described as a covenant document sent on a mission to the church to bring about God's redemptive action.[25] Vanhoozer claims, "The most important reason for doing theology in accord with the canon, then, is that Scripture is a divine *covenant* document before it is an ecclesial constitution."[26] The concept of covenant provides, for Vanhoozer, the single greatest reason why the search for divine authorial intent must be central to the project of scriptural interpretation. It also provides the greatest reason that Scripture is authoritative over the church. God uses Scripture to address the church, and hence "The canon is a rule and criterion . . . precisely because of its place in the divine economy of redemption."[27] Since Scripture functions as a covenant document, Scripture can even be said to constitute the church, just as in all covenants God called and constituted a people for relationship.[28]

This refocusing of the discussion specifically on the economy of redemption allows Vanhoozer to make a substantive contribution to scriptural hermeneutics which will move beyond simply the relationship between author, text, and reader to a discussion of God's unique use of Scripture. This First Theology now forms a starting point for all Vanhoozer's hermeneutics, and allows Vanhoozer to locate Scripture more precisely in the economy of redemption. Rather than focusing almost exclusively on epistemological concerns about the nature of meaning and literary theory, Vanhoozer now focuses on the way in which the triune God has graciously used Scripture to call and sanctify a people in covenant relationship. Whereas Vanhoozer previously explained interpretation as a morally responsible quest for the (human) author's meaning, he now claims that "the interpretation of Scripture is the means by which human discourse *participates in* the 'strange new world of the Bible'—the

24. Vanhoozer, *Remythologizing Scripture*, 30.
25. Vanhoozer, *The Drama of Doctrine*, 205 and 30, respectively.
26. Ibid., 133.
27. Ibid., 147.
28. Ibid., 135, "It is the divine drama—the communicative action of the triune God creating and covenanting with what is other than God—that gives rise to the church, and not vice versa."

divine discourse of the blessed Trinity."[29] As Vanhoozer's communicative/covenantal ontology focuses on God's ongoing use of Scripture to invite readers into covenant relationship, interpretation is now viewed as a participation in the relational life of God.

Dual Authorship and the Sufficiency of the Literal Sense

Throughout his career, Vanhoozer insists on the sufficiency of the literal sense of Scripture to communicate the author's intended meaning. However, since Vanhoozer affirms both human authorship and divine authorship of Scripture, he must develop a theory of dual authorship to show how God's communicative action both emerges from and supervenes upon the collection of human texts in a way that does not change their meaning. Throughout his work, Vanhoozer uses the philosophical tool of speech-act theory to specify both how the various human authors communicate the content of Scripture and how God supervenes canonical illocutions upon human speech-acts in a way that respects the communicative action of each. While Vanhoozer's later work places more emphasis on God's use of Scripture in the economy of redemption than on a particular theory of authorship, this later work still relies on his earlier use of speech-act theory to account for God's authorship of Scripture. This section will show how Vanhoozer moves from human to divine authorship while insisting on the sufficiency of the literal sense of Scripture.

Determinate Meaning in Human Authorial Speech-Acts

Speech-act theory provides Vanhoozer with the conceptual tools needed to locate determinate meaning in a text and connect it to the author. More importantly, in the case of Scripture, speech-act theory will allow Vanhoozer to suggest that God is involved in both the authorship of Scripture and in bringing about the response of the reader. As a result, a brief analysis of the parts of a speech-act and the way in which they establish meaning is necessary.

Speech-act theory proposes that all speech acts have three parts: locutions (the words themselves), illocutions (the stance taken by the

---

29. Vanhoozer, *Remythologizing Theology*, 80.

author, i.e., commanding, requesting, etc.) and perlocutions (the effect produced by the author's communication). Following this structure, Vanhoozer defines a text as a written "complex communicative act with *matter* (propositional content), *energy* (illocutionary force) and *purpose* (perlocutionary effect)."[30] Yet while each component of the speech act is necessary to a text, Vanhoozer locates the meaning of the text in the locutions and illocutions only. Meaning can be discovered in texts because the author encodes that meaning in the text by means of locutions and illocutions.

Vanhoozer describes the literal sense as the combination of locutions and illocutions intended by the author within the context of the whole communicative act. It is the illocutions, however, which are finally decisive for establishing the meaning of the literal sense (a detail quite essential for understanding Vanhoozer's move from human speech-acts to divine speech-acts in Scripture).[31] Interpretation takes place when a reader moves from discerning the locutions to "inferring illocutionary intent from the evidence, which includes both the primary data (the text) and secondary considerations (context)."[32] Vanhoozer emphasizes not only that texts have determinate meaning, but also that there is ultimately only one right interpretation of a speech act.[33] While interpreters can never have complete confidence that they have attained the one right interpretation, Vanhoozer argues that it is a faulty conclusion to abandon the search for determinate meaning.[34] Vanhoozer's paradigmatic example

---

30. Ibid., 228.

31. Vanhoozer ("From Speech Acts to Scripture Acts," 178) defines the literal sense as "the sum total of those illocutionary acts performed by the author intentionally and with self-awareness." Yet Vanhoozer (*Is There a Meaning in This Text?*, 310–11) also insists, "The literal sense, I maintain, is not a matter of locutions alone; every utterance has an illocutionary force as well (e.g., assertive, directive, expressive, etc.). . . . To ignore the role of illocutions is to succumb to 'letterism,' or to what could also be called 'locutionism.'"

32. Vanhoozer, "From Speech Acts to Scripture Acts," 183.

33. Vanhoozer (*Is There a Meaning in This Text?*, 302) suggests that ultimately, "There is one determinate meaning in light of which the many interpretations must be judged inadequate or incorrect." Vanhoozer ("The Semantics of Biblical Literature," 85) suggests that meaning and truth are ultimately united in God, and thus all interpretations are oriented toward, though will never completely reach, the fullness of meaning/truth.

34. Against the deconstructionists, Vanhoozer (*Is There a Meaning in This Text?*, 334) writes, "The argument, 'If no absolutes, then skepticism,' is fallacious. Between 'all' and 'nothing' stands 'some.' Hermeneutic rationality yields *some* literary knowledge."

here is the interpretation of legal documents (a will, for example) where the thought process of the author must be reconstructed in order to understand the communicative act intentionally preserved by writing.[35] The reader must use the locutions in order to move to the illocutions, and hence to the meaning of a text.[36]

Vanhoozer further shows the importance of illocutions by likening interpretation to translation. Good translation, Vanhoozer claims, occurs when the illocutions and perlocutions are preserved as the locutions are changed. This produces "an 'equivalent response' in a new context."[37] While something is always added and lost in translation, "Moral interpretation respects and responds to the illocutions of the text in the way intended by the author."[38] Through this explanation, it is possible to see how closely tied authorial intent remains to meaning. The very ability to grasp meaning depends on one's ability to grasp the illocutionary efficacy of the text while using different locutions. In the structure of language, "illocutions 'supervene' on locutions," so that, "One can perform an illocutionary act only on the basis of locutions—words, sentences—though illocutions cannot be reduced to locutions."[39] The literal sense is understood by moving from the words of the text to the authorial intent which created those words and supervened on them in an illocutionary stance.

Interpretation, then, is the art of grasping the meaning inscribed in the text, not creating meaning in dialogue with the author. Since meaning is bound to the illocutions and locutions of a text, meaning is codified in the text by the author and is not added to by the text's perlocutionary effect. Vanhoozer articulates this distinction between meaning and

---

35. Ibid., 332.

36. Christology provides a pivotal analogy for Vanhoozer's understanding of the literal sense. Vanhoozer (ibid., 357n143) claims, "One cannot read divine revelation off of the body of Jesus. It is only in other contexts, on higher descriptive levels, that we can see Jesus as the Christ and as the Son of God. 'Christ' supervenes on 'Jesus.' His divinity cannot be reduced to his humanity, but it cannot be discussed apart from it either." In the same way, one must move from locutions to supervening illocutions to understand the literal sense.

37. Ibid., 387. Vanhoozer further claims, "In order to preserve the nature and content (proposition and illocution) of the message, however, it is often necessary to change the form (locution)."

38. Ibid., 335. Vanhoozer claims, "What we are after as readers is not an interpretation that perfectly corresponds to the text (whatever that might mean), but rather an interpretation that adequately responds to it. In responding to the text we allow the text to complete the purpose for which it was sent."

39. Vanhoozer, "From Speech Acts to Scripture Acts," 178.

perlocutionary effect in various ways, at times distinguishing between "meaning" (the product of the illocutions and locutions of the author) and "significance" (the "effects that the text produces in its community of readers)," and at other times between the "literal sense" ("what it meant to the author and the original audience") and the "ecclesiastical sense" ("what it means to us today in the community guided by tradition or by the Spirit").[40] In Scripture, while "perlocutionary effect," "significance" and "ecclesial sense" may continually change based on the response of the church, the determinate meaning of the text remains unaffected.

Vanhoozer suggests further that to associate perlocutionary effect with meaning would be to make both a philosophical mistake and a theological mistake. Philosophically, to allow for "confusion" between illocutionary efficacy and perlocutionary efficacy would be a *"confusion of text and commentary,"* and hence would be just "another version of the affective fallacy."[41] Meaning must be set (i.e., determinate) before perlocutionary effect is able to occur.[42] Theologically, it is immoral to confuse "textual meaning with its [perlocutionary] effects," because this would prohibit the interpreter from genuinely being confronted by the voice of the other in the text.[43] Vanhoozer argues, "The task of an ethics of interpretation, I submit, is to guard the otherness of the text: to preserve its ability to say something to and affect the reader, thus creating the possibility of self-transcendence."[44] For Vanhoozer, assuming that determinate meaning exists is a necessary prerequisite for any communication. To enter the process of communication, interpreters must trust that the "illocutionary intent is usually recognizable" in all texts.[45] As a result, the

40. Ibid., 408-09.

41. Ibid., 386 (cf. 409). For a good definition of the affective fallacy, see Wimsatt and Beardsley, *The Verbal Icon*, 21, who define the "Affective Fallacy" as "a confusion between the poem and its *results* (what it *is* and what it *does*).... It begins by trying to describe the standard of criticism from the psychological effects of the poem and ends in impressionism and relativism."

42. Vanhoozer (*Is There Meaning in This Text?*, 427), clarifies that there exists both an illocutionary efficacy and a perlocutionary efficacy in Scripture. The "illocutionary efficacy" intended by the author (which "is a matter of meaning") and "perlocutionary efficacy," the effect the text has on the reader (which does not affect that meaning).

43. Ibid., 386.

44. Ibid., 383.

45. Ibid., 427. Vanhoozer argues that the "external clarity" of Scripture is similar to the "external clarity" of all texts. Notice that all textual meaning is placed on an equal playing field here: "The suggestion that either the church *magisterium* or the

isolation of meaning from perlocutionary effect is necessary to preserve moral reading.

Divine Authorship and the Sufficiency of the Literal Sense

God's supervening illocutions: Vanhoozer makes his move from human authorship to divine authorship by claiming that God supervenes divine illocutions on human speech acts, thus bringing canonical meaning to completion. Since God acts upon the biblical texts in this way, the whole canon can be considered a unified speech act, of which God is the primary author. Vanhoozer explains the unity of Scripture by suggesting that God's illocutionary stance supervenes upon the many locutions and illocutions of the human writers, thereby making the Scriptures God's speaking action. Vanhoozer calls this supervening action, which becomes apparent at the level of the whole canon, the canonical sense of Scripture. Understanding the full meaning of any author can best occur as one examines the speech act (the locutions and the illocutionary stance of the author) in its whole context; e.g., an author's whole text in the context of its genre, with the cultural situation of the author, etc. In Scripture, while individual authors wrote the individual texts of Scripture as speech acts, the fullest meaning emerges at the level of the canon where the whole of Scripture can best be understood as God's unified speech act. Thus the "*canon as a whole becomes the unified act for which the divine intention serves as the unifying principle.*"[46] God's speech act is best understood within the whole canonical context. Vanhoozer explains:

> A text must be read in light of its intentional context, that is, against the background that best allows us to answer the question of what the author is doing. For it is in relation to its intentional context that a text yields its maximal sense, its fullest meaning. *If we are reading the Bible as the Word of God, therefore, I suggest that the context that yields this maximal sense is the canon taken as a unified communicative act.* The books of Scripture, taken individually, may anticipate the whole, but the canon alone is its *instantiation.*[47]

Spirit's illumination is a prerequisite for understanding would call this presumption into question."

46. Ibid., 265.
47. Ibid.

Since this "fuller meaning ... emerges only at the level of the whole canon," Vanhoozer argues that the fuller sense, the literal sense, and the canonical sense are all ways of referring to the same unified, divine speech act of God.[48] Ultimately, Vanhoozer suggests, the literal sense is the canonical sense as the canon provides the full context for understanding God's communicative act.

Since Vanhoozer has emphasized the moral obligation of the reader to respect the meaning encoded by authors, Vanhoozer must also explain how God can supervene God's own speech act on human speech acts without doing interpretive violence to the intended meaning of the human authors. In order to show that "[t]*he divine intention does not contravene the intention of the human author but rather supervenes on it,*" Vanhoozer suggests that the greater context of Scripture further specifies the meaning of the individual human authors. On this account, the individual texts were determinate in meaning as individual human speech-acts, yet were indeterminate in meaning as parts of the canonical whole in which God's speech-act comes to light.[49] With the closure of the canon, these texts gained a certain determinacy as God's speech act supervened upon them and their determinate canonical meaning was established. Vanhoozer explains,

> What this means is that the literal sense—the sense of the literary act—may, at times, be indeterminate or open-ended. However—and this is crucial—the indeterminacy we are considering is intended; moreover, it is a definite feature of the meaning of the text. . . . If there is a *sensus plenior*, then, it is on the level of God's gathering together the various partial and progressive communicative acts and purposes of the human authors into one "great canonical Design."[50]

God's supervening action upon the human speech-acts first providentially brought about a certain indeterminacy in the original texts which would order them toward their full, determinate meaning in the

---

48. Ibid., 264. The "fuller sense," for Vanhoozer (ibid., 313), is "the literal sense, taken at the level of its thickest description." This "thickest description" is the whole canon (see Vanhoozer, "Body Piercing," 292).

49. Vanhoozer, *Is There Meaning in This Text?*, 265. Using Brevard Childs's canonical approach, Vanhoozer claims that "a work's potential is its capacity to function in future circumstances, a capacity that for Childs is precisely the canonical function" (313).

50. Ibid., 314.

context of the canon as God placed a unifying, divine illocutionary stance upon the canonical whole. As the canon was closed, those providentially indeterminate texts could be recognized as a unified speech act of God with a stable, determinate meaning.[51]

Scripture as God's unified generic speech-act: Genres are a common literary structure which makes communication possible, and God used precisely this human structure to extend covenant to human beings.[52] Vanhoozer argues that meaning is always structured by a particular genre, since authors must choose a particular genre in order to establish a particular illocutionary stance. For example, "In choosing to write in the narrative genre, authors choose to take up a stance . . . an ideology, a 'worldview.'"[53] This means one cannot understand God's speaking action in Scripture without attending to the human speech-acts structured by their particular genres. Both form and content are essential "elements in the divine drama of revelation and redemption," as God has used just these forms (genres) to communicate just this message (Christ) to just this covenant people (the church).[54] Literary forms "are the indispensable means of conforming our minds to the 'divine genius' of Scripture. For the way God communicates, and the point of view that gets communicated, 'is as much part of the story as the events it tells.'"[55] Ultimately, God's communicative action in Scripture is that of "offering a theologically thick description of Jesus Christ" and bringing believers to be covenantally incorporated into him.[56] Such a "thick description" requires God's use of many genres, as each genre provides an aspect of God's testimony

---

51. Ibid., 313.

52. Adonis Vidu (Review of *Is There a Meaning in This Text?*, 211–12) claims that for Vanhoozer, "Genres are essential to Vanhoozer's hermeneutics because they provide the key to the illocutionary aspect of the literary act. One of Derrida's charges against determinate meaning is that each text becomes decontextualized by its being fixed in writing. The text therefore floats from one context to another, missing any anchor for its meaning. However, if Vanhoozer is right, genre creates a shared literary context, the context of a practice with its history and virtues. What writing pulls asunder, genre joins together."

53. Vanhoozer, *Is There a Meaning in This Text?*, 341.

54. Vanhoozer, "The Apostolic Discourse and Its Development," 194.

55. Vanhoozer, *Remythologizing Theology*, 190.

56. Vanhoozer (*The Drama of Doctrine*, 68) adds, "It is precisely by responding to the various illocutions in Scripture—by believing its assertions, by trusting its promises, by obeying its commands, by singing its songs—that we become 'thickly,' which is to say covenantally, related to Christ."

about Christ.[57] This "thick description" of Christ, for Vanhoozer, includes "not only promise but other aspects of the covenant—stories, stipulations, sanctions—that together constitute the relationship between God and his people."[58] As a result, the content of the covenant could not be adequately communicated without precisely the many genres represented in the canon.

Yet although Scripture contains a plurality of genres through which human authors propose their illocutionary stances, Scripture can itself be described as a unique genre at the level of the canonical whole. The "various literary forms" may be "taken together" at the level of canon where they yield a larger illocutionary stance.[59] As Chris Spinks has noted, Vanhoozer suggests that the whole canon operates something like a "super-genre," displaying its own divine illocutionary stance.[60] Vanhoozer proposes the phrase "canonical illocution" to show "what God is doing by means of the human discourse in the biblical texts *at the level of the canon.*"[61] This overarching stance, as a canonical illocution, is "something that comes to light only on the canonical level, when the divine playwright speaks in and through the various human authorial voices."[62] For Vanhoozer, identifying this supervening illocutionary stance provides the key to articulating what the Bible finally is, and thus allows the theologian to formulate a theology of Scripture. Vanhoozer identifies this unique "macrogenre" as "divine address" or "theodrama," and suggests that God's illocutionary intention is that Scripture function as a covenant document for the church. "Covenant is the social situation

---

57. Vanhoozer (ibid., 287) argues, "Each literary form in the canon . . . renders true testimony to the truth of Jesus Christ. . . . What God is doing in Jesus Christ for the salvation of the world is Scripture's ultimate propositional content, though Scripture proposes this content for our consideration in many ways, through diverse forms."

58. Vanhoozer, *The Drama of Doctrine*, 137. Vanhoozer agrees with Ricoeur that although Scripture should be seen as a unified narrative, the genre of narrative must not be allowed to overrun other genres within Scripture (273).

59. Vanhoozer, *Is There a Meaning in This Text?*, 342. Vanhoozer suggests that "genre . . . describes the illocutionary act *at the level of the whole*, placing the parts within an overall unity that serves a meaningful purpose" (341). God's supervening illocution is variously suggested to be: "confessing faith" (349), "proclaiming God's salvation" (342), "testifying to Christ" (342), "bearing witness" (349), or "providing guidance for future generations" (380).

60. Spinks, *The Bible and the Crisis of Meaning*, 100.

61. Vanhoozer, *The Drama of Doctrine*, 179.

62. Ibid., 287.

to which the various language games of Scripture broadly correspond . . . the many canonical practices represent and render the real in Christ, the shape, and hope, of glory."[63] Vanhoozer uses the phrase "generic illocution" to distinguish between "what an author is doing at the level of the whole text," and "every genre in Scripture" that "performs its distinct illocutionary act (or acts)."[64] Consequently, Vanhoozer suggests all of Scripture ought to be viewed ultimately as God's unified speaking action which mediates the New Covenant to the church through the use of all of the individual human speech-acts.

Vanhoozer contends, then, that God's speaking action (generic illocutionary stance) becomes apparent at the level of the canon as God supervenes upon the many human speech-acts and unifies them into one determinate canonical whole. Vanhoozer insists that this model respects the determinate meaning codified in the human speech-acts, yet brings them to their full determinate canonical meaning, which transcends the individual human speech-acts. Yet as we will see in the next section, this model seems to locate God's speaking action entirely in the past, as it appears to have ceased with the completion of the canon. Vanhoozer's persistent tension will be to show how God not only spoke, but continues to speak through God's use of Scripture in the economy of redemption.

Inscribed vs. Ongoing Communication: a Persistent Challenge?

When Vanhoozer speaks of "theological interpretation" of Scripture in his later work, he always associates it with the recognition of "divine action," a shorthand description of God's speaking action in the text.[65] Vanhoozer affirms both that God spoke in determinate speech acts that are codified in the canonical sense of Scripture, and he also insists that

---

63. Ibid., 220.

64. Ibid., 283.

65. Vanhoozer, *Dictionary for Theological Interpretation of the Bible*, 20. While it is right, Vanhoozer believes, to explore meaning behind, in, and in front of the text, secular hermeneutics "stops short of a properly theological criticism to the extent that it brackets out a consideration of divine action." In fact, Vanhoozer claims that reading to understand God can be considered the only legitimate primary purpose of Scripture: "the principal interests of the Bible's authors, of the text itself, and of the original community of readers was theological: reading the Scriptures therefore meant coming to hear God's word and to know God better" (ibid., 22).

God currently speaks to readers by means of the Scriptures. It is precisely in the relationship between past and present speaking that a certain tension exists in Vanhoozer's work. Overall, it appears that Vanhoozer wants to place greater emphasis on God's present speaking than his model will allow, as his emphasis on the determinate meaning of Scripture tends to confine God's speaking action to the past.

God's speech-acts as closed, past events: Much of Vanhoozer's early project places emphasis decidedly on the side of God's past speaking action rather than God's present speaking action. As the canonical speech-acts are closed and determinate, Vanhoozer's early work could be summarized by saying that God spoke in the Scriptures and the Spirit now *applies* this determinate meaning to readers today. Drawing a distinction between meaning and application, Vanhoozer claims that meaning is encoded in the text, while application continues. Attributing the Spirit's role to that of perlocutionary effect of the text, Vanhoozer argues that the Spirit applies the already-determinate meaning of Scripture's literal sense to the reader. Vanhoozer supplies his axiomatic claim that "the Spirit is tied to the written Word as significance is tied to meaning," in order to show that "the role of the Spirit is to serve as the Spirit of significance and thus to apply meaning, not to change it."[66] The Spirit does not contribute to illocutionary meaning, but instead "renders the Word *effective*."[67] Both the Son and Spirit cannot be responsible for meaning, Vanhoozer suggests, because attributing meaning to the Spirit would make the Spirit a "rival author" setting "Spirit against Word."[68] Instead, suggests Vanhoozer, "*The Spirit's role in bringing about understanding is to*

---

66. Vanhoozer, *Is There Meaning in This Text?*, 265. This separation of perlocutionary effect from meaning allows Vanhoozer, to say Spirit has the role of "bringing about understanding is to witness to what is other than himself (meaning accomplished) and to bring its significance to bear on the reader (meaning applied)" (413). Spinks (*The Bible and the Crisis of Meaning*, 92) has noted that Vanhoozer's safeguarding of the term "meaning" becomes very difficult to defend as it is extended "from sentence to text to canon while all the while maintaining authorial intention, both human and divine," so that "Vanhoozer's term 'meaning' seems to have to bear a good deal of weight as it moves to incorporate the whole of Scripture." This tension in determinate meaning will only grow throughout Vanhoozer's later work, as he seeks to keep his early understanding of meaning and claims that the meaning of Scripture includes the Spirit's perlocutionary effect and extends to the whole economy of redemption.

67. Vanhoozer, *Is There Meaning in This Text?*, 413.

68. Ibid., 427.

witness to what is other than himself (meaning accomplished) and to bring its significance to bear on the reader (meaning applied)."[69]

Since Scripture is complete in meaning (locutions and "illocutionary success"), but indeterminate in bringing about the appropriate response in the reader ("perlocutionary success"), it is naturally the Holy Spirit who accomplishes the canon's intended response.[70] Practically, this means that the Spirit "ensures that [the illocutionary acts] are recognized for what they are," by means of "conviction," "illumination," and "sanctification."[71] Vanhoozer's proposal ties the work of the Spirit to the Scriptures, for it suggests a model in which the Spirit primarily works in Scripture rather than the practices of the church or in the created order.[72] It also ties speaking to the past, as present speaking can only be described analogously as the Spirit merely applies what is determinatively spoken in the plain sense of Scripture. The close association between locutions and illocutions in speech-acts and determinate meaning seems to be at the heart of the problem, since the more strongly Vanhoozer argues that the canon possesses determinate meaning as a closed speech-act, the more difficult it is to show that such speaking is ongoing.

God's ongoing speaking action: In his later work, Vanhoozer works to show that God does have an ongoing *speaking* role in Scripture, insisting quite clearly that the "biblical text is . . . the locus and medium of God's continued speaking."[73] Vanhoozer even suggests, "To call the Bible God's word, then, is to [recognize it as] . . . ongoing triune communicative action."[74] Yet Vanhoozer seeks to identify the Spirit with ongoing speaking action without abandoning either an insistence on the closed,

---

69. Ibid., 412.

70. Vanhoozer ("The Apostolic Discourse and Its Development," 197) claims, "The external testimony of the apostles is fixed; the internal testimony of the Spirit is free."

71. Vanhoozer, *Is There a Meaning in This Text?*, 428 and 412 respectively.

72. This model seeks to locate the Spirit's work primarily in Scripture and only secondarily in creation and in the church. On the one hand, Vanhoozer, "The Spirit of Understanding," 227, criticizes Tracy and Ricoeur for associating the work of the Spirit more with the universal work of creation than with Christology, believing that such a model will de-emphasize the particularity of Christianity (the claim is developed fully in *Biblical Narrative*, ch. 9, esp. 248–57). On the other hand, Vanhoozer (*The Drama of Doctrine*, 226) criticizes postliberals for their tendency to "confine the Spirit to the church by making the Spirit's work a function of community reading practices," believing that this will de-emphasize the authority of Scripture.

73. Vanhoozer, "Triune Discourse," 65.

74. Ibid., 67.

determinate nature of God's unified canonical speech-act, or an insistence that the Holy Spirit does not change the meaning of the text. In his later work, Vanhoozer expands his discussion of divine speech to include present speaking in two distinguishable ways.

The first way is through the development of a "communicative ontology" which allows Vanhoozer to call each kind of communicative action by God a "subset of something even bigger: the economy of communication."[75] In this schema, Vanhoozer emphasizes that the "economy of communication terminates not in the text but in us."[76] Consequently, the Spirit is said to speak as the Spirit "does not change the substance of the word but removes... the cloud of unknowing—that prevents illumined readers from acknowledging the textual truth that is already there by virtue of the Spirit's inspiration."[77] Here speech-act theory is set in the background (though determinate meaning is not abandoned) and emphasis is placed on the Spirit's ongoing work of conforming readers to God. Here "Scripture exists" not so much to transmit truth as "to engraft and insert readers into the economy," and on this account it appears that the Spirit has not "spoken" unless this transformation of the reader takes place.[78] While God's speaking action is past, closed, and determinate with the closure of the canon, yet a second continued communicative action takes place when the Spirit illumines the reader to the truth of Scripture.

Vanhoozer explicitly incorporates the tools of speech-act theory into his "economy of communication" in engagement with Barth. Where Barth was reticent to call the Bible the Word of God, Vanhoozer suggests that Scripture *is* the Word of God in regard to its locutionary and illocutionary dimensions, yet Scripture *becomes* the Word of God in regard to its perlocutionary and interlocutionary dimensions. Vanhoozer employs the tools of speech-act theory to argue (against Barth) that Scripture is God's speech-act (and therefore is revelation) and (with Barth) that Scripture is God's present speaking action (i.e., that God presently speaks by means of it). Vanhoozer claims that,

> The Bible *is* the word of God insofar as its inspired witnesses— which is to say the inspired locutions and illocutions—really present Jesus Christ. Yet the Bible also *becomes* the word of God

75. Ibid., 68.
76. Ibid., 74.
77. Ibid., 75.
78. Ibid., 78.

when its illumined readers receive and grasp the subject matter by grace through faith, which is to say, when the Spirit enables what we might call illocutionary uptake and perlocutionary efficacy.[79]

On this account, God's speaking action in Scripture must be regarded both as past and determinate, and as ongoing action as the Spirit enables "illocutionary uptake" and "perlocutionary efficacy."

The second approach to explaining God's present speaking in Scripture is Vanhoozer's claim that the "meaning potential" of Scripture is realized in the whole context of the economy of redemption. Following Ricoeur, Vanhoozer suggests that the scriptural texts contain a surplus of meaning that can be "further specified" without changing Scripture's meaning.[80] As the Spirit "continues to lead the church into all truth," Vanhoozer suggests it can be expected that "God may do new things with the canonical script" as the "church continues to translate and interpret" the Scriptures.[81] This allows Vanhoozer to maintain that while "Christian doctrine is the realization of canonical potential," yet "[a]uthority ultimately remains with the canonical text."[82] On this account, Scripture's divine meaning is still somewhat indeterminate, as it is continually subject to further specification (though not change) until the conclusion of the economy of redemption. Vanhoozer again specifies his position in terms of Speech-act theory, claiming, "The human locutions and their semantic content do not change, but the divine illocutions and their historical referents . . . do."[83] Thus the original meaning of a text does not change, but is intended by God to find further specification in the larger context.[84]

---

79. See Vanhoozer, "A Person of the Book?," 57.

80. See Vanhoozer, "Ascending the Mountain," 781–803.

81. Vanhoozer, *The Drama of Doctrine*, 349 and 344 respectively.

82. Ibid., 352. Vanhoozer describes this as a textual "surplus of meaning." More will be said about this in the final chapter.

83. Vanhoozer, "Ascending the Mountain," 792. Vanhoozer (ibid., 784), argues that the real debate in figural reading is not about the semantic content of a text (the "what" or *meaning* of a text, which Vanhoozer sees as clear and relatively determinate in most cases), but about the ultimate referent of the text (what Vanhoozer calls the "'about what' of meaning"). Using the Song of Songs as an example, Vanhoozer (ibid., 785), argues that the semantic content of the text is quite clear, but disagreement arises in determining whether the text's ultimate referent is intended to be the celebration of human conjugal love, the relationship between God and Israel, or the relationship between Christ and the church. In this way, the meaning does not change, but the referent is "further specified."

84. Ibid., 792. This is very similar to Vanhoozer's earlier claim (*Is There a Meaning*

God's use of scripture for self-communication 23

Persistent Challenge: Does God Presently Speak in Scripture? Vanhoozer, then, insists that God supervened a unified canonical speech-act on the texts of Scripture, thereby having spoken in Scripture. At the same time, Vanhoozer insists that the Spirit presently speaks in Scripture. However, it is less than clear that such an account can be held without tension using the tools Vanhoozer uses. First, a tension still exists in Vanhoozer's broader "communication" model. As we have just seen in dialogue with Barth, Vanhoozer continues to closely associate God's speech-acts with revelation, thereby practically distinguishing "speech" from other forms of "communication."[85] Even when Vanhoozer does distinguish God's revelatory actions from God's verbal speaking action, Vanhoozer still insists that when God acts in a revelatory way, God will disambiguate the revelatory act with a speech-act.[86] When the speech-acts are brought into such close proximity with God's past, closed revelatory action, it becomes difficult to describe other communicative action as speech.

Furthermore, it is not clear that the Spirit's communicative action could be described as "speech" on Vanhoozer's own account. Vanhoozer uses speech-act theory to show that speech-acts are indeed *actions* in the public sphere.[87] And Vanhoozer emphasizes that all God's actions are communicative. Yet this does not mean that all the Spirit's *actions* are to be considered *speech*. In fact, Vanhoozer often seems to argue that the Spirit's effective action should *not* be considered speech. Vanhoozer has followed Wolterstorff in criticizing Barth for calling the Spirit's effective action speech, arguing that for Barth the Spirit only "grabs" the reader "by the content of what God has already said [in Jesus Christ]. I find no reason to call this 'speech.'"[88] Yet a close examination of the verbs Vanhoozer employs to describe the Spirit's speaking action shows that Vanhoozer always describes the Spirit's ongoing work as effective action

in this Text, 423), yet there Vanhoozer clearly distinguished between meaning and significance (as shown above). Here Vanhoozer is trying to avoid this distinction.

85. Vanhoozer, "A Person of the Book?," 56–57.

86. See Vanhoozer (*Remythologizing Theology*, 213). "Only speech disambiguates behavior. Only God's word disambiguates God's deed."

87. Vanhoozer, *Is There Meaning in This Text*, 209, cites Searle, *Expression and Meaning*, 29, to show that speech is considered action as persons "do" certain things with language: "We tell people how things are, we try to get them to do things, we commit ourselves to doing things, we express our feelings and attitudes and we bring about changes through our utterances."

88. Interestingly, Vanhoozer "A Person of the Book?," 55, citing Wolterstorff, *Divine Discourse*, 68.

rather than speech, thereby describing the Spirit's action in precisely the same way Barth has described it. For example, Vanhoozer claims that the Spirit "enables" the reader to grasp the "illocutionary uptake," thus resulting in the communicative act of "perlocutionary efficacy" of the text upon the reader.[89] The Spirit "makes public . . . inner-trinitarian communication," "draws" the church to Father and Son, "pours out" their love, "communicates . . . eternal life," "persuades," and "removes . . . the cloud of unknowing."[90] Elsewhere Vanhoozer claims that the Spirit does not "go beyond" Scripture or "add new words," but "enables," "advocates," "executes," "effects," and is the "means through which" God's speech is conveyed to human beings.[91] The Spirit's present communication, then, is not so much speaking, as it is bringing about the desired response in the individual when the Scriptures are read. Of course, Vanhoozer's argument is that his model ties the Spirit's present action much more to the *words* of Scripture than does Barth (who ties the action to the *event* of Christ), and this is why the Spirit's action may be considered speech for Vanhoozer while it cannot for Barth.[92] For Vanhoozer, so long as the Spirit's effective action takes place by *means of the scriptural texts*, that action can be considered speech. Still, while this action should be considered *communicative*, it is still not *speech* in the way that God's supervening illocutions on the canonical texts are considered speech. Consequently, tension still remains between Vanhoozer's argument for God's past speech in the closed, determinate canonical sense and God's present speech in Scripture. Here de Lubac's sacramental model, which is very close to Vanhoozer's communication model, may provide resources to ease this tension.

Second, Vanhoozer's proposal that Scripture's meaning emerges only in the context of the whole economy of redemption (and is therefore presently relatively indeterminate in meaning) makes much room for the Spirit's present speaking action, yet it is not clear that Vanhoozer fully commits himself to this model. As Vanhoozer develops this proposal, he suggests, "We too 'figure' in the story [of Scripture]. . . . We have been transferred into the story of Jesus Christ, emplotted into his narrative, drafted into the drama of redemption."[93] Here Scripture's ultimate refer-

---

89. Ibid.
90. Ibid., 57, 63, and 75.
91. Vanhoozer, *The Drama of Doctrine*, 199.
92. Vanhoozer, "A Person of the Book?," 55.
93. Vanhoozer, "Ascending the Mountain," 797.

ent includes present readers in participation with Christ and extends to the whole economy of redemption. Consequently, the "Spirit's intended transfigural meaning . . . *includes the reader's transfigurartion.*"[94] This fits well with Vanhoozer's claim that the Spirit "continues to lead the church into all truth," and that "God may do new things with the canonical script," as it places significant emphasis on God's ongoing speaking action.[95]

However, in the same article Vanhoozer appears to move back to his earlier insistence that canonical meaning is closed and determinate, as he identifies the "fuller sense," which he describes as the "literal sense, taken at the level of its thickest description," with the canon.[96] Consequently, "It is not that new meaning has been added, but rather that the original meaning has finally achieved its Christological *telos*," with the completion of the canon.[97] On this account, it seems that the canon alone is the context in which God's speech-act becomes clear. Vanhoozer specifically conflates these two distinct options when he claims that "the typological meaning *is* the literal meaning of the discourse when viewed in *canonical, which is to say redemptive-historical context.*"[98] Yet the "canonical" context cannot be exactly the same as the "redemptive-historical" context, since the canonical context is closed and the redemptive-historical context includes all present and future readers who participate in Christ. Vanhoozer seems to waver between an insistence that God's speech-act is closed, clear, and determinate in the canonical Scriptures (i.e., that the literal sense is the canonical sense), and a proposal in which the full context of God's speaking action is the entire drama of redemption (which includes the present reader in Scripture's meaning).[99]

---

94. Ibid., 792.

95. Vanhoozer, *The Drama of Doctrine*, 349 and 344, respectively.

96. Ibid., 313. Vanhoozer at times seems to base his whole argument for divine authorship on the ability to specify God's speech-act within the canon. Vanhoozer ("Body Piercing," 292) writes, "If one takes divine authorship of Scripture seriously, then literal interpretation must have recourse to the canonical context, for the meaning of the parts is related to the whole of Scripture. The literal sense of Scripture as intended by God is the sense of the canonical act (the communicative act when seen in the context of the canon)."

97. Vanhoozer, "Ascending the Mountain," 792.

98. Ibid., (emphasis mine).

99. Vanhoozer (ibid., 793) insists that evangelicals must recover a participatory model of scriptural reading in which they understand that the "redemptive-historical context" of Scripture includes "both text and contemporary readers." Vanhoozer (ibid., 788) also suggests that using figural reading is a matter of enlarging "our notions

I regard both Vanhoozer's establishment of a communicative ontology and his suggestion that Scripture's meaning becomes finally determinate in the whole economy of redemption as significant proposals which will further the theological interpretation of Scripture. Furthermore, I will show in the next section that de Lubac's project is in fundamental agreement with both, and that his model provides a number of resources that could further dialogue between evangelicals and Catholics on the theological interpretation of Scripture. I will then suggest that the apparent tensions between Vanhoozer and de Lubac are not so much about God's communicative action or a debate about the legitimacy of the spiritual sense of Scripture, but about different understandings of meaning (chapter 2) and disagreement about God's use of the church in the economy of redemption (chapter 3).

HENRI DE LUBAC: CHRIST'S PRESENCE IN SCRIPTURE AND THE NECESSITY OF THE SPIRITUAL SENSE

Writing a generation before Vanhoozer, de Lubac's chief concern was to develop an understanding of scriptural interpretation which, on the one hand, steered clear of the neo-Thomist error of reducing Scripture to a set of propositions that could be used for proof-texts and a record of miracles (which reduced Scripture to a book of evidence for apologetics) and, on the other hand, steered clear of an over-dependence upon the historical critical method to discover the meaning of Scripture (which reduced Scripture to a bare historical record). To confront both these errors, de Lubac emphasizes the indispensability of the spiritual sense of Scripture. De Lubac's insistence on the spiritual sense of Scripture is grounded in God's use of the scriptural texts to mediate the singular mystery of the Christian faith revealed in Jesus Christ. For de Lubac, Christianity is unique among religions in its historical grounding, as God has entered into human history for self-revelation. This revelation is divided into a covenant of promise (Old Testament) and a covenant of fulfillment (New Testament). This twofold structure of letter and spirit characterizes de Lubac's understanding of the relationship between nature and the supernatural, and hence his understanding of all reality from a Christian

of historical context, recognizing that later readers also figure among the divine addressees."

perspective.[100] De Lubac emphasizes that the transcendent mystery of the supernatural, though always beyond the grasp of the human intellect, is nonetheless revealed in its entirety in Christ. Christ is then mediated to readers through sacramental realities through which he has chosen to make himself known. Hence Scripture is a sacramental reality used by Christ, who is present in it through the Spirit. Because Christ actively uses the Scriptures for self-mediation to readers to draw them into participation in the mystery, a spiritual sense of Scripture exists that transcends the letter.

De Lubac's *Ressourcement* project returns to the exegesis of the early church to find resources used by the Fathers to move beyond these reductive alternatives of modernism and neo-Thomism. De Lubac finds in the church fathers a commitment to understanding the meaning of all history through Christ, and he finds their traditional fourfold hermeneutic of Scripture the means by which this mystery was kept from reduction.[101] De Lubac writes that the Fathers "did have a sense of biblical history, or even of universal history, because they held on to its principle of discernment in the Mystery of Christ, the absolutely ultimate final cause. The doctrine of the four senses, through which this mystery has found its expression . . . provid[ed] the foundation for the objective sense of history and by that the very fact *giving history its proper value*."[102] From his earliest work, *Catholicism* (1938), de Lubac emphasizes the indispensability of a spiritual sense of Scripture which highlights Scripture's unified meaning in Christ, Christ's self-mediation through Scripture, and the infinite mystery revealed in Christ. All of de Lubac's subsequent works on the interpretation of Scripture, including his four volume *Medieval Exegesis* and his work on Origen *History and Spirit* affirm the christological center of Scripture as establishing the necessity of the spiritual sense of Scripture.

---

100. For a good treatment of the relationship between nature and the supernatural for de Lubac and the consequences this has for his whole theological project, see Milbank, "Henri De Lubac," 76–91, where he presents a clear description of the issues involved without his more idiosyncratic reading reflected in Milbank, *The Suspended Middle*.

101. See Henri de Lubac, "On an Old Distch."

102. De Lubac, *Medieval Exegesis*, 2:71–72 (emphasis original).

Establishing a First Theology: Christ as Subject and Object of Scripture

The center of de Lubac's scriptural hermeneutics is the premise that Christ is at the same time both singular object and subject of Scripture. As object, "Jesus Christ brings about the unity of Scripture, because he is the endpoint and fullness of Scripture. Everything in it is related to him. In the end he is its sole object."[103] The goal of scriptural exegesis, then, is to look to the reality of Christ and read all Scripture in light of him as object. Yet to exegete Christ in Scripture is not simply to read Scripture in light of some new doctrinal principle or teaching, but to participate in Christ's presence, as Christ stands as subject of Scripture. As Subject, "Inasmuch as he is the exegesis of Scripture, Jesus Christ is also the exegete. He is truly Scripture's Logos, in an active as well as a passive sense."[104] Christ is always active in the process of exegesis, mediating himself through the texts of Scriptures to readers. "Christ's exegesis," De Lubac claims, "does not consist of words first and foremost. It is actual. It is Action. . . . The mysteries of Scripture are 'revealed in action.'"[105] This action is both the action of God and the action of the interpreter. Scripture cannot be understood without participation in Christ because Christ, as subject of Scripture, must incorporate the reader into the mystery in order for it to be understood. Without participation, the reader could only understand things about Christ, and would miss the reality of the one to whom the whole Scripture points. Yet participation is only possible as Christ incorporates readers into his body, the *totus Christus*, through reading.

For de Lubac, the relationship between the Testaments can be described neither simply by a doctrine of progressive revelation nor by the assumption that there is a spiritual dimension which transcends the letter, but only by the active presence of Christ unifying them. It is this unification of all Scripture in Christ that makes the Christian Scriptures unique among religious books. De Lubac recognizes that all religions of the book claim that the reality to which their text points is greater than the words themselves, and every religion "fancies that there is some hidden meaning" in their religious texts.[106] Yet de Lubac's claim is that the

---

103. De Lubac, *Medieval Exegesis*, 2:237.

104. Ibid., 2:238.

105. Ibid. De Lubac (ibid., 2:239) claims that Christ is "exegete, in principle, from the moment of his Incarnation," in the sense that he is the unified mystery.

106. De Lubac, *The Sources of Revelation*, 88.

Christian Scriptures are unique because Christ, as object of Scripture, gave meaning to both Testaments by entering into history and unifying them within himself. And they are unique because Christ, as subject of Scripture, continually mediates himself through them in a unique manner. The event of Christ goes far beyond the assumption that Old Testament letter points to a deeper spiritual reality. The event of Christ goes far beyond progressive revelation, as it "offers the spectacle of a discontinuity that has no equal, which makes the traditional idea of allegory, understood in its most profound essence, irreplaceable."[107] Christ reorients all of Scripture toward himself. The Christian faith, for de Lubac, is not a religion of the book, but a religion of the Word. The movement from letter to spirit in the Christian Scriptures is unique because it is grounded in the "definitive" and "eternal" act of Christ which unifies the Testaments. Hence, "in fulfilling" the Old Testament, the act of Christ "gives it new life and renews it. It transfigures it. It subsumes it into itself. In a word, it changes its letter into spirit."[108] Thus the event of Christ that unifies Scripture establishes the unique character of Christian reading, and a properly Christian reading of Scripture could never be grounded in general hermeneutics. It is the movement from the literal sense to the spiritual sense (which de Lubac calls allegory), which insures that all Scripture is read as a unified whole. De Lubac claims,

> Thus, using "allegory" as a means of going beyond the literal significance of Old Testament texts and finding in them the mysteries then being revealed in the flesh by the New was a way of showing the indissoluble unity of the two Testaments. Hence, the relationship of history to allegory, of fact to doctrine or of the figure to the truth was the link between the two parts of Scripture and the witness to its profound unity.[109]

Christ, the great allegory, is the ground upon which all subsequent allegorical interpretation of particular passages can be legitimated. The more resolutely the reader approaches the text presupposing the unity of the Testaments in Christ, the more Christian will be the disclosure yielded by the interpretation.

For de Lubac, the spiritual sense of Scripture can be distinguished as allegory, tropology and anagogy, which are the threefold means of

107. De Lubac, *Medieval Exegesis*, 1:234–35.
108. Ibid., 1:228.
109. De Lubac, "On an Old Distch," 123–24.

approaching the singular mystery. The three spiritual senses of Scripture are not so much different ways to read the text as they are mutually complementary aspects of reality which result from participation in the unified mystery, the union between God and human beings in Christ. The whole structure of Christian reality is the movement from sign to the unified Christian mystery viewed in three aspects: as the radical transposition of the OT in the advent of Christ (allegory), as the transformative participation of the individual in the body of Christ (tropology), and as the eschatological union of the *totus Christus*, Christ and church (anagogy). The literal sense discloses the mystery, which must be illumined in three intrinsically related ways. There is an integral movement from one sense of Scripture to the other, which de Lubac calls a "living evolution," so that the senses of Scripture, while distinguished from one another, cannot be separated from one another.[110] De Lubac writes, "Each sense leads to the other as its end . . . a unity of source, and a unity of convergence."[111] The fourfold nature of scriptural interpretation is really the fourfold understanding of all of Christian reality. Only the Christian Scriptures can be interpreted in a fourfold manner, because they are the privileged witness to the revelation of the whole mystery of Christ who, coming in history, transformed the meaning of history, and invites individuals to share in this salvation history and await the fulfillment of history.[112] None of these senses of Scripture could be removed from the Christian understanding of reality without the collapse of the integral Christian vision. It is impossible to practice one of the spiritual senses in isolation from the others, just as it is impossible to practice faith, hope, or love in isolation from the others or to understand the mystery of Christ without one of his three advents (Christ's historical advent, Christ's spiritual birth in the soul of the believer, and Christ's future bodily return to earth).[113]

---

110. De Lubac, *The Sources of Revelation*, 221. This de Lubac (*Medieval Exegesis*, 2:203) also described as a "living development" or an "organic unfolding."

111. de Lubac, *Medieval Exegesis*, 2:26. "But in Scripture itself, one professes that there is no dissociation of the two senses. The spirit does not exist without the letter, nor is the letter devoid of the spirit. Each of the two senses is in the other—like the 'wheel within the wheel.' Each needs the other. With those two they constitute 'the perfect science.'"

112. See ibid., 1:8.

113. One way de Lubac (*Medieval Exegesis*, 2:138–40) highlights the intrinsic unity of the spiritual senses is to relate them to the three advents of Christ. Christ's advent in history radically transformed the meaning of the OT history and creating the spiritual reality of the church (allegory); Christ is born daily in the soul of the individual

Since Christ (both as subject and object) is the meaning of Scripture, all three senses are parts of this christological meaning.

Divine Presence and the Indispensability of the Literal and Spiritual Senses

Christ's use of Scripture as both its subject and its object necessitates both the literal and spiritual senses of Scripture. Christ was revealed in history, and Christ builds his church into eschatological union with himself through the matrix of history. In the economy of redemption, history participates in the infinite mystery, and consequently the history of God's redemptive acts (biblical history) cannot be understood simply by natural historical study. Because Scripture is used by Christ to mediate the infinite mystery, and because readers participate in this mystery in scriptural reading, a spiritual sense of Scripture must be distinguished but not separated from the literal sense. This section will explain the various ways in which de Lubac describes the literal and spiritual senses of Scripture.

The Literal Sense

While many Protestants worry that de Lubac's insistence on the spiritual sense will relegate the literal sense to a position of mere relative importance and discourage good exegetical work, de Lubac insists that the literal sense has an indispensable role in all scriptural interpretation. The letter of Scripture is the indispensable starting point for all Christian reading for two essential reasons.[114] First, without the literal sense, Christianity would be unintelligible. Christian faith is a uniquely histori-

---

believer, causing an interiorization of the mystery (tropology), and Christ will return in glory at the end of time (anagogy). Another way de Lubac often highlights their unity is by showing their correspondence to the threefold Pauline theological virtues: faith, hope and love. Allegory is the Christian faith, tropology corresponds to the love that is the interiorization of the Christian faith, and anagogy corresponds to the hope of the final consummation of the Christian faith (see *The Sources of Revelation*, 221).

114. Besides these two characteristics of the letter that make it indispensable for Christian faith, de Lubac notes several other less essential characteristics about the literal sense for premodern interpreters. First, the literal sense is the way for beginners to enter the Scriptures, as it does not require conversion to be understood. Second, the literal sense provides moral lessons for readers (see de Lubac, *Medieval Exegesis*, 2:44–45 and 2:70, respectively). The distinction of this understanding of morality from tropology will be seen later.

cal faith, and the literal sense narrates the historical events of salvation history.[115] De Lubac insists that "redemption has not been accomplished in the imagination, but in time and in factual reality," so that "our whole salvation in fact is worked out in . . . history."[116] The narrative structure of the literal sense is the means by which this history is rendered to readers. Second, the letter is the indispensable means by which the Spirit presently communicates with readers. It is precisely as God's redemptive action in Scripture is mediated to believers that the Spirit speaks to them. Summarily, de Lubac claims, "The spirit is not separate from the letter but is contained and, at least initially, hidden within it. The letter is both good and necessary, for it leads to the spirit: it is the instrument and the servant of the spirit."[117] This necessary movement from history to spirit is often described as a sacramental relationship, in which "the letter is 'the sacrament of the spirit.'"[118]

Uses of the letter: Yet while de Lubac affirms the necessity and importance of the literal sense, it is not always clear exactly what he means when he refers to the "letter" of Scripture. De Lubac at times suggests quite varied understandings of the letter, often leaving the reader to discern from the context exactly what he meant by the term. Throughout de Lubac's work, at least four different meanings of the "letter" of Scripture appear. First, the literal sense often means *the Old Testament Scriptures*

---

115. D'Ambrosio (*Traditional Hermeneutic*, 173) notes that the "letter" and "history" were basically "synonyms in the patristic and medieval exegetical tradition," and de Lubac emphasizes that the "letter" refers to "objective facts or events in history."

116. De Lubac, *Medieval Exegesis*, 2:46–47. Hence de Lubac (*Paradoxes of Faith*, 145) states strongly, "Christianity is not one of the great things of history: it is history which is one of the great things of Christianity." De Lubac (*Medieval Exegesis*, 2:75) realizes that many premoderns practiced a tendency "to pass rapidly over this 'letter,' so as to have more time to give to the exploration of the 'mystery,'" yet he insists that this as a problem merely in practice, and does not illegitimate the move from the literal to the spiritual sense.

117. De Lubac, *The Sources of Revelation*, 87.

118. Ibid., 14. De Lubac often likens the letter of Scripture to wax that holds honey (the spiritual sense). (See, for example, de Lubac, *Medieval Exegesis*, 2:162–5 and *The Sources of Revelation*, 87.) A number of theological and anthropological analogies are also given to show the indispensability of the letter in leading to the divine reality. De Lubac uses the analogy of the relationship of the Son to the Father in the Trinity (the Son is the indispensable means to know the Father), the soul to the body in a human being, and the human nature to the divine nature in Christ (See *The Sources of Revelation*, 14; *Medieval Exegesis*, 2:45 and 2:60–61, respectively). These are, of course, just analogies, but they show the intrinsic nature of the relationship of the literal sense of Scripture to the spiritual senses of Scripture.

before the advent of Christ. In this usage, the letter corresponds to the Old Testament, while the Spirit corresponds to the New Testament. Here the letter was preparation for the Spirit and contains the Spirit, so that the economy of Old Testament history was transposed by the economy of New Testament grace.[119] Second, the literal sense often means *the Old Testament read without Christian faith*. De Lubac's classic text to illustrate this kind of reading is Paul's analogy between Moses' veiled and unveiled face and the veiled letter and Spirit (2 Cor 3:15–17). The Jewish exegete, by refusing to read in light of Christ, would only read the "mere letter."[120] Using only his secular methodology, the secular exegete could only access the "mere letter," since this is all that can be discerned using the tools of secular historical research.[121] As the letter was not allowed to operate as a sign which points to the spiritual reality, for both Jew and secular historian it becomes a "mere letter."[122] Third, the literal sense often designates *the historical events of salvation history*. As de Lubac follows the medieval formula, the letter "delivers us facts" of history.[123] Fourth, the literal sense often simply means *the plain sense of the text*. God, as divine author, had overseen the pattern of words in such a way that the meaning that they render is reliable. Context alone appears to be the guide to which of these four uses is primarily in view.

While some of de Lubac's ambiguity in defining the "letter" of Scripture can be attributed to the flexibility of the patristic usage of the term, part of the ambiguity lies in de Lubac's relishing of paradoxes in the relationship between letter and spirit. Overall, de Lubac appears to be more

---

119. De Lubac (*Medieval Exegesis*, 2:225) claims, for example, that "Scripture has two meanings. The most general name for these two meanings is the literal meaning and the spiritual ('pneumatic') meaning, and these two meanings have the same kind of relationship to each other as do the Old and New Testaments to each other."

120. De Lubac, *Medieval Exegesis*, 2:51, 2:53–54, 2:60.

121. Ibid., 2:81. This is the picture of the modern commentators who, de Lubac says, "consider the Bible 'as a book that interests them, but which does not concern them.'"

122. D'Ambrosio (*Traditional Hermeneutic*, 182) claims that the letter that kills is "that attachment to the literal sense that blinds the interpreter to the spirit hidden within it . . . the obstinate refusal to go beyond the *littera sola*." Williams (*Receiving the Bible in Faith*, 154) notes that the central problem by those who create a "mere letter" was that the letter "was restricted in scope. It failed to acknowledge the inner potential that would find its actuality in the Gospel and, explicitly or implicitly, denied the affirmation that would be later integrated into the Creed: that these things happened in fulfillment of the Scriptures."

123. De Lubac, *Medieval Exegesis*, 2:44.

interested in emphasizing the relationship of letter to spirit than he is in providing a precise definition of the literal sense. The letter is described in a variety of ways that de Lubac feels are advantageous in illuminating the way in which the letter hides, contains, and discloses the spirit. Only the specific context will help the reader discern which meaning is intended.

The Spiritual Sense

As we have seen, de Lubac insists on the historical character of Christian faith as one of the unique features of Christianity. De Lubac insists that it is this characteristic of "the history of redemptive events" which is "the characteristic that most markedly differentiates the Bible from so many other sacred scriptures," even "for the unbelieving observer."[124] In his classic work, *Catholicism*, de Lubac emphasizes the historical, and hence social nature of the Christian faith, showing that "if the salvation offered by God is in fact the salvation of the human race . . . any account of this salvation will naturally take a historical form—it will be the history of the penetration of humanity by Christ."[125] Due to Christianity's uniquely historical character, Scripture must first be a record that "delivers us facts," and to participate in Christian faith we are "obliged to believe in a whole series of facts that have really come about."[126] It is precisely this uniquely historical character of Christian faith that causes de Lubac to insist on the spiritual sense, which he calls allegory. Like the letter above, de Lubac assigns the term allegory a number of different meanings depending on his purpose. The most common of these will be explored in this section.

Allegory as the meaning of history: If history discloses the mystery, allegory is the mystery disclosed in its various aspects. Allegory is thus the intended completion of history. All historical events, if they are to be understood, need a principle of reference, without which they remain merely random events. Allegory is the meaning of history, for it shows that all history is unified in Christ. De Lubac claims, "At the summit of history, the fact of Christ supposed history, and its radiance transfigured

---

124. De Lubac, "On an Old Distich," 122–23.

125. De Lubac, *Catholicism*, 141.

126. De Lubac, *Medieval Exegesis*, 2:44. De Lubac ("On an Old Distich," 114) adds that Christian "religion is first of all a historical fact. God has intervened in human history: the first thing to do is to learn the history of his interventions from the Book where they have been recorded by the Holy Spirit."

history."[127] It is in this sense that allegory is, as the Old Distich says, first of all "what you must believe ... doctrine, the very object of faith."[128] This "theological sense of history," de Lubac claims, is the only kind which really has resources to understand the whole of history, since it has "recourse to the final causes" which can allow the interpreter to understand the individual parts.[129] As a result, far from undermining the historical importance of Scripture, the spiritual sense was actually "providing the foundation for the objective sense of history and by that very fact *giving history its proper value*."[130] Thus, de Lubac claims, "If it is . . . a dive into the 'mystery,' it in no way follows that it is, as it has been accused of, a 'flight from history.'"[131]

De Lubac never tires of stressing the unique historical character of Christian allegory as opposed to the allegory used by classical writers, claiming that, "Biblical allegory is . . . essentially *allegoria facti*," not allegory based on the words alone, like other instances of ancient allegory.[132] A fundamental difference existed between Christian allegory and pagan allegory, as Christian allegory was always a unification of history in an

---

127. De Lubac, "On an Old Distich," 105. Hence allegory, de Lubac claims, was a very useful and necessary tool to "construct . . . the edifice of the faith" and show "how all of biblical history bears witness to Christ" (107).

128. Ibid., 114. De Lubac (*Medieval Exegesis*, 2:109), explains that the "content" of allegory "is exactly 'the doctrine of the holy Church.' The allegorical sense of Scripture is 'The Catholic sense.'"

129. De Lubac, *Medieval Exegesis*, 2:71. For de Lubac "This is why, if any not merely partial and relative but total, comprehensive, and absolutely valid explication of history is truly possible, this explication can only be theological. Only faith anticipates the future with security. Only an explication founded upon faith can invoke a definitive principle and appeal to ultimate causes." De Lubac calls this "total exegesis" and "theology itself" and even "spirituality" (77).

130. De Lubac, *Medieval Exegesis*, 2:72 (emphasis his). This is a happy alternative to the immanentism that de Lubac sees lurking in many secular histories, which he calls "absolutized History" (2:71).

131. Ibid., 100. To show the great difference between Christian allegory and pagan allegory, de Lubac asks, "Where would one find, in the facts of history, or only in the thought or imagination of the Greek allegorists, the irruption of some 'new testament' analogous to that of the Christians, an irruption which one day would have turned the ancient exegesis of the Homeric poems upside-down by overturning the very being of their exegete? Where would one find . . . anything even remotely resembling the opposition between the *oldness* of the letter and the *newness* of the spirit?" (104).

132. Ibid., 88. See also de Lubac, "Hellenistic Allegory and Christian Allegory," 165–96 for de Lubac's most pointed description of the difference between Christian allegory and pagan allegory.

actual historical event, as opposed to pagan allegory which sought to reconcile fictitious stories and myths with "timeless philosophical truths."[133] The Christian use of allegory was developed from the Apostle Paul, who saw his own allegory grounded in real historical events.[134] While the allegorical sense is the doctrinal sense, it can never operate apart from the foundation of the historical (literal) sense. Wherever there is spirit, there is also history. For de Lubac, Christian allegory was based in history and saw history as essential, while pagan allegory was often an attempt to escape something embarrassing in history. The spiritual reality cannot be disclosed in Scripture without attention to the literal sense.

Allegory as movement from nature to supernatural: The realm of allegory brings the reader into a qualitatively new dimension which is imperceptible to the unbeliever. The rule of thumb seems to be that if a secular historian could notice the historical correspondence based on his or her own secular tools, that observation does not yield an allegorical reading. De Lubac insists that in this movement exists an "infinite qualitative difference" exists, which, if diminished, would "make out of the allegorical sense, which is a *spiritual* sense, a new literal sense; and this would practically negate the interiority of the Christian mystery."[135] Boersma suggests that for de Lubac the movement from letter to spirit can best be described as a sacramental relationship. This means "The sacramental character of history implied that it pointed beyond itself not just in a horizontal, historical, but also in a vertical sense. The natural-supernatural relationship should provide the pattern for the relationship between history and spirit."[136] No method, then, can move the exegete from history to spirit. This movement is made by God, as the reader places herself in the place of submission to receive the mediation of God's revelation by Scripture.

De Lubac's emphasis on the entrance into a new dimension of reality with the spiritual sense can be illustrated in his dissatisfaction with the terms typology and *sensus plenior*. Typology could be defined as an

---

133. D'Ambrosio, *The Traditional Hermeneutic*, 99.

134. De Lubac ("On an Old Distich," 123) claims that "even if allegory has a certain value, it alone does not provide the doctrine to be believed." For Paul's establishment of a distinct Christian practice grounded in history and not in words, see especially de Lubac, "Typology and Allegorization," 129–64.

135. De Lubac, *Medieval Exegesis*, 2:98–99. Thus de Lubac claims, "Faith is the light 'that makes one see the light of the spirit in the law of the letter.' . . . We are therefore 'to be imbued in the faith through allegory.'"

136. Boersma, *Nouvelle Theologie*, 183.

instance recorded in Scripture where an earlier historical event in salvation history is recognized to prefigure a later historical event of salvation history. Typology, de Lubac feels, falls short of the radical newness of allegory because typology is grounded only in historical correspondence and not in the definitive revelation of God in Jesus Christ.[137] The very uniqueness of Christian allegory is grounded in the radical newness of the Event of Christ giving meaning to all historical events. As a result, typology "does not have a foundation of its own, typology by itself says nothing about the dialectical opposition of the two Testaments nor about the conditions for their union. It does not explain the unique passage from prophecy to Gospel."[138] Typology, then, taken on its own, could only diminish understanding of the radical newness of Christ, because typology "lacks the ability to show that the New Testament is something other than a second Old Testament which . . . would leave us completely within the thread of history."[139] Typology without allegory, then, would leave the reader in the realm of nature and consequently without apprehension of the mystery or personal incorporation into it.[140]

The movement to a supernatural dimension in the biblical texts forces the reader to relinquish control over the meaning of the text. De Lubac resists any attempt use a conception of *sensus plenior* to "constitute a 'scientific demonstration of the harmonies of the two Testaments,'" as this approach will always attempt to capture knowledge at a natural level and will never advance to the level of faith.[141] De Lubac insists that when

---

137. Notice that for de Lubac (*The Sources of Revelation*, 144) "Scriptural allegory provides a justification for typology, provides a foundation for it and contains it within itself." Thus de Lubac is not arguing against typological reading; he is only showing that typology falls short of allegory in showing Christian newness.

138. Ibid. Typology, claims de Lubac "has the drawback of referring solely to a result, without alluding to the spirit or basic thrust of the process which produces that result," and consequently "it stops the spiritual impulse at the half-way mark" (145).

139. Ibid., 144.

140. Typology, claims de Lubac, "does not express the connection between spiritual understanding and the personal conversion and life of the Christian" (ibid., 144–45).

141. Ibid., 150–51. *Sensus plenior* refers to the deeper meaning intended by God to the text written by the human author. This deeper intended meaning comes to light in the reading community only through further revelation (e.g., the Old Testament meaning revealed in Christ), or through a deepening understanding of revelation in the church (e.g., the progress of doctrine). (See, for example, Brown, *The Sensus Plenior of Sacred Scripture*.) De Lubac's concern (*Sources of Revelation*, 151) is that the *sensus plenior* "presupposes a transposition which is impossible or unseemly without 'newness of spirit.'" Consequently, while the goal of *sensus plenior* was to show the

reading Scripture, "In order to receive it, it is not enough . . . to 'press hard,' to 'seek'; it is also necessary to 'pray,' to 'implore.'"[142] This is because the only adequate movement to the spiritual sense is one that takes place "on the level of faith," which "cannot be something purely technical or purely intellectual," but is "a gift of this Spirit."[143]

Allegory as conversion: Since the passage to allegory brings scriptural reading to a qualitatively new dimension, de Lubac insists that spiritual meaning "'stems totally from the Spirit' inasmuch as it presupposes an entire grasp of the history of salvation as directed toward Jesus."[144] Yet this qualitatively new dimension is not simply an intellectually apprehended theological presupposition. The reader must not think that the event of Christ in history provided the singular historical clue which would allow the secular historian to now decipher all history without personal faith. De Lubac claims that in Scripture, "To stop at the objective datum of the mystery would be to mutilate it, to betray it."[145] Since the Christian mystery cannot be understood without participation, allegory is essentially the process of conversion.[146] De Lubac shows this desire to read first for conversion rather than mastery of the text as he claims that for the premoderns, "It was an undefined understanding, precisely because it was an approach to the depths of God. It was not a matter merely of a text being explicated, but of mysteries being explored."[147] As a result, de Lubac emphasizes that it is not guaranteed that those most knowledgeable will understand allegory. He claims, "But it is not ordained by God that the most learned will inevitably be the most believing, nor the most spiritual; nor that the century which sees the greatest progress realized in scientific exegesis will, by that fact alone, be the century with the best

---

gradual recognition of God's communication in Scripture, it cannot incorporate the radical newness of Christ without moving from the realm of observation to the realm of faith (ibid., 152).

142. Ibid., 152–53.

143. Ibid., 152.

144. Williams, *Receiving the Bible in Faith*, 143, citing de Lubac, *History and Spirit*, 390.

145. De Lubac, *Medieval Exegesis*, 2:134.

146. De Lubac, *The Sources of Revelation*, 20–21, cited in Murphy, "Henri De Lubac's Mystical Tropology," 186. De Lubac (*Medieval Exegesis*, 2:117) writes, "To pass from history to allegory or from the letter to the mystery or from the shadow to the truth, is without a doubt always to pass to spiritual understanding: but it is also, thereby, 'to be converted to the faith.'"

147. De Lubac, *Medieval Exegesis*, 1:34.

understanding of Holy Scripture."[148] Allegory, then, is more than reading the Scriptures as a unified whole; it is personal participation in the mystery.

Allegory as the threefold spiritual sense: Since allegory includes an already/not yet tension, allegory can be described in its three aspects, allegory, tropology, and anagogy. Tropology and anagogy are not additional senses of Scripture, but are intrinsic aspects of the spiritual sense. Tropology is application of the mystery to the individual believer in the ongoing process of conversion. Tropology does not move beyond allegory, but gives allegory specification in the individual. Anagogy is the anticipation of the union of the four senses of Scripture in the eschatological return of Christ. At present, allegory, although it is the full revelation of the mystery, can only be described as an "image" and a "promise" of what is to come.[149] Tropology also is inherently ordered toward anagogy, since this is the full incorporation of all individuals into the *totus Christus*.[150] Anagogy unifies the literal sense with the spiritual senses, as Christ returns in glory within history to unify all history within himself. Hence all three spiritual senses are really one unified Christian vision of reality, imparted by Christ, and participated in through the Spirit. The fourfold structure of apprehending the Christian mystery stresses that because the unified mystery can never be fully comprehended, there will always be "an incurable character of non-fulfillment which marks all spiritual understanding ... there will always be new aspects of doctrine to bring to light and new applications of it to be adduced" as the Scriptures are studied.[151]

Allegory as the totus Christus: The Christian mystery disclosed in allegory is the union of the triune God with human beings, and the incarnation of Christ has as its goal the union with church as body. Since the "Mystery of Christ ... is also the mystery of ourselves and our eternity,"[152] the "whole content of the Bible" is the mystery of Christ and the church.[153]

---

148. De Lubac, *The Sources of Revelation*, 157.

149. Ibid., 182.

150. Ibid., 186–87.

151. De Lubac, *Medieval Exegesis*, 1:29.

152. Ibid., 1:222. Because the mystery is precisely that union between God and human beings, de Lubac also, in a secondary way, describes the human person as mystery as well. The human being is the one created for, enabled, and called into this relationship as partaker of the mystery. In this way, de Lubac can, at times, speak of the human being as mystery.

153. De Lubac, *Medieval Exegesis*, 2:90. One of de Lubac's most frequent uses of

In the scope of salvation history, then, "This ecclesial body . . . must thus be said . . . to be 'truer' than the [incarnate body], because it constitutes a more perfect, fuller realization of the divine design."[154] Emphasizing the *totus Christus* does not in any way depreciate the value of the Incarnation, but instead shows this unique and transformative event in light of its completion. De Lubac shows that at times premodern exegetes understood the object of allegory to be Christ, yet at other times they speak of the object as the church, and at times they do not distinguish between them. De Lubac likens this difference in approach to the distinction drawn in contemporary Christology between "Christology from above" and "Christology from below."[155] For the premoderns, one could consider the *totus Christus* from the perspective of Christ as head, or from the perspective of church as body, but both must be considered in relation to each other. De Lubac explains that, "The matter of holy Scripture is the whole Christ, head and members,"[156] and because "Christ and the Church are just one great mystery," one cannot really consider one reality without the other, without risking abstraction.[157]

Since the mystery revealed is the *totus Christus*, the church is included in the allegorical meaning of Scripture. De Lubac explains that, "For a long time, allegory was taken by theology to mean, and often in the broadest sense, the mysteries of Christ and of the church as they appeared in Scripture."[158] As D'Ambrosio claims, "The fact that biblical allegory has the mystery of the Church as part of its very object means that the Church and its tradition must necessarily be a principle of interpretation."[159] God has both ordained the events recorded in Scripture to disclose the church as mystery and has ordained that the church, by participating in the mys-

---

mystery is the usage taken from Paul about the relationship of Christ and the church in Ephesians 5. De Lubac claims, "[A]s Saint Paul said, Christ and the Church are just one great mystery: this is the mystery of their union. Now the whole mystery of Scripture, the whole object of *allegoria*, resides in this. This enables one to discover everywhere the 'deeper mysteries about Christ and his body'" (2:92).

154. De Lubac (*History and Spirit*, 412) claims, "The assumption of individual flesh has a unique importance, of course, because it constitutes the point where God inserts himself into our humanity. But it is not an end in itself. Its goal is to allow the assumption of the Church."

155. De Lubac, *Medieval Exegesis*, 2:92.
156. Ibid., 2:93.
157. Ibid., 2:92.
158. De Lubac, *The Sources of Revelation*, 12.
159. D'Ambrosio, *Traditional Hermeneutic*, 189.

tery, is the only institution that can understand the disclosed mystery. Furthermore, since the allegorical sense includes the church and can only be understood by the church, it follows that allegory can only be understood within the church. The church, as that institution that participates in the mystery, is the only one which has an intuition of the mystery, and this intuition toward which the church yearns allows the church to sense which interpretations are legitimately part of its faith. Hence, "The 'true' meaning of the Scriptures, their complete and definitive meaning, can really be nothing other than the meaning 'which the Spirit gives to the Church.'"[160] This means that while all readers may have access to the literal sense of the text, only those who participate in Christ can participate in the spiritual sense of Scripture, since the spiritual sense *is* the mediation of Christ through the Spirit.

De Lubac contends, then, that Christ uses Scripture to bring the church to its completion as the *totus Christus,* and that the reader's participation in Christ takes place as the reader moves from the literal sense to the spiritual sense. De Lubac insists that this model values the literal sense of Scripture and the historical nature of the economy of redemption, as the event of Christ establishes the historical center of the Christian faith. Yet as we will see in the next section, this model may fail to describe adequately God's governance of the scriptural texts, as it tends to move too quickly from analysis of scriptural texts to contemplation of scriptural events. De Lubac's persistent tension will be to how God uses Scripture to structure Christian understanding of the events of history, and thus *how* Christ uses Scripture for self-mediation.

Inscribed vs. Ongoing Communication: A Persistent Challenge?

For de Lubac, the text possesses a quasi-sacramental character as it is used by Christ to mediate the mystery. Since the letter of Scripture discloses the spiritual sense, and since the spiritual sense is inaccessible without the work of the Spirit, the very distinction between letter and spirit shows that God must use the Scriptures in a unique way for communication. In fact, it would be fair to say that for de Lubac, the spiritual sense of Scripture *is* God's communicative action. Conversely, God's presence in and communication through the texts *is* the spiritual sense of Scripture.

---

160. De Lubac, *The Sources of Revelation,* 114.

Since the spiritual sense of Scripture is God's communication through the texts, the category of *ongoing inspiration* dominates de Lubac's work. The Spirit's inspiration of Scripture takes three discernible forms in de Lubac's work: the Spirit's ongoing mediation of the presence of Christ through the text, the Spirit's transformation of present readers to receive Christ, and (much more faintly) the Spirit's inspiration of the original authors in the literal sense.

Inspiration as ongoing mediation of Christ: To speak of inspiration in the spiritual sense is to speak tautologically, since de Lubac insists that the spiritual sense is inaccessible without the active presence of the Spirit to the reader. When de Lubac speaks of inspiration, his focus is usually on the ongoing aspect of inspiration, in which the Spirit continues to mediate the mystery to the believer by means of the spiritual sense of Scripture. This spiritual mediation is perhaps *the* defining characteristic of de Lubac's whole hermeneutical project, as the very distinction of "letter" and "spirit" emphasizes the Spirit's involvement in the text *beyond* the letter. In a summary statement, de Lubac emphasizes,

> It is not only the sacred writers who were inspired one fine day. The sacred books themselves are and remain inspired. It can and must be said of them, with especially good reason, what Saint Augustine said of all the beings of creation: "God did not create them and then depart from the scene. They come from him and exist in him."[161]

This kind of ongoing inspiration is best described as sacramental presence. In fact, there is such a close connection between Christ's sacramental presence in Scripture and the continued inspiration of the Holy Spirit in Scripture that ongoing inspiration can only be understood in light of de Lubac's understanding of the incorporation of the Logos in Scripture.[162] In *History and Spirit*, de Lubac claims, "In his Scripture as in his earthly life, Origen thought, the Logos needs a body; the historical

---

161. De Lubac, *Medieval Exegesis*, 1:81. Significant also is de Lubac's discussion of Origen's understanding of inspiration. D'Ambrosio (*Traditional Hermeneutic*, 146) shows that while Origen "focused upon the objective inspiration of the Book itself," de Lubac shifts emphasis onto the ongoing aspect of inspiration and emphasizes the Spirit's indwelling of the text.

162. For de Lubac, the Spirit is always the Spirit of Christ. Wherever Christ is incorporated (Scripture, Eucharist, church), the Spirit is always present mediating the mystery. Distinguishing between the work of Christ and the work of the Spirit was not much of a priority for de Lubac, as he seems to see the Spirit as the mediating agent of Christ wherever Christ is present.

meaning and the spiritual meaning are, between them, like the flesh and the divinity of the Logos."[163] Just as the Spirit prepared a physical body for the Logos so that God's revelation could take place, so the Spirit prepares a literary body for the Logos so that God's revelation could become effective in the church. The Spirit is the active agent in both, and the Spirit uses the physical and literary bodies to manifest the mystery which transcends them both. Scripture, then, is characterized by the continual presence of God, just as was the humanity of Christ. De Lubac emphatically claims,

> Within the Scripture, God resides; by the Scripture, God makes himself known; the mystery of the Scripture is the very mystery of the Kingdom of God.... Thus Scripture is not merely divinely guaranteed. It is divinely true. The Spirit did not merely dictate it. The Spirit immured himself in it, as it were. He lives in it. His breath has always animated it. Scripture is "fertilized by a miracle of the Holy Spirit."[164]

Since Christ and the Spirit of Christ are continually present in Scripture, communication to the believer is always available through the movement from letter to the spirit of Scripture.

Inspiration as transformation of readers: De Lubac rarely speaks of the Spirit's present inspiration of texts without also speaking about the Spirit's present inspiration of readers. De Lubac insists that "the Word of God . . . speaks to us still" in Scripture, "reaching the depth of our souls as the limits of the universe."[165] The divine speaking action that takes place in Scripture is a twofold action: It is a disclosure of the mystery to the reader and a transformation of the reader which enables understanding. Notice the twofold action by God in this extended quote:

> It is the same God who gives us scripture and makes it understood; what appear to be two successive acts on his part are in reality but one. The Spirit communicates to the sacred text a limitless potentiality, which therefore entails degrees of profundity which can go on and on. No more than this world was Scripture,

---

163. De Lubac, *History and Spirit*, 104. Boersma (*Nouvelle Theologie*, 161–62), suggests a close link between "Incarnation and the inspiration of Scripture" and claims that "the medieval mindset had realized that at the divine level much more was at stake than just a comparison [between text and human flesh]," since ultimately Christ is the Object of both, and both are used by the Spirit to reveal Christ.

164. De Lubac, *Medieval Exegesis*, 1:82.

165. Ibid., 2:81.

that other world, created once for all: the Spirit "creates" it still, as if every day, to the extent that he "opens" it. Through a wondrous and precise correlationship, *he "expands" it to the extent that he expands the understanding of him who receives it.*[166]

God gives Scripture, opens it for understanding, and uses it to move the individual soul toward union with God. On the one hand, Scripture "expands" to the reader, and on the other hand, the reader is "expanded" to Scripture.[167] Speaking, then, is the drawing of the individual into the unified mystery, and takes place as one enters into the spiritual sense. De Lubac claims that Scripture "is not a document handed over to the historian or thinker, even to the believing historian or thinker. It is a word, which is to say, the start of a dialogue. It is addressed to someone from whom it awaits a response . . . a return movement."[168] This speaking is inaccessible at the level of the letter, yet it animates readers and draws them into participation in Christ.

Inspiration as providential ordering of texts: While never denying inspiration of the original texts, de Lubac's emphasis lies clearly on the Spirit's ongoing action within the texts. De Lubac is unhappy that theories about inspiration in the original authors or texts are often developed for apologetic reasons to safeguard God's past action in the text.[169] Furthermore, de Lubac continually worries that believers will see the inspired Scriptures simply as a warehouse of dogmatic propositions of divine origin which need only to be discovered and applied in the church.[170]

---

166. Ibid., 2:225–26. De Lubac further claims, "The Word of God never stops creating and burrowing within a man who makes use of his capacity to receive it, so that the understanding which also believes can grow indefinitely" (2:223, emphasis mine).

167. Ibid., 2:224. De Lubac claims, "Scripture . . . 'moves forward with those who read it.' . . . Scripture, which contains God's revelation about himself, is, we might say, expandable—or penetrable—to an infinite degree." Yet at the same time, de Lubac suggests, "As a result of the revealing unction of the Spirit, our mind is expanded for the understanding of the Scriptures" (2:157).

168. De Lubac, *History and Spirit*, 346–47.

169. See, for example, de Lubac (*The Sources of Revelation*, 62–63) is dissatisfied that in contemporary "treatises on hermeneutics . . . there is much more discussion about the inspiration of the sacred writers than about the inspiration of Scripture."

170. Ibid., 225–26. De Lubac sees this problem in Protestant theology, in which only the literal sense is accepted and the ongoing speaking action is the application of certain dogmatic truths in the text to the contemporary church. He also sees this problem in Catholic neo-Thomism, as many theologians suggested that the church could continually find hidden dogmatic truths in Scripture which the Spirit originally placed in the text to be found by the church at the proper time.

Both tendencies, De Lubac thinks, ignore the intrinsic unity between letter and spirit. To avoid this error, de Lubac emphasizes the passage to the spiritual sense as the moment when the communicative action of God takes place.

Yet, while de Lubac's emphasis is on the ongoing aspect of inspiration in the spiritual sense, he occasionally hints at the inspiration of the letter of Scripture as well. In order to distinguish de Lubac's approach from Vanhoozer's, it will be helpful to distinguish between inspiration as *providential ordering* of Scripture and inspiration as *authoring* of Scripture. De Lubac typically seems to view inspiration of the literal sense as God's *providential ordering* of the texts to lead readers to the events of history. De Lubac does seem to believe that the Spirit *providentially insured* the literal sense to be a reliable rendering of God's action in history, yet he never develops if and how the Spirit ought to be seen as the *author* of the literal sense.[171] This lack of clarification on divine authoring of the literal sense seems to be closely linked to de Lubac's ambiguity about the literal sense itself. The literal sense records history, and thus leads readers to the historical events where the Spirit draws them into mystery. De Lubac never specifies exactly how the texts themselves narrate exactly what God has providentially ordered, and consequently how the human authors were inspired by the Divine author to communicate this truth.

Persistent challenge: specifying the relationship between texts and events: De Lubac's lack of focus on the texts themselves arises from his insistence that allegory is grounded in events of history, not texts. When de Lubac claims that "the letter is 'the sacrament of the spirit,'" he insists that the letter refers "not Scripture as text, but sacred history as contained in Scripture . . . since spiritual meaning is not the meaning of words but the meaning of things."[172] Furthermore, de Lubac insists that "to discover

---

171. There are occasional hints that de Lubac might describe the Spirit as having an integral role in the authorship of the text in such a way that the texts themselves have a certain role in salvation history beyond merely leading readers to events. One hint at this is the causal role of the Spirit assigned to difficult passages. De Lubac (*Medieval Exegesis*, 2:74–76) notes it was assumed the Holy Spirit placed difficulties into the literal sense so readers would be humbled and would be required to think more deeply into the truths of Scripture (See Wright, "The Literal Sense of Scripture"). Another hint is de Lubac's suggestion that the Holy Spirit actively inscribed moral lessons in the texts during their composition (De Lubac, *Medieval Exegesis*, 2:64). Admittedly, however, these are quite undeveloped, and it is unclear that de Lubac really thought of the literal sense as being "authored" by God.

172. De Lubac, *The Sources of Revelation*, 14–15n10.

... allegory, one will not find it properly speaking in the text, but in the realities of which the text speaks; not in history as recitation, but in history as event . . . allegory is indeed in the recitation, but one that relates a real event."[173] Wright shows that de Lubac makes a key distinction between "history in the objective sense as a past event and history in the subjective sense as a report of that past event by witnesses."[174] In this schema, historical referents (what de Lubac calls objective history—the events themselves) are typically given priority over textual sense (what de Lubac calls subjective history—scriptural witness to those events).[175] Yet hermeneutical discussions center on the *textual rendering* of the event, and de Lubac must say more about how texts mediate the events of history. When the great act of Christ transformed history, it transformed a *certain* history—a history recorded through the inspiration of the Holy Spirit in the literal sense. A fundamental ambiguity exists throughout de Lubac's writings about the relationship of the scriptural texts to the historical events they signify.

In fact, three distinct positions can be seen in de Lubac's work about the relationship between text and event.[176] On what may be considered his standard account, de Lubac speaks of the text as merely pointing to historical events, which, in turn point to spiritual realities. De Lubac claims, for example, that "the text acts only as spokesman to lead to the historical realities; the latter are themselves the figures, they themselves contain the mysteries that the exercise of allegory is supposed to extract

---

173. De Lubac, *Medieval Exegesis*, 2:86.

174. Wright, "The Literal Sense of Scripture," 262, referring to de Lubac, *Medieval Exegesis*, 2:44.

175. De Lubac (*Medieval Exegesis*, 2:44) distinguishes between "on the one hand, the deeds recounted and, on the other, the report of these deeds."

176. Articulating de Lubac's understanding of the transition from letter to spirit is complicated by several factors. Overall, de Lubac's delight of paradoxes to describe the relationship between letter and spirit makes systematization difficult. Spirit is at times opposed to the letter and described as the fulfillment of the letter in the same discussion. Second, de Lubac desires to represent the breadth of the whole Christian tradition, and therefore provides a wealth of quotes, which are difficult to reconcile systematically. Third, a genuine ambiguity exists in de Lubac's own thought between the relationship between the letter of the text and the events of history, which make it unclear what meaning of the "letter" de Lubac is referring to. Fourth, the relationship between letter and spirit must be seen in light of de Lubac's whole understanding of Christian reality in all its various forms: the relationship of nature/supernatural, church as divine and human, sacramental presence, in which "letter" and "spirit" provide a short-hand for nature and the supernatural.

from them."[177] This would suggest a providential relationship between text and event only, as God has preserved an adequate and reliable witness about historical events so that the events may render spiritual realities. The literal sense, then, as text, would simply be a providentially ordered witness to history.

Yet a second and more robust understanding can be discerned, in which the spiritual reality is intrinsically contained in the text itself. Following Origen, de Lubac calls Scripture an "incorporation" of the Logos, claiming, "The Logos is already truly incorporated there; he himself dwells there, not just some idea of him, and this is what authorizes us to speak already of his coming, of his hidden presence," a "presence that [is] actualized anew each time this Scripture illumines us."[178] While defending Origen's understanding of eucharistic presence, de Lubac claims that while the Eucharist "truly contains the Body and Blood of Christ . . . in a subsequent, more elevated and profound and, therefore, 'truer' sense, Scripture is the Body and Blood of the Logos."[179] The Logos dwells in Scripture as mystery, analogous to the way the Logos dwells in the flesh of Christ.[180] On this account, de Lubac seems to agree that texts, unified by Christ, provide access to the Logos as mystery because they are words

---

177. Ibid., 2:86.

178. De Lubac, *History and Spirit*, 389. It is important to note that de Lubac makes a clear distinction between the Logos's presence in the incarnation and the Logos's incorporation in Scripture, as he emphasizes that "the Logos is . . . not, properly speaking, incarnated [in Scripture] as he is in the humanity of Jesus."

179. Ibid., 415.

180. Ibid., 393. De Lubac spends much time exploring Origen's concept of the two incarnations of the Word (though, as noted above, de Lubac makes an essential qualitative difference between Scripture and incarnation). Just as the Word was clothed flesh, so also the Word descends to the Scriptures. Significantly, de Lubac (*Medieval Exegesis*, 2:60–61), records Origen's claim that this dual "incarnation" (using Origen's term) "is here something more than a comparison; 'letter' and 'flesh' are not only alike in that they are both likened to a 'veil'; for, according to Scripture itself, one can say that 'the Word of God has been incarnated in two ways,' since at bottom it is one and the same unique Word of God who descends into the letter of Scripture and into the flesh of our humanity." Here Scripture *as text* houses the Logos. De Lubac strengthens this sacramental allusion by claiming, "Already in its literal sense, or in its 'body,' Scripture expresses something of the Logos, just as something of him is glimpsed through the flesh of Christ" (De Lubac, *History and Spirit*, 416). Furthermore, while de Lubac never himself claims that the Word was present in Scripture before the incarnation, he records Origen's claim that even before the incarnation, the Word was present in Scripture and "the function of Scripture is to reveal this Logos." On this account, the text of Scripture itself, as the dwelling place of the Logos, intrinsically discloses the mystery.

that render the Word. Thus Scripture has the same role in disclosing the second Person of the Trinity as does the humanity of Christ. When the mystery is viewed in terms of its historical revelation, the great act of Christ, the event has priority over the text. Yet when the mystery is viewed in terms of the reality revealed, the Logos, both text and incarnation are seen as efficacious signs.[181]

Yet a third position can be discerned, which is distinct from both text as mere "spokesman" and text as sacramental embodiment of the Logos. At times de Lubac seems to have in mind a double movement which takes place from words to events to spiritual reality. Words really signify and make present the events of history, and the events, in turn, really signify and make present the mystery. For example, De Lubac suggests that for Origen, history takes a "new mode" when written down in Scripture, so that the past events "survive today . . . as signs and mysteries. . . . for the purpose of our 'edification.'"[182] This "new mode" is not simply the record of events, but the providentially ordained record of salvation history. The letter preserves the event, and hence participates in the flow of history from past to present. The purpose of this recorded history is to "pass on," and hence, "'In following the trail of truth in the letter of Scripture', we 'will thus be served by history as by a ladder.'"[183] The "ladder" de Lubac refers to allows the reader to climb from text to event to spirit. De Lubac seems to be suggesting that the human authors themselves are caught up into the events of salvation history as they recorded sacred history, so that the mystery is disclosed through "both" the events themselves and the written record of the events. Hence de Lubac claims that although "the human authors of the holy Books have died," and "the events that they have reported have passed away," yet still "the Word of God was expressed through both."[184] In this way, texts, authors, and events are all drawn as integral and indispensable parts into salvation history, so that the texts themselves are used as mediation of the Logos, and not just the

---

181. It is important here to again note that for de Lubac, the mystery is singular. There is no incompatibility between disclosure of the Logos and disclosure of Christ, as both ultimately are aspects of the same mystery. Christ is the definitive revelation of God in history, yet the Logos is always working in history to incorporate believers into the mystery.

182. De Lubac, *History and Spirit*, 322, noted by Wright, "The Literal Sense of Scripture," 264.

183. Ibid., 323.

184. De Lubac, *Medieval Exegesis*, 2:81. See also Wright, "The Literal Sense of Scripture," 264.

events to which they point. On this account, not only does God order the texts of Scripture in a providential way, but they also participate in the mystery as uniquely mediating the events of salvation history to readers.

Understandably, de Lubac is less concerned with hermeneutical theory than he is in showing *that* God uses both text and history to mediate the mystery. Yet, the role of the text in mediating this history is a pressing issue that must be addressed in order to develop an adequate hermeneutical program. De Lubac's lack of clarity about the relationship between text and event leads indirectly to a tension that practically tends to detract from the literal sense of Scripture. First, de Lubac is more concerned about the church's illumination of the mystery through allegory than he is on the church's regulation of careless allegorical interpretation.[185] While de Lubac admits that many allegorical interpretations have been inadequate and should be quickly dismissed, he also insists that interpreters "not confuse them with what they are intended to signify"—the great Allegory of Christ.[186] So long as the interpretation fit within the analogy of faith, it should be appreciated as being a "Christian" reading. This fundamental stress on illumination over regulation is further seen in de Lubac's tacit acceptance of *allegoria dicti* (allegory based on the correspondence of words). De Lubac argues forcefully that *allegoria facti* (allegory based on the correspondence of historical events) is distinctly Christian while *allegoria dicti* is not, as the Christian understanding of

---

185. De Lubac believes that the Spirit always resides in the Scriptures to disclose the mystery to the church. De Lubac's whole project of recovering the wealth of traditional insights illustrates his emphasis on doctrinal maximalism (D'Ambrosio, *Traditional Hermeneutic*, 59, for example, claims that de Lubac's ultimate goal is "to help Christians enter into sanctifying communion with the divine principle of tradition which is the Holy Spirit.")

186. De Lubac, *The Sources of Revelation*, 143. De Lubac agrees that there was need for some control on allegory. Wood (*Spiritual Exegesis and the Church*, 49–50) assembles several of de Lubac's criteria for limiting allegory. First, "divine revelation" both in the sense that the New Testament explicitly authorizes a particular allegory and in the sense that there is "unanimous agreement" among the Fathers about such an interpretation (49). Second, the analogy of faith is helpful, because it points to the one, unified meaning of Scripture (50). Third, and most importantly, allegory should only be *allegoria facti* (allegory of the events of history) and not *allegoria verbi* (allegory based on a correlation of terminology). This third principle is most important, as it kept the allegory always based in and dependent upon history, rather than being based in the imagination of the commentator (50). Unfortunately, I would suggest that none of these rules have been followed consistently either by the tradition or by de Lubac himself, and it is this misuse of allegory that has often made it appear an arbitrary hermeneutical principle.

allegory is established on real historical events rather than from relationships drawn between figures in the text.[187] However, in practice de Lubac does not discourage *allegoria dicti*, provided that it is grounded on *allegoria facti*, the great allegory of Christ.[188] As D'Ambrosio claims, "So long as *allegoria facti* is given first place, and the theological principles that establish its validity granted, [de Lubac] regards the use of verbal allegory as a matter of indifference."[189] *Allegoria dicti* may be fanciful and imaginative, but it is not harmful to Christian faith so long as it directs the imagination toward the great act of Christ. So long as the mystery is being contemplated, de Lubac tends to view literary rules as a matter of lesser importance. Vanhoozer would likely suggest that if de Lubac were clearer about the way in which the text structures as well as mediates our knowledge of the event, he would better be able to regulate *allegoria verbi* by showing that the texts of Scripture do form a plain canonical sense that resist arbitrary interpretation.

CONCLUSION: PERSISTENT CHALLENGES AND DIALOGUE

In light of the previous analysis, it seems that Vanhoozer's literal, canonical sense may be much closer to de Lubac's spiritual sense than is typically thought. Both Vanhoozer and de Lubac insist that reading the bare literal sense is insufficient for reading the bible as Scripture, and both insist that readers must employ a First Theology that will allow them to hear the voice of God in Scripture rather than simply the collection of human words. Both Vanhoozer and de Lubac strongly agree that the activity of theological interpretation of Scripture ought to occur in the realm of grace rather than nature.[190] Vanhoozer's model suggests that the transition from nature to grace occurs by employing a schema of divine

---

187. See de Lubac, "Hellenistic Allegory and Christian Allegory," 165–96.

188. D'Ambrosio, *Traditional Hermeneutic*, 186. As D'Ambrosio claims, "Thus, in the ancient exegetical tradition, the various *allegoriae dicti* are ordinarily pressed into the service of the one great *Allegoria facti* by means of the analogy of faith" (193).

189. Williams, *Receiving the Bible in Faith*, 171.

190. Vanhoozer (*Dictionary for Theological Interpretation of the Bible*, 20) argues that suggesting readers to participate in the realm of grace rather than nature is not yet to make a judgment about whether grace "opposes, crowns, or outflanks reason"; but is simply to "establish theological interpretation as dealing with issues outside the realm of nature."

authorship to Scripture, a First Theology, which will allow them to seek God's speaking action in Scripture and participate in the Spirit's ongoing transforming work. By taking God's speaking action as his point of departure, Vanhoozer seeks to describe God's communicative action as both past and determinate and as present and participatory. Vanhoozer's insistence that, "There are no shortcuts. The drama-of-redemption approach takes the detour of sanctification," quite clearly brings out both the necessity of the Spirit's governance and the necessity of human participation which must attend scriptural reading.[191] De Lubac's model suggests that the transition from nature to grace occurs in the transition from the literal sense to the spiritual sense, as de Lubac insists that even the right theological presuppositions cannot, by themselves, lead to right reading without the active and ongoing communication by the Spirit. By taking Christ's active self-mediation through Scripture as his point of departure, de Lubac is able to insist upon the indispensability of a spiritual sense of Scripture, in which encounter with and participation in the living, present Christ is ultimately the meaning of Scripture. Both, then, suggest that scriptural meaning cannot be understood without participation in God's redemptive action.

Furthermore, Vanhoozer's understanding of the perlocutionary effect of Scripture is quite close to de Lubac's understanding of the spiritual sense of Scripture. For both authors, God uses the text to mediate self-revelation to human beings and the Spirit acts to incorporate readers into Scripture's story and transforms them into the body of Christ. Both authors refer to the Spirit's ongoing communicative work as speaking, yet both typically employ a number of actions verbs other than speaking to explain the Spirit's work in the lives of readers. Vanhoozer's recent emphasis on the Spirit's ongoing speaking action, then, is quite consistent with de Lubac's insistence on the spiritual sense of Scripture.

Were Vanhoozer to embrace the logical conclusions of his communicative ontology, his project may be even closer to de Lubac's work. One such implication of Vanhoozer's "economy of communication" is that the Spirit communicates through a number of channels, including sacraments, the leadership of the church, lives of the saints, etc.[192] This broad model of communication appears to be very similar to de Lubac's sacramental model, as it shows that all of God's actions to human be-

---

191. Vanhoozer, "A Drama-of-Redemption Model," 178.
192. Vanhoozer, *Remythologizing Theology*, 412.

ings (i.e., everything in the economy of redemption) could be considered communicative actions. Yet Vanhoozer never distinguishes these different kinds of communicative action. Instead, Vanhoozer's focus always moves to Scripture as God's unique (and perhaps only?) *speaking* action, and his defense of a communicative ontology often appears to be simply an apologetic backdrop for establishing that God can speak and has spoken in Scripture, so that Vanhoozer can then get on with the task of describing how Scripture operates as God's normative speaking action.[193] Vanhoozer appears to be holding two models of God's communicative action: a broad model in which God *communicates* through a number of creaturely realities in the economy of redemption, and a narrow model in which God's *speaking action* is past and determinate in the canon of Scripture. Vanhoozer often seems to revert back to his narrow model when he attempts to emphasize the uniqueness and authority of Scripture. This will be explored in the next chapter.

Another implication of Vanhoozer's "economy of communication" model would be a greater appreciation for God's use of the church to recognize, develop and safeguard scriptural meaning. If canonical meaning potential is realized only in the whole economy of redemption, and if this canonical meaning potential is ordered by God, then God must use the church as part of God's communicative action. This leads de Lubac to claim that "the meaning of Scripture is Christ and the Church," and such a conclusion seems in line with Vanhoozer's recent work.[194] Yet as we will see, Vanhoozer is quite hesitant to describe God's use of the church as a normative or authoritative instrument of divine self-communication. This will be the topic of chapter three, as I will suggest that the real issue for Vanhoozer is the problem of authority, and it is this concern to safeguard Scripture's determinate meaning which prevents him from fully accepting the implications of his own communicative ontology.

As de Lubac starts with Christ's active presence in the scriptural texts and employs categories of sacramental mediation rather than analysis of

---

193. Notice that Vanhoozer (ibid., 30) suggests that remythologizing theology "is a way of viewing God, Scripture, and hermeneutics in terms of their mutual implications.... Scripture is an element in the triune God's communicative action; interpretation is the way the church demonstrates her understanding of what God is saying and doing in and through Scripture by right theodramatic participation." It is unclear what role God's communicative action in other creaturely realities may have in relationship to Scripture.

194. De Lubac (*Medieval Exegesis*, 2:93) assures us that "The matter of holy Scripture is the whole Christ, head and members."

God's use of scripture for self-communication 53

literary theory to explain Christ's self-mediation, de Lubac is able to bypass Vanhoozer's difficulty of relating God's past speaking action to God's present speaking action. Yet this emphasis on sacramental presence comes at a price, as de Lubac's lacks precision in specifying both the nature of the literal sense and God's use of it for self-mediation. De Lubac's difficulty arises in his lack of specification about the relationship between texts and event, and therefore in his lack of specification about the way in which God uses the literal sense of Scripture to structure Christian understanding of the mystery. Vanhoozer insists that because God uses the closed canon to regulate all subsequent interpretation of the mystery, some explanation of either God's inspiration of the human author or of divine authorship of the literal sense must be articulated. If what is "in the text" is what has been set apart by God as the normative and authoritative means to participating in spiritual reality, then attention must be given to God's past action codified in the canon. As we have seen, de Lubac never really provides a complete discussion of the role of the human authors, choosing instead to emphasize the ongoing aspect of inspiration in texts and readers.[195] Here Vanhoozer's emphasis on God's supervening upon the unique and varied speech-acts of the human authors articulates a better model for understanding just how they participate in the economy of redemption. The Scriptures are a diversity of texts of many genres written by numerous authors, and while they all form a unified witness to Christ, they are all called into the economy of redemption to communicate in a particular way about the Christian mystery. Vanhoozer's emphasis on a relatively clear and determinate plain canonical sense of Scripture does not undermine de Lubac's project, but simply provides conceptual tools with which to both regulate allegory and allow readers to more fruitfully encounter God's speaking action in the text. Were de Lubac to focuses more clearly on God's use of the literal, canonical sense of Scripture as God's specific structuring of Christian understanding about God, his project may look more like Vanhoozer's.

---

195. Williams (*Receiving the Bible in Faith*, 171) highlights this problem as he critiques de Lubac's understanding of the original authors: "As one magnifies the importance of the overall biblical gestalt as the object of God's intention and a primary medium of the Spirit, so the significance of what the human authors of individual books intended to convey diminishes. Their intention, as with any human effort, is part of the particular historical context that is now gone; it must pale to some degree when contrasted with an opportunity to discern the movement of the divine plan borne by the Spirit."

CHAPTER 2

Vanhoozer's Covenantal Ontology and de Lubac's Sacramental Ontology

Different Models of Christ's Self-Mediation in the Economy of Redemption

INTRODUCTION

In the last chapter we examined the way in which Vanhoozer and de Lubac both seek to show that God's use of Scripture is the foundational norm for all subsequent hermeneutical reflection. God's use of precisely this collection of texts for self-mediation to readers is what makes Scripture unique, and all rules for reading should be developed from this assumption. Vanhoozer's understanding of God's speaking action through a clear, determinate canonical sense of Scripture, and de Lubac's understanding of God's speaking action through a three-fold spiritual sense of Scripture both arise from the same desire to articulate God's present speaking action in Scripture as an invitation to readers to relationship with the triune Persons. The comparison of both projects in light of this theological starting-point has made it possible to identify the close similarities between Vanhoozer's canonical sense of Scripture and de Lubac's three-fold spiritual sense of Scripture, and to identify certain areas where each project could strengthen the other.

However, this comparison between Vanhoozer and de Lubac has also highlighted a more substantial difference between the two theologians: where Vanhoozer understands Christ's self-mediation primarily through speech-acts, de Lubac understands Christ's self-mediation primarily through sacramental signs. In order to better articulate God's use of Scripture in the economy of redemption, it will be necessary to examine the conceptual framework (ontology) by which each author understands the triune God's self-mediation to human beings. Here Vanhoozer's communicative or covenantal ontology will be compared with de Lubac's sacramental ontology in order to better articulate how God uses Scripture and to show the impact of ontology on scriptural interpretation.

Both Vanhoozer and de Lubac strongly resist what Heidegger called "ontotheology" (i.e., in reducing God to the highest link in the chain of being), yet they seek to overcome the problem in quite different ways.[1] Both begin with the assumption that only God can make God known, and that God has revealed himself in Jesus Christ. Yet from here, the projects differ. Vanhoozer begins with the assumption that the very possibility of revelation is dependent upon the sufficient perspicuity of that revelation. The very term *revelation* implies, for Vanhoozer, that God has revealed himself clearly enough to be understood. This leads Vanhoozer to argue that not only that revelation has occurred in history, but that this revelatory action in history must be disambiguated by God's revelatory speaking action so that the meaning of that action would become clear. God's revelatory words must always accompany God's revelatory action. This, for Vanhoozer, establishes Scriptures as the starting point for understanding God, as they are God's authorized explanation of God's action in history.

De Lubac, on the other hand, begins with an emphasis on the infinite nature of the Christian mystery. This mystery, which de Lubac describes as the whole drama of redemption (the triune God establishing relationship with human beings), is infinite, and although it is *reasonable*, it can never fully be grasped by human reason. As a result, de Lubac argues that while the Christian mystery is revealed fully in God's historical action in

---

1. See Vanhoozer, *Remythologizing Theology*, 8; and de Lubac, *The Discovery of God*, 11.

Christ, human understanding of and participation in this revealed mystery comes through sacramental signs which Christ uses to mediate the mystery. Christ, the incarnate Logos of God, uses the primary sacramental mediators of Scripture, church, and Eucharist to incorporate human beings into the mystery. The difference in emphasis between revelation as clear communication and revelation as participation in infinite mystery will cause Vanhoozer to focus on the intelligibility of revelation mediated through adequately clear, determinate speech-acts, while de Lubac will focus on the infinite character of revelation mediated through sacramental signs.

VANHOOZER'S COMMUNICATIVE/COVENANTAL ONTOLOGY AND GOD'S USE OF SCRIPTURE

In the first chapter we saw that the center of Vanhoozer's scriptural hermeneutics is what he calls the "Scripture Principle," the Christian preunderstanding or First Theology that the Bible is the Word of God. "Theology's first principle is God in communicative action," states Vanhoozer, and the "Scripture principle maintains that the Bible itself is ultimately a species of divine discourse."[2] It is as Vanhoozer provides a rich description of this Scripture principle that he develops his communicative ontology. Later in his career, Vanhoozer admits that his early work did not adequately show how "God is involved in the production and reception of the Bible in a way that is so qualitatively different that it makes of biblical interpretation a special case."[3] This early work failed

---

2. Vanhoozer (*The Drama of Doctrine*, 63–68) claims this is said to be held by the early church, and is grounded theologically in the concept of God's covenant communication. Vanhoozer (ibid., 205) claims "The church has traditionally acknowledged the Bible's self-attestation as the word of God. It follows that the various biblical texts are forms of divine discourse and should thus be counted as figuring among the divine repertoire of communicative action." Vanhoozer ("The Apostolic Discourse and Its Development," 197) argues that the practice of the church is the primary reason Scripture should be understood as God's word. There he claims, "Suffice it to say that the church has taken the apostolic discourse as authoritative precisely because it communicates the word of God."

3. See Vanhoozer's "Preface to the Tenth Anniversary Edition." Vanhoozer claims "I am as guilty as anyone of procrastinating in the prolegomenal fields. In *Is There a Meaning in this Text*, I tilled the textual ground with small conceptual tool (e.g., speech acts) and heavy hermeneutical equipment (e.g., Paul Ricoeur). I buttressed my hermeneutical approach by calling it 'theological,' but the appeal was too cavalier" (*Remythologizing Theology*, xiii).

Vanhoozer's covenantal ontology and de Lubac's sacramental ontology

to appreciate adequately the uniqueness of Scripture because it focused too much on human authorship and literary theory, and gave too little attention to God's use of Scripture in the economy of redemption. In his later work, *Remythologizing Theology* (2010), Vanhoozer moves beyond hermeneutics to develop an ontology of God as pure self-communicative action.[4] This development of a communicative ontology forms a turning-point in his hermeneutical method, as it allows Vanhoozer to begin his hermeneutical project specifically from an understanding of the triune God as being-in-communication and work out the implications of this doctrine of God for scriptural interpretation, rather than beginning with general hermeneutics and working toward theology proper. It is this location of Scripture in the doctrine of God which allows Vanhoozer to develop his argument for God's use of Scripture in the economy of redemption.

Reclaiming the Christian Claim that God Speaks

For Vanhoozer, affirming that God can and does speak is part of the essence of the Christian faith, and starting theology from God's self-communication rather than human experience is the only way to rightly talk about God.[5] Vanhoozer argues that the Christian faith depends on God's actually taking up human symbols and using them for communicative purposes. God's communicative acts, of course, are not necessarily equivocal to human speech acts, although for communication to take place God must use symbols which are able to effectively communicate.[6]

---

4. Vanhoozer (*Remythologizing Theology*, xiv) claims, "The recent interest in theological hermeneutics, together with the church's recovery of the practice of interpreting the Bible in the context of God's triune activity, welcome though these be, must be matched by an equal attention to the nature of the God of whose communicative activity the Bible is an ingredient."

5. Vanhoozer (ibid., 206) claims, "From the fact that God dialogues with human beings we may infer at the very least that he has the capacity to communicate. From the incarnation of the Word we may further conclude that God has the capacity to communicate *himself*. God's presence is thus in the first instance personal, agential, and communicative rather than merely spatial, substantive, or metaphysical."

6. Vanhoozer (ibid., 210) specifies, "It is not self-evident that 'employing vocal cords' is an essential element in speaking. . . . It is entirely possible that God could achieve fundamentally the same result by other means." Vanhoozer introduces the distinction between "*mode of action*" and the "*action done*" to show that God can perform the same action, although in a different way. Vanhoozer (ibid., 210–11) notes, "It is therefore legitimate to say 'God (literally) speaks' (because he performs

Vanhoozer defines communication as "interaction by means of mutually recognized signals," and "manipulation of symbols by one person to stimulate meaning in another person," or "social interaction through messages."[7] For God to act in the economy of redemption, God must be able to perform speech acts, i.e., to communicate and take up illocutionary stances in the public realm.[8] Vanhoozer suggests that, "A great deal of God's communicative work . . . involves language," and this kind of communicative action must be developed.[9]

To establish the primacy of God's speaking action for all understanding of God, Vanhoozer sets forth a "communicative ontology (i.e., a set of concepts with which to speak of God-in-communicative-action)" of the economy of redemption.[10] Vanhoozer is aware of contemporary tendency of postmodern readers to be suspicious of all systems of "ontology" and "metaphysics." Consequently, Vanhoozer suggests that the goal of his project is "not ontotheology but theo-ontology, not general but special (remythologized, biblically governed) metaphysics."[11] Ontotheology (a "unified system of thought that employs concepts such as Supreme Being or Unmoved Mover as conceptual stopgaps to prevent infinite metaphysical regress") must be expelled and replaced by "theo-ontology" ("*A 'theodramatic' metaphysics* [which] *provides a systematic account of*

communicative acts via words, which is what 'speaking' ordinarily means) even though 'speaks' is not being used univocally with regard to God and human beings (because the mode of God's speaking may be extraordinary)."

7. Ibid., 212.

8. Here Vanhoozer (ibid., 213) invites readers to "Consider the alternative" and recognize that if God does not "literally perform speech acts, we cannot say that God commands, blesses, promises, warns, etc." and the "whole history of Israel would be unintelligible." Vanhoozer (ibid., 210) heightens the intensity of this claim by arguing, "The stakes could not be higher: to the extent that one refuses to ascribe specific (communicative) acts to God's personal agency, one revises what the Bible and Christian faith are primarily about."

9. Ibid., 277.

10. Ibid., xv. Observing that recent theologians have said much about God's self-communication, Vanhoozer finds it surprising that very few have actually explained what self-communication means. Vanhoozer (ibid., xiii), claims, "Western theologians as diverse as Thomas Aquinas, John Owen, Karl Rahner, and Karl Barth freely employ the notions of communication and self-communication in the contexts of divine revelation and/or redemption, yet usually without explicit analysis. Finally, few theologians have made use of the available linguistic, philosophical, literary, and rhetorical resources conceptually to elaborate the nature of God's communicative action."

11. Ibid., 222.

the categories needed to describe what God has said and done to renew all things in Jesus Christ through the Holy Spirit.")[12] Ontotheology is "bad" metaphysics because it "imposes a system of categories on God without attending to God's own self-communication," and must be replaced by a "good" metaphysics of theo-ontology, which is a "descriptive metaphysics," which "derives its system of categories from the train of God's own communicative action (i.e., theodrama)."[13] Vanhoozer's goal, then, is to show that Scripture is God's "communicative agency," and hence to show that the texts of Scripture must be the foundation for a human understanding of all reality.[14]

Vanhoozer suggests that the way to respond to the problem of "ontotheology" is to "remythologize" theology. Remythologizing theology involves a shift in metaphysical focus from "motional causality" to "communicative agency."[15] This shift to communicative agency will eliminate the understanding of God based in motional causality as simply the highest being in a causal chain, and will instead stress that we know God through God's self-revelation, in the categories of "revelation, Incarnation, resurrection."[16] Consequently a communicative ontology would emphasize the "absolute distinction" between God and creatures and would describe the God/world/Scripture relationship in terms of an "economy of communication."[17] Metaphysics, in this model of communicative agency, would become simply "the attempt to reflect on subjects, human and divine" who are actively communicating themselves according to their being.[18]

Remythologizing theology requires that conceptual "categories are generated by (or, if borrowed from elsewhere, revised in light of) the divine self-presentation in the gospel of Jesus Christ and its canonical

---

12. Ibid., 8 and 222, respectively. "Ontotheology" is also defined by Vanhoozer as a "unified system" developed "from below" which projects God as the greatest Being in our conceptual schema. Ontotheology arises from "totalizing" metaphysics, the "underlying assumption that there is one set of categories, accessible to unaided human reason, which applies both to the world and to God, created and uncreated reality."

13. Ibid., 8n27.

14. Ibid., 24.

15. Ibid., 24–25.

16. Ibid., 222.

17. Ibid., 26.

18. Ibid., 222 and 25 respectively.

attestation."[19] While Vanhoozer recognizes that Christian theology cannot abandon a holistic system for understanding reality, he insists that such a holistic quest must start from God's self-revelation in Christ and Scripture rather than from some correlational system of truth.[20] Remythologizing theology means articulating just such an ontology that proceeds from God's self-communicative action rather than first configuring a metaphysics into which God and Scripture are placed.[21] Vanhoozer declares,

> [Remythologizing theology] is a way of viewing God, Scripture, and hermeneutics in terms of their mutual implications, all coordinated by the notion of communicative action: the triune God is the ultimate communicative agent of Scripture; Scripture is an element in the triune God's communicative action; interpretation is the way the church demonstrates her understanding of what God is saying and doing in and through Scripture by right theodramatic participation.[22]

The project of remythologizing theology can be best understood in contrast to the post-Enlightenment tendency to demythologize God's communicative acts.[23] Demythologizing is generally defined by Vanhoozer as "a strategy for translating biblical statements about God into existential statements about human being."[24] Vanhoozer uses Bultmann and Feuerbach as interlocutors in order to contrast his own project of

---

19. Ibid., 183.

20. Vanhoozer (ibid., 199) believes Barth was correct in his emphasis that any ontology of God must be based (*a posteriori*) on God's own self-revelation in Jesus Christ, and only from there move to philosophy. Yet Vanhoozer (ibid., 217) suggests that "faith that stops its search for understanding short of ontology risks falling back into mere mythologizing. By contrast, remythologizing renews and revitalizes . . . by letting Scripture serve as our primary interpretative framework."

21. When Vanhoozer (ibid., 7) suggests that Christians must "remythologize" theology, he is not speaking of the reinstitution of mythical language for Scripture, but of Aristotle's "mythos" or "emplotment," whereby God institutes "one overall plot, the story of God's self-presentation in the history of Israel and Jesus Christ," yet making this "unified self-presentation" clear to readers through the "many voices speaking in diverse (literary) registers."

22. Ibid., 30.

23. Vanhoozer (ibid.) claims that "*remythologizing is best defined in contrast to demythologizing as a type of first theology*" (emphasis his).

24. Ibid., 15.

remythologizing with their project of demythologizing.[25] Bultmann is described as a "soft" demythologizer because he insists that God still "encounters" the believer, in his/her "inner life," while Feuerbach is a "hard" demythologizer, in that everything said about God is merely the projection of the ideal self. Hence, "On [Feuerbach's] view, the secret of reading is authoring: what appears to be the creation of an author—meaning—is actually the invention (projection) of the reader."[26] It is this quality of projection (allowing existential concerns to dictate language about God), which remythologizing seeks to reverse.[27] On the contrary, Vanhoozer suggests that "remythologizing" theology supposes that we know God because God has first revealed himself to us (in Christ and Scripture), and thus becomes the "material principle at the heart of first theology (i.e., what must God be like if he is actually the speaking and acting agent depicted in the Bible?)."[28] All theology must start by attending to God's speaking action in Christ and Scripture, since remythologizing Scripture means *"taking Christ, together with the Spirit-breathed canon that the living Word commissions, as the chief means of God's self-presentation and communication."*[29]

Conceptual Tools: Post-Barthian Thomism

Vanhoozer has argued that metaphysics should not begin with a system of causality but by understanding God as Pure communicative action.[30]

---

25. Ibid., 16–20.

26. Ibid.

27. Vanhoozer's use of Feuerbach as paradigmatic demythologizer is not to associate contemporary revisionist theologians with Feuerbach as much as it is to apply a lesson learned from Feuerbach to contemporary theology: any speech about God that *starts from our* own experience rather than God's self-communication has the potential to lead us away from what God has, in fact, communicated about Godself. Vanhoozer is, then, highlighting the difference between two trajectories, the trajectory of demythologizing (represented by Feuerbach and Bultmann), and the trajectory of remythologizing (uncompleted by Barth, approached by Ricoeur, and advanced by Vanhoozer).

28. Ibid., 23.

29. Ibid., 29 (emphasis his).

30. Vanhoozer (ibid., 217) believes Aquinas was correct in his emphasis that "being is not a static substance but a dynamic, existential act," and that this revised ontology will call for a more modest metaphysics of God as Being-as-self-communicative-action that starts from God's self-revelation rather than God as First Cause, which starts

The use of speech-act theory as a philosophical tool allows Vanhoozer to draw God's speaking and God's acting very close together, as speech-act theory shows that persons really perform actions in the community of persons with their requests, promises, demands, etc. As God's action and God's speaking are brought conceptually close, Vanhoozer is able to develop a metaphysics that focuses on communication over causality.[31] This, Vanhoozer believes, will provide a conceptual framework for understanding the God/world relationship without proposing God as the first cause in a great causal chain. Instead, since "God renders his identity through his communicative action," God is to be understood first from his self-revelation to human beings primarily in Christ and secondarily in Scripture.[32] Vanhoozer's communicative ontology emerges as he brings Barth's emphasis on revelation together with a Thomistic understanding of communication into a unique and constructive proposal.

Vanhoozer insists that all Christian metaphysics and ontology begin with, and remain chastened by, revelation. Describing himself as a "post-Barthian Thomist," Vanhoozer follows a form of Aquinas's metaphysics combined with Barth's Christology.[33] Vanhoozer agrees with Aquinas's description of God's being as pure act. However, Vanhoozer wishes to emphasize that *communication* instead of *causality* is the proper starting point for metaphysics. In shifting emphasis from casuality to communication, Vanhoozer intends to "bring out a communicative sense to which the church has not sufficiently attended."[34] Vanhoozer begins by agreeing with Aquinas's claim that to be is to act, as well as W. Norris Clarke's claim that "Action is the self-revelation of being; every being, insofar as it is in act, is self-communicative."[35] This brings Barth and Aquinas very close, since Barth attempted to overcome an idea of God as perfect being by beginning with God as act. This initial correlation of God's being with God's action allows Vanhoozer to move from God's action to God's

---

from a system of philosophical logic.

31. Ibid., 28, thesis 3.
32. Ibid., 29, thesis 7.
33. Vanhoozer's claim to be a "post-Barthian Thomist" (ibid., 222), has taken its cue from Ricoeur's claim to be a "post-Hegelian Kantian" (see Ricoeur, "Biblical Hermeneutics").
34. Vanhoozer, *Remythologizing Theology*, 28 (see thesis 4 and n. 109, respectively). Vanhoozer stresses that he does not wish to entirely dismiss the notion of God as cause; rather, he wants to personalize the notion.
35. See ibid., 24–25, citing Clarke, *Explorations in Metaphysics*, 37.

Vanhoozer's covenantal ontology and de Lubac's sacramental ontology 63

self-communication. To be is to act and to act is to communicate. Following Clarke, Vanhoozer claims that "it is the very nature of real being... to pour over into action that is *self-revealing* and *self-communicative*."[36] Vanhoozer further follows Clarke's suggestion that "All action is communication, and all communication is action."[37] In other words, being-in-action always is being-in-communication.[38] As a result, for Vanhoozer, being-as-pure-act is being-as-pure-communicative-act. Once again utilizing the resources of speech-act theory, Vanhoozer suggests that God, both in essence and in personal relations, is communicative. Vanhoozer claims that,

> God is the communicator, communication, and communicatedness. The triune God is the agent, act, and effect of his own self-communication. As Voice, the Father is the speaking subject who initiates the process of communication. As Word, the Son is what the Father speaks, the content of the communicative act. As the Breath that accompanies and conveys the Father's Word, the Spirit is the channel or medium of the communicative act as well as its efficacy.[39]

Vanhoozer suggests that Aquinas's metaphysical system can best be employed today after it has been chastened by Barth's priority of revelation over reason.[40] Remythologizing "has Thomistic ambitions yet is tempered by Barthian anxieties: we begin with faith in revealed truth and proceed to reason, sometimes with the aid of philosophical concepts."[41] Vanhoozer believes that his most important "Barthian anxi-

---

36. Vanhoozer, *Remythologizing Theology*, 224, citing Clarke, *The One and the Many*, 32.

37. Vanhoozer, *Remythologizing Theology*, 224, citing Clarke, *Explorations in Metaphysics*, 9. Vanhoozer (*Remythologizing Theology*, 225) cites Clarke (*Explorations in Metaphysics*, 215) who claims that being as "intrinsically self-communicative" is "one of the few great fundamental insights in the history of metaphysics."

38. Vanhoozer, *Remythologizing Theology*, 225. Human persons are the best example of this, because persons are most authentically "being" as they are self-communicative. Humans only analogously reflect the personhood of God. Thus Vanhoozer claims, "God is God in large part because his communicative capacity far outstrips that of humans. In particular, God has the ability to 'communicate' his own life to others, through Word and Spirit, thereby establishing communion and fulfilling his word" (207).

39. Ibid., 261.

40. Ibid., 222.

41. Ibid.

ety" is Barth's insistence on Christology as the starting point for God's self-communication.[42] This "post-Barthian Thomism," then, agrees with Barth's "conviction that any ontology of the divine must be *a posteriori* (after the fact or event of Jesus)" and from Aquinas's "notion that being is not a static substance but a dynamic, existential act."[43] Consequently, Vanhoozer will develop a creative combination of both Aquinas's conception of God as pure act and Barth's focus on God's self-communication. Vanhoozer sees his own project as an advancement of "Barth's unfinished task of rethinking God's being on the basis of his revelation in 'word' and 'act.'"[44] The way to finish Barth's project, Vanhoozer suggests, is to "includ[e] other instances of divine speaking and acting alongside the Incarnation."[45] Practically, this means including Scripture in the economy of God's speaking and acting. The contents of the biblical texts, as well as the diverse forms in which they are recorded, ought to be seen as "part of a prior economy of divine self-projection."[46] As a result, to remythologize theology is "to put our discourse of *what is* under the discipline of the biblical accounts of God's speaking and acting."[47] Remythologizing means "rendering explicit the implicit 'metaphysics' of the biblical *mythos*. Its aim is to let the biblical texts govern one's understanding of being, not to deploy an independently derived concept of being to govern

---

42. As Vanhoozer (ibid., 222) sees it, the key difference between Aquinas and Barth is that "Aquinas asks what God the creator must be given the existence of creation while Barth asks what God must be given the history of Jesus Christ." The other noted difference is that "Aquinas employs a single conceptual scheme, that of Aristotle, while Barth is more eclectic" (ibid).

43. Ibid., 217.

44. Ibid., 31.

45. Ibid., 207. Vanhoozer feels "Barth unnecessarily delimits the set of divine communicative acts by making divine ontology a function of the incarnate life of Jesus alone." On Barth's account, since God is God's self-revelation, Scripture cannot be considered God's self-communication, lest God be identified with Scripture (bibliolatry). Vanhoozer (ibid., 211) responds that Barth, in equating revelation only with the event of Jesus Christ, may "overlook other things that speakers do with their words. . . . It is not clear on Barth's account how God can do the things the Bible depicts him as doing (i.e., commanding, warning, promising) if he is not the agent of properly verbal communicative acts as well as of the revelatory act of incarnation." Speech act theory, then, provides Vanhoozer with resources to describe God as a properly speaking agent, and one who is able to speak in Scripture.

46. Ibid., 197.

47. Ibid., 182.

one's reading of the biblical texts."[48] For Vanhoozer, the whole trajectory of contemporary revisionist theology provides a wrong direction for theology because revisionist theologians begin from human experience.[49] Through Barth and Aquinas, Vanhoozer develops the conceptual means to insure that theology "is ultimately governed by the biblical accounts of God's self-presentation in speech and act."[50]

Divine Action as Communication: God's Speech in Christ and Scripture

Having established the conceptual scaffolding for his communicative ontology, Vanhoozer employs it to show Scripture's place in the economy of redemption. Here Vanhoozer seeks to show that Scripture is ultimately more a species of the economic triune communicative action than a product of human discourse. While the focal point of the economy of redemption "consists in what God has done and is doing in Christ, the Scriptures, as testimony to this act, are themselves caught up in it and become a means for God for building up his church in Christ through the power of the Spirit."[51] Clearly Vanhoozer's program of remythologizing aims at establishing the theological priority of Scripture over church, sacraments, etc. in the economy of redemption. Vanhoozer's argument for God's use of Scripture based on God's communicative action is developed in several moves which are organized here in logical (if not sequential) progression.

First, God is author of all things. Vanhoozer defines authorship very broadly as "a convenient shorthand for the notion of verbal

---

48. Ibid., 183.

49. Vanhoozer (*Remythologizing Theology*, 182) draws a dividing line between those theologians who (wrongly) "seek to speak of God on the basis of nature" and human experience, and those theologians who (rightly) "believe that speaking well of God is ultimately possible only on the basis of God's own communication." Vanhoozer includes nearly everyone else on the revisionist trajectory as those who begin their discussion of God based in nature rather than God's self-revelation, including Elizabeth Johnson, David Tracy, Jurgen Moltmann, Wolfhart Pannenberg, and Robert Jensen.

50. Ibid., 223. Vanhoozer describes the choice before theologians in his familiar either/or construal: "Should theologians derive their understanding of *actus* from God's communicative action or should they understand God's communicative action against the background of an independently derived general conception of being-in-act? Put differently: is theology merely a regional instance of a general metaphysic?" (220).

51. Vanhoozer, *The Drama of Doctrine*, 418.

communicative action" in general, although the term "verbal" is much broader than simply human words when applied to God.[52] Consequently, when applied to God, "'Authoring' covers what God does as creator, reconciler, redeemer, and perfecter, and so serves as a metaphor for the economic Trinity as well: *the Father 'authors' in Christ through the Spirit.*"[53] God is even the "author" of God's own Being.[54] The advantage of attributing authorship to God, Vanhoozer suggests, is that it provides a way of explaining "God's relation to the world, and to Scripture, in terms of an 'economy of communication,'" which, in turn, "enables us to better conceive . . . the absolute distinction between Creator and creation."[55] Vanhoozer uses the analogy of being to relate human scriptural statements about God to the nature of God himself, allowing Vanhoozer to make a distinction between "literal" and "univocal" speech. The claim that God speaks is a "literal," although not "univocal," claim.[56] To literally say God speaks or acts is to affirm that God does not simply do so "figuratively."[57] But this does not limit God to speaking or acting in exactly the same way humans speak or act. In its broadest sense, "To communicate is to 'share' or 'make common.'"[58] This means that God can communicate or author in a number of ways that are only analogously speech-acts. For God to speak is for God to "bring about a change . . . by an act of will, decision, or intention."[59] For example, God can "'communicate' his own life to others."[60] The economy of redemption, then, is best called an economy of communication, and God's causal communicative action may best be described as authorship.[61] Authorship, then, serves as a broad general description for God's self-communicating action.

---

52. Ibid., xiii.
53. Ibid., 26.
54. Ibid., 206.
55. Ibid., 26.
56. Ibid., 210–11.
57. Ibid., 211n118.
58. Ibid., 206.

59. Ibid., 210. Notice the broad range of communication in Vanhoozer's claim about God's authoring action: "Trinitarian authorship also proves helpful in conceiving divine providence in terms of God's sustaining, cooperating with, and governing the world through, the properly *communicative* means of Word and Spirit" (28).

60. Ibid., 207.
61. Vanhoozer (ibid., xiii) refers especially to Aquinas, Rahner, and Barth.

Second, God's revelatory action must be explained by speaking action. Authorship, as it has been described up to this point, can cover nearly all God's actions in the economy of redemption. Yet while all God's actions may be described as communication, not all God's actions can be described as revelation. Since Vanhoozer has argued that what is known about God is known on the basis of God's revelation, Vanhoozer must distinguish God's revelatory activity from God's other analogous communicative acts. Employing his terminology of God's literal yet analogical speaking action, Vanhoozer first argues that the revelation of the Word in the person of Jesus Christ is God's speech-act. "Jesus Christ, as God's self-revelation, is God's literal (though accommodated) speech, a communication that indirectly—because through a human form—communicates God's being."[62] Yet this is still analogous speech, and at this point Vanhoozer makes another crucial step. Vanhoozer argues that God's revelatory action in the world must be backed up by explanatory communication, or else it would remain too ambiguous to be useful. Vanhoozer argues that, "Without an event of divine speaking, we are unable to say either *who* is acting or *what* this person is up to: 'behavior unaccompanied by speech remains inherently ambiguous.'"[63] Crucial acts of God in redemptive history, such as the Exodus event, would remain ambiguous, were it not for God's speech-act which accompanied it.[64] Even the "event of Jesus Christ is ultimately unintelligible apart from other speech acts—namely those of the prophets and apostles."[65] It is clear at this point that Vanhoozer's argument has moved from a general theory of authorship as God's action toward all creation to a more specific application of analogous speech-acts in revelation to a very specific claim that God can, and must, use human words to communicate. God's revelatory acts in history will be disambiguated with God's subsequent use of human words to explain those acts. When God acts in a decisive (revelatory) way, God will also provide a speech act (Scripture) to explain the action.

Third, God gives Scripture an active communicative role in the economy of redemption. At this point, Vanhoozer's general ontology of

---

62. Ibid., 195.

63. Ibid., 209. Vanhoozer is citing Mitchell, "Revelation Revisited," 182. See also Vanhoozer's claim (*Remythologizing Theology*, 213) "Only speech disambiguates behavior. Only God's word disambiguates God's deed."

64. Vanhoozer, *Remythologizing Theology*, 214.

65. Ibid., 209. (Notice that Vanhoozer does not mention tradition as a way of making the event of Christ intelligible.)

authorship has been narrowed to a much more specific claim that God's revelatory action will be disambiguated by God's use of human words. Yet Vanhoozer still must show why the Scriptures should be considered God's own speaking which disambiguates revelation rather than simply a collection of human speech-acts which witness to divine revelation. Vanhoozer furthers his argument from Speech-act theory that God can and does speak with an argument about God's "missional" use of Scripture. Scripture "is a rule and criterion . . . precisely because of its place in the divine economy of redemption."[66]

Vanhoozer locates Scripture in the economy of redemption by comparing the mission of Scripture to the economic missions of Son and Spirit. God exists as self-communicative act, eternally communicating among the Persons of the immanent Trinity. Yet, Vanhoozer claims, "When directed *ad extra*, the communicative action of God is perhaps better termed *mission*. Hence the economy of communication is ultimately missional: divine communicative action involves the 'sendings' (*missio*) of Son and Spirit."[67] In this context, Vanhoozer proposes that Scripture has itself been given a mission for redemption analogous to the missions of the triune Persons, and that "*Scripture's mission is tied up with the Trinitarian missions of the Son and Spirit.*"[68] Vanhoozer states that "Scripture, like the Son, is sent on a mission," and draws an "*analogia missio*" between God's use of a human being in Christ (incarnation) and God's use of the texts of Scripture ("inscripturation") based on three similarities: "(1) both are species of triune communicative action—embodied in the case of Jesus, verbalized in the case of Scripture;" (2) both aim to draw communicants into the new covenant community; and (3) both are accompanied by the Spirit and require the Spirit in order to complete their respective missions."[69]

It is the Spirit's very mission to extend Christ's communicative action through the use of Scripture.[70] Through the Spirit's sanctifying action,

---

66. Vanhoozer, *The Drama of Doctrine*, 147.

67. Ibid., 261.

68. Ibid., 60. Vanhoozer argues that the missions of Word and Spirit must be closely connected because "Word without Spirit is powerless; Spirit without Word is directionless. . . . The canon is the Spirit's chosen means to mediate the covenant and foster the communion that obtains between Christ and the church" (199).

69. Ibid., 70.

70. Vanhoozer (ibid., 228) claims that the "Spirit's sanctifying work in producing Scripture is thus the completion and perfection of Jesus' communicative action; it is in

the "books that make up the Bible, and the very words that make up the various books, are taken up into the economy of divine communicative action."[71] Scripture exists, then, as communicative act sent on an economic mission through which the Word and Spirit carry out their respective missions today. As a result, "Scripture does not simply recount action; it is part of the action . . . it contributes to the realization of God's purposes for the world. . . . Scripture is thus a collection of statements—and promises, commands, warnings, and so on—all on their respective missions."[72]

Fourth, God uses Scripture as a covenant document to the church. In the end, it is the theological concept of covenant which does most of the heavy lifting in establishing Scripture as God's unified speech-act.[73] While Vanhoozer has used speech-act theory to show how God can be considered a speaker and author, Vanhoozer realizes that he needs a distinctly theological argument, not simply a philosophical construct, to show that the Scriptures should be granted authority as God's speech act (the whole point of remythologizing, after all, is to start with God's self-communication!). Vanhoozer "remythologizes" his own argument as he unites the theological concept of covenant with speech-act theory to show that a covenant is a specific kind of speech act.[74] Vanhoozer's basic claim is that "*the Bible is a divine communicative act that exists for the sake of covenantal relations.*"[75] Describing Scripture as God's covenant document leads to several significant conclusions for Vanhoozer.

---

this way that the Spirit is the literary executor, as it were, of the word of Jesus Christ."

71. Ibid., 228.

72. Ibid.

73. Vanhoozer's use of covenant in his later work is significantly different from his earlier construction. In his early work, Vanhoozer argued that precisely because all language is covenantal, Scripture imposes a demand on its readers to read to understand the intentions of its human authors. Now, Vanhoozer significantly softens this argument, claiming, "While discourse in general creates a quasi-covenantal situation inasmuch as speakers and hearers assume certain obligations in the process of communicating, this is particularly the case when the discourse is *explicitly* covenantal" (ibid., 67). While language does create a structure of rights and obligations, it is precisely because God has authored Scripture for use as the covenant document in the economy of redemption that Scripture has authority in the church.

74. Vanhoozer (ibid., 64) appeals to Austin, who "listed 'making a covenant' as one of the things we do with words: 'Our word is our bond.'" (See Austin, *How to Do Things with Words*, 10.)

75. Ibid., 68.

First, the concept of covenant allows Vanhoozer to show that Scripture is ultimately one unified speech-act. If Scripture is a document of covenant, God must be the primary speaker, and the words must be considered to be God's own communication.[76] The Christian must enter the interpretive process understanding that "inspired Scripture" is "the discourse therefore of *one single speaker* . . . a *single body* of discourse, which serves the consistent purpose of a single authoritative agent."[77] Although God "employs a plurality of human voices to communicate what he was doing in Christ to reconcile the world to himself, the canonical Scriptures must be understood to be a unified speech act of God."[78] Readers must understand the diverse scriptural speech-acts as a "rainbow of divine communicative acts" presented through the various genres of Scripture, unified in one covenantal speech-act, and sent on a mission to the church.[79]

Second, the concept of covenant gives Vanhoozer his most substantive reason to equate Scripture with revelation. When establishing covenant, God always "takes the communicative initiative to enter into covenantal relation," and "this covenant-making involves both oral and written communicative acts on God's part."[80] Vanhoozer argues that God enters into real obligation to humanity through Scripture, and that this equates Scripture with revelation.[81] Real obligation between God and hu-

---

76. In Vanhoozer's early work he suggested that "genre . . . describes the illocutionary act *at the level of the whole*, placing the parts within an overall unity that serves a meaningful purpose. It follows that genre is the key to interpreting communicative action" (Vanhoozer, *Is There a Meaning in This Text?*, 341). Vanhoozer suggests in his later work that the whole canon operates something like a "macrogenre," which he calls "divine address" or "theodrama," as descriptions that allow for the existence of other genres within them. In his later work Vanhoozer retains this argument and enriches it with an understanding of God's use of Scripture as mission.

77. Vanhoozer, *The Drama of Doctrine*, 231.

78. Vanhoozer, *Remythologizing Theology*, 26.

79. Vanhoozer, "First Theology," 35.

80. Vanhoozer, *Remythologizing Theology*, 263.

81. Vanhoozer's discussion of the canon as God's communicative covenant document takes place in dialogue with Barth, who had argued that Scripture cannot be God's word because God's freedom cannot be tied to human language. Vanhoozer responds that if Barth had started from the assumption that the Bible is the document preserving God's covenant with human beings, Barth would likely not have difficulty accepting that God could, in freedom, enter into obligation with human beings by extending God's self-communication to the Bible. Vanhoozer's argument (ibid., 136–40) against Barth runs like this: First, God can enter a covenant only by communicative

man beings occurs because "[t]o covenant is to enter into a personal relationship structured by divine promises to behave in certain ways and to do certain things."[82] In every covenant recorded in Scripture, Vanhoozer claims, "The words . . . were the communicative medium by which the people approached God and vice versa, so much so that to engage the words of Scripture is to engage God in communicative action."[83] Scripture, then, cannot be considered simply a witness to revelation used by God, but must itself be revelation as it is the document by which God communicates covenant and thereby enters into real obligation with human beings.

Implications of a Communicative Ontology

Vanhoozer's later work begins with a doctrine of God as pure communicative act and builds an argument for the role of Scripture in the economy of redemption, which is based on a more general communicative ontology. Specifically, Scripture plays a role of covenant document sent on a mission, which extends the missions of Son and Spirit by disambiguating God's revelatory action in history. In Vanhoozer's communicative ontology, several emphases should be noted which will be brought into dialogue with de Lubac.

First, Vanhoozer's communicative ontology places a priority on closed, determinate speech-acts over other forms of communicative action. Although Vanhoozer initially describes God's communicative action as a general description for all God's acts toward creatures, Vanhoozer's subsequent claim that revelatory actions must be accompanied by God's speaking action shows a practical tendency to view God's revelatory action in history as incomplete without speech-acts. This will be better

---

action (136). Second, the canon is the documentation of these covenantal initiatives, it "'documents' our covenantal privileges and responsibilities" (137). Third, the canon was completed because the new covenant needed a written, binding witness (138). Fourth, God still ministers the covenant today through the Scriptures (139). Fifth, the canon constitutes the community with whom God has committed Godself to covenant relationship (140). These five points together build a strong case that God indeed could bind his freedom to human communicative acts in Scripture.

82. Ibid., 136.

83. Ibid., 263. Vanhoozer ("Triune Discourse," 65) claims, "The Bible is the God-ordained means of communicating the terms and the reality of the covenant whose content is Jesus Christ. The Son is both the promise of God and the obedient response of humanity."

seen in contrast to de Lubac, who gives conceptual priority for the events of salvation history over the textual record of those events. Vanhoozer's claim that only verbal speech-acts disambiguate revelatory action provides a foundation for his identification of Scripture with revelation.

Second, Vanhoozer's emphasis on clear and determinate speech-acts moves his project quickly (perhaps a bit too quickly) from a communicative ontology to a covenantal ontology. Vanhoozer's communicative ontology, taken by itself, is a broad proposal which shows how God incorporates created realities into the economy of redemption, and it thereby possesses conceptual resources for articulating God's self-mediation in a plurality of forms (sacraments, the church, etc.). For example, within the schema of a communicative ontology, Vanhoozer has claimed that because "The *analogia communication* need not always be verbal," the church "participates in and continues Jesus' communicative actions through the preaching of the word and the administration of the sacraments."[84] Furthermore, Vanhoozer specifically describes sacraments as "communicative actions, less speech-acts than acts that speak, but acts that communicate all the same."[85] On this broad account of communicative ontology, God communicates in Scripture, sacraments and the church in a way that is very close to the account presented in de Lubac's sacramental ontology. Practically, however, Vanhoozer's more specific covenantal ontology often takes priority over his more general communicative ontology. It is telling that Vanhoozer, in dialogue with Hans Boersma about the Nouvelle theologians, specifically calls his own ontology "covenantal" rather than "communicative."[86] It is this move from a communicative ontology to a covenantal ontology which makes Scripture qualitatively distinct as it alone is associated with revelation. This focus on the unique, covenantal role of Scripture, unfortunately, tends to close off discussions of God's use of other creaturely realities such as church and sacraments for the communication of God's speech acts. Specifically, if God could supervene the over the human speech-acts of Scripture, it would seem that He could do so in the creeds and conciliar pronouncements of the church as well. And if God could communicate

---

84. Vanhoozer, *The Drama of Doctrine*, 74. Vanhoozer claims that "baptism and the Lord's Supper are means of grace precisely because they are able to draw us into the pattern of Jesus' own communicative action" (75). How the sacraments exercise this causality is never discussed.

85. Ibid.

86. See Vanhoozer, "Ascending the Mountain," 781–803.

self-presence to readers by means of Scripture, it would seem that God could do so through sacraments as well. It is unclear, then, on Vanhoozer's account, why doctrinal statements made by the church could not also be incorporated into the economy of communication and themselves seen as God's speech-acts, even if they are not part of Scripture as covenant document. It is possible to affirm with Vanhoozer that "[i]n attending closely to Scripture we not only read about God but confront God in one mode of his self-presentation" without denying that in the church and Eucharist we also encounter God in other modes of self-presentation.[87] There appears to be no necessary reason why Vanhoozer's more specific covenantal ontology should lead to the neglect of God's communicative action in other created realities. De Lubac's construction of a sacramental ontology in which Scripture, church, and Eucharist play mutually constitutive roles in the economy will bring this difficulty into clearer focus.

DE LUBAC'S SACRAMENTAL ONTOLOGY AND GOD'S USE OF SCRIPTURE

In the last chapter we saw that the center of de Lubac's scriptural hermeneutics is the claim that Christ is both subject and object of Scripture, the one who unifies the covenant of promise (Old Testament) and the covenant of fulfillment (New Testament), and the one who mediates himself to the church by means of Scripture. Consequently, for de Lubac, the spiritual sense of Scripture is equivalent to Christ's self-communicative action. This chapter will discuss de Lubac's sacramental ontology, which provides the conceptual scaffolding for understanding how Christ uses Scripture for self-mediation to the church. This section will explore the way in which the infinite mystery of God, revealed in Christ, is mediated to human beings through sacramental signs.

Reclaiming a Christian Sense of Revealed Mystery

Central to de Lubac's hermeneutical project is the belief that the object of Christian faith is a unified "mystery" to which believers ascend, but never fully grasp. De Lubac, like Vanhoozer, builds his ontology in a

---

87. Vanhoozer, *The Drama of Doctrine*, 189. See also Vanhoozer, "*The canon is that field of dialogical action wherein the church not only reads about but is confronted by God himself in communicative presence and action*" (229, emphasis his).

way that shuns what Heidegger called "onto-theology" (i.e., making God merely the highest link in the causal chain).[88] Yet where Vanhoozer begins his ontology with God's communicative action in Christ and Scripture, de Lubac begins with the paradoxical understanding of the human being in relation to Mystery, which de Lubac calls the "mystery of the supernatural."[89] On de Lubac's account, the human being exists in a state of paradox that arises from being both a human animal and being created in the image of God. God is always already and inescapably implicitly present to and sensed by the human being, as the "divine operation constitutes the very center of man."[90] This implicit knowledge of God is described by de Lubac as "an 'image', an 'imprint', a 'seal,'" or the "mark of God" upon human beings.[91] This inescapable natural desire for God gives rise to at once a recognition and suppression of God. Humans implicitly recognize God, yet, because they cannot attain to God by their own reason, they simultaneously desire to suppress the idea of God. De Lubac claims, "It is only natural that the idea of God should be, at one and the same time, ready to emerge and yet menaced with suffocation; for mankind—made in the image of God, though sinful—while destined to grope its way slowly up, is nevertheless obsessed from the first moment of its awakening by a call from above."[92] Humans reduce this paradox either by denying the existence of God, or by constructing onto-theological systems of being that will reduce God to human apprehension.

For de Lubac, the Christian mystery is a reality so great that it can be participated in but can never be comprehended. De Lubac argues that this mystery, "Not having been conceived or formed by us, can never be mastered by us. Truly, we never possess it; it is it which possesses us.

---

88. See de Lubac, *The Discovery of God*, 11. De Lubac specifically claims, "God is not the first link in the chain of being" (42). Interestingly, de Lubac uses Xenophanes and Moses where Vanhoozer uses Feuerbach and Barth in order to make the same argument: humans either begin with experience and build an understanding of God as the ideal image of themselves, or they begin with God's self-revelation and participate in the infinite mystery of triune relationship (41).

89. For a good overview of the relationship between nature and the supernatural for de Lubac and the consequences this has for his whole theological project, see Milbank, "Henri de Lubac," 167–84. See also ibid., xxxiv, where de Lubac argues that "all the ideas that bear upon the reality of our being in relation to God" are paradoxical.

90. De Lubac, *The Discovery of God*, 16.

91. Ibid., 13.

92. Ibid., 25. As Davis ("The Call of Grace," 187) puts it, the paradox is that "God's call is only heard in response to it since the call founds the possibility of response."

We do not measure it; we are measured by it."[93] This understanding of mystery is influenced by the Christian philosopher Maurice Blondel who made a careful distinction between an *enigma*, an "impasse, a moment of confusion, a stumbling block to thought," which ought to be but has not yet been solved, and a *mystery*, which "by contrast, is not something that eludes but something to be found and entered into; it does not describe the state of knowledge at the end of data but rather the state of being confronted by Truth."[94] The scientific and philosophical disciplines are structured to solve enigmas, yet they do not possess the right tools for approaching mystery. Blondel had explained that philosophy could take a person to the point of encounter with the very mystery of existence, yet it could not bring about that encounter.[95] Blondel claims,

> We will use this word "mystery" in order to signify a revealed truth that the human spirit, left to its own resources, would not have been able to discover and identify with certainty. [It is] a secret that, even once revealed, remains impenetrable in its depth. Yet, it is not without useful significance, illuminating and profitable for us. [It is] a speculative and practical teaching which, in this *clair-obscur* moment where faith and reason have to cooperate, allows us to know and achieve our true and entire destiny.[96]

Mystery is infinitely beyond human apprehension, yet it is (paradoxically) inscribed inescapably on every human being. It is unavoidable to the rational mind, yet it remains out of reach of the rational mind without the revelation of Jesus Christ.

Thus far in the discussion, it appears that two mysteries can be discerned in de Lubac's work. On the one hand, the mystery is often described as the triune God which infinitely surpasses our understanding. On the other hand, the mystery is sometimes described as the existential

93. Ibid.

94. English, *The Possibility of Chrisian Philosophy*, 64. Blondel was perhaps the most influential philosophical influence on de Lubac, as Blondel's proposal for a distinctly Christian philosophy sets forth many of the distinctive features de Lubac finds central to his own hermeneutical project.

95. For example, Blondel ends his doctoral thesis by claiming, "There is no middle ground or neutrality: not to do as if it were true, is to do as if it were false. . . . But philosophy can go no further, nor can it say, in its own name alone, whether it be or not" (*Action*, 466).

96. Blondel, *La philosophie*, 1:14, cited in English, *The Possibility of Chrisian Philosophy*, 65.

reality of the supernatural penetrating the natural realm, constituting human beings with a natural desire for God. Yet these two mysteries are really one mystery, the union of the triune God with human beings, or, as de Lubac calls it, the "Whole of the redemptive Action."[97] This infinite and unified mystery is revealed completely in Jesus Christ and can only be explicitly known through revelation.

Yet although the mystery is ultimately one reality, human beings cannot understand infinite mystery as a unified whole, and consequently the revelation of the mystery must be mediated to human beings in various aspects. This means that although the mystery was revealed fully in Jesus Christ, is necessarily expressed in its various aspects, primarily through sacramental signs and always through paradoxical truths. De Lubac insists that it is only by concession (a positive one, to be sure), that the believer separates those different aspects.[98] In a key paragraph, de Lubac claims,

> Under its form of action and under its form of revelation, as reality and as the object of faith, this unique and total Thing carries one and the same name in Scripture and in Christian Tradition: it is *mystery*. It is already a first abstraction, therefore, to separate completely the gift and the revelation of the gift, the redemptive action and the knowledge of redemption, the mystery as act and the mystery as proposed to faith. It is a second abstraction to separate from this total revelation or this "Whole of Dogma" certain particular truths, enunciated in separate propositions, which will concern respectively the Trinity, the incarnate Word, baptism, grace, and so on. Legitimate and necessary abstractions, we repeat—for the mind can only preserve the total truth by actively exercising itself on it and according to its own laws.[99]

It was a gracious concession by God to allow the whole mystery, revealed in Jesus Christ, to be mediated to human beings in various aspects. These various aspects, however, will always appear paradoxical, as

---

97. De Lubac, "The Problem of the Development of Dogma," 274.

98. Ibid. Consequently the various expressions of the mystery are parts of the singular mystery. De Lubac (*The Splendor of the Church*, 16) claims, "The Christian mystery, which is the object or content of faith, is in itself one. It offers itself for our adherence, under the multiplicity of the formulae which have accumulated with the centuries, as the one total reality, which these formulae 'enclose on all sides, without ever exhausting it or dividing it.'"

99. De Lubac, "The Problem of the Development of Dogma," 275.

they will always remain partial expressions of a mystery beyond comprehension.[100] Jesus Christ is the ultimate paradox, as "God has become for us . . . a mystery. . . . [I]n Christ God has become the Being who in his inner life as in his free designs has consented to become an object of our knowledge."[101] Consequently, theology will always be fundamentally paradoxical, as it seeks to speak about the supreme paradox, the incarnation of the mystery in the person of Jesus Christ. De Lubac claims in *Catholicism*,

> The whole of dogma is thus but a series of paradoxes, disconcerting to natural reason and requiring not an impossible proof but reflective justification. For if the mind must submit to what is incomprehensible, it cannot admit what is unintelligible, and it is not enough for it to seek refuge in an "absence of contradiction" by an absence of thought. It finds stimulation, then, in its very submission. Despite its natural laziness it is almost obliged to delve beneath these superficial contradictions and to penetrate into those deeper regions where what was hitherto a stumbling-block becomes darkness visible.[102]

The preservation of paradox in theology is what keeps human beings confronted and confounded by the mystery which has been revealed in Jesus Christ. Paradox appears because the mystery to which both (seemingly incompatible) sides of the paradox point is so great that two seemingly incompatible assertions may be considered true at the same time.[103] Since all truths about mystery (i.e., all scriptural assertions, doctrine, etc.) are paradoxical in nature, the natural human tendency is to reduce it to what can be understood. This tendency arises from a desire to resolve and master, rather than embrace and participate in mystery, yet

---

100. For de Lubac, paradox refers to the very structure of reality, so that "Paradoxes: the word specifies, above all, then, things themselves, not the way of saying them" (*The Church*, 62). D'Ambrosio (*Traditional Hermeneutic*, 63) claims, "The great methodological sin for de Lubac is one-sidedness," which would eliminate one side of tensions between nature and the supernatural, and hence creation and redemption, etc.

101. De Lubac, *The Church*, 14.

102. De Lubac, *Catholicism*, 182.

103. One example of this may be the supposed dilemma of God's sovereignty and human freewill. This is a paradox (as it seemingly cannot be reconciled), yet is not irrational. De Lubac's own example (*Paradoxes of Faith*, 12) is purgatory, where the soul is suffering yet joyful. The supreme paradox of the Christian faith is the incarnation (see ibid., 8 and 10). As we will see in the next chapter, the church is also a great paradox, as it is simultaneously holy and sinful.

such facile attempts at resolution reduce theology to bare propositionalism, fundamentalism, and ultimately heresy.[104] Consequently, de Lubac says, "Paradox is the search or wait for synthesis. It is the provisional expression of a view which remains incomplete, but whose orientation is ever toward fullness."[105] Paradoxes "do not sin against logic, laws remain inviolable: but they escape its domain."[106] Instead, theology's paradoxical structure must remain unresolved because it points to a mystery (the triune life) in which the paradox is finally reconciled.[107]

It is this emphasis on the infinite character of the Christian mystery, a singular reality given through revelation and approached through participation without ever being fully comprehended by reason, which leads de Lubac to develop his sacramental ontology. De Lubac argues that mystery must always be mediated in its various aspects through God's use of sacramental structures. De Lubac points out that the Latin word "sacrament" really means "mystery," and hence that visible things can be given a sacramental role in mediating the mystery.[108] As a result, de Lubac will suggest that all Christian realities used by God have a fundamentally sacramental structure, so that an intrinsic relationship exists between the visible sign and disclosure of the mystery.

On de Lubac's account, God has given Scripture the role of sacramentally mediating the revelation of Christ to readers so that they may understand and participate in the Christian mystery. Scripture "contains all revelation" and is an indispensable means by which human beings encounter mystery.[109] Yet because Scripture mediates mystery, it is not

---

104. See de Lubac, *The Mystery of the Supernatural*, 175: "When it is between two truths of faith that the ultimate harmony cannot be seen, to choose one and reject the other then becomes heresy properly so called. We have a series of classic examples of this in the great Trinitarian and Christological heresies."

105. De Lubac, *Paradoxes of Faith*, 9.

106. Ibid., 12.

107. De Lubac (*A Brief Catechesis on Nature and Grace*, 72–73), claims, "For every statement of the faith . . . as regards us it necessarily consists of two views, the two apparent objects of which seem at first to be opposed to each other, not to say contradictory. These two views tend to coale at an infinite distance upon a single object, but the intuition of this unity escapes us."

108. De Lubac, *Medieval Exegesis*, 2:20. De Lubac (2:20–21) claims, "In Latin *mysterium* serves as the double for *sacramentum*. . . . The two words are often simply synonyms," and following Augustine de Lubac calls the *sacramentum* the "exterior component, the 'envelope.'"

109. De Lubac, *Medieval Exegesis*, 1:25.

simply a storehouse of facts about God's action in history culminating in Jesus Christ, but "Scripture . . . 'moves forward with those who read it'" and is "expandable—or penetrable—to an infinite degree" because it is the locus of God's self-mediation.[110] This means that the process of scriptural interpretation, while it must include close attention to Scripture's historical detail and textual structure, and while it must include systematization of Scripture's theological propositions about the nature and activity of God, cannot be limited such activities. Rather, on de Lubac's account, the principle purpose of scriptural interpretation is the incorporation of the reader into the story of Scripture where she finds her identity through participation in the infinite mystery of God revealed in Jesus Christ.[111]

Conceptual Tools: The Blondelian Synthesis

De Lubac's *Ressourcement* project proposes a middle way between what he saw as two reductive approaches to the interpretation of Scripture. On the one hand, neo-Thomists had reduced the mystery through "extrinsicism." Extrinsicism could be defined as use of the historical evidence of Scripture primarily as an instrument of apologetics to prove a spiritual reality, rather than seeking to understand the revelation brought about by, or contained in, the historical event.[112] In extrinsicism, historical events were regarded as merely extrinsic signs which point toward, but are not intrinsically related to, the spiritual reality that is assumed.[113] Theologians who tended toward extrinsicism tended to dismiss the historical develop-

---

110. De Lubac, *The Sources of Revelation*, 224.

111. See the section, "The Causal Role of Scripture in the Economy" in the next chapter for a deeper analysis of de Lubac's explanation of tropology as incorporation into the mystery.

112. D'Ambrosio (*Traditional Hermeneutic*, 6) claims that neo-Thomism, as de Lubac understood it, "has virtually no historical sense. In an existentialist world, it remains resolutely essentialist and objectivist, oblivious to human subjectivity. . . . Hardened by its Scholastic categories, neo-Thomism remains basically incomprehensible to most people and is thus incapable of offering them spiritual and doctrinal nourishment."

113. Blondel, "History and Dogma," 227 (emphasis his). As Blondel claims, in extrinsicism "historical facts are merely a vehicle, the interest of which is limited to the apologetic use which can be made of them." The result, Blondel claims, is that "the relation of the sign to the thing signified is extrinsic, the relation of the facts to the theology superimposed upon them is extrinsic, and extrinsic too is the link between our thought and our life and the truths proposed to us from outside" (228).

ment of the Scriptures, and tended to use historical evidence primarily for its apologetic value.[114] Typical in theological method at the time was what Voderholzer calls an "'instruction theory' of revelation," where Scripture was truncated to a set of propositions, a major proposition taken from Scripture and a minor proposition taken from philosophy, and through deductive reasoning certain true propositions could be made about the content of Christian faith.[115] This method, which saw Scripture primarily as a divinely revealed collection of propositions to be developed for the instruction of the church, necessarily downplayed the importance of God's revelation in history and hence disregarded the uniquely historical character of Christian revelation.

On the other hand, the liberal Protestant movement and some Catholic "modernists" had reduced the mystery through "historicism." Historicism could be defined as the reduction of the content of the Christian faith to only what is in principle observable to the secular historian. Whatever content of Christian faith cannot be demonstrated through the scientific methods of secular history was regarded suspiciously, since it was not able to be defended by historical evidence. The result was that Christian faith began to be viewed as only a historical or social reality, without any relationship to a transcendent reality. Eschatology was reduced to the more observable category of human progress, and God was often reduced to the ideal image of humanity.

In formulating a response to these reductive alternatives, de Lubac relies heavily on Blondel's proposal to re-identify the role of tradition as the "living synthesis" which unifies God's past action in history with the present Christian faith.[116] Blondel suggests that both extrinsicism and historicism, though completely opposed to each other, are really two sides of the same coin. Neither approach is useful for apprehending the

---

114. Ibid., 230. At first, Blondel claims, the use of higher criticism in Scripture was tolerated, since it appeared that the whole of the Scriptures remained a reliable historical testimony. Crisis occurred when criticism yielded so many difficulties that the authority of Scripture as a whole was questioned. For, if the dogmatic credibility of Scripture was based on the proofs that its historical facts yielded, historical criticism was seen to be able to topple the credibility of the whole Christian faith. De Lubac ("Apologetics and Theology," 94) adds that the result of this approach was inevitable, as theology was "defeated by better-armed opponents competing on their own terrain," as theologians attempted to establish the reasonableness of the Christian faith by means of secular sciences.

115. Voderholzer, "Dogma and History," 649–50.

116. See Blondel, "History and Dogma," 224–41.

reality of Christian faith, as both have disconnected spiritual reality from historical event.[117] Both errors were attempts to reduce the paradoxical nature of mystery to apprehension by human reason, as both reduce the revelatory action of God in history; extrinsicism by limiting God's revelatory action to the proof that can be adduced from it, and historicism by limiting God's revelatory action to the 'facts' which the secular historian can ascertain. To move beyond these reductions, Blondel makes a key distinction between *secular history*, the historian's construction of the past by whatever tools are available, and *real history*, the whole reality of life which always transcends what can be reconstructed by the secular historian.[118] Just as the fullness of lived reality in any society transcends the texts, customs and norms which the community finds to be expressions of its identity, so Christianity as a lived reality transcends the sum of all aspects of the Christian faith which can be observed. Blondel argues that because "the Christian facts do not, by common consent, suffice for Christian beliefs," limiting Christian faith to the conclusions of a historical discipline necessarily proscribes the reality of Christian faith.[119]

Blondel's argument is basically this: Just as the secular historian, simply by uncovering facts about a particular society, cannot expect to understand the fuller dimension of lived reality in that society, so much the more the secular historian cannot expect to understand the full spiritual reality of the Christian faith through a collection of 'facts' about the Christian faith alone. If every society has a lived reality (a "real history") that transcends the sum of its collectable facts, infinitely more does the Christian faith transcend what is observable through the facts collected by a secular historian, because the Christian community participates in the mystery of the triune God as a spiritual reality. Blondel suggests that this lived reality, the participation of the church in the triune mystery, is the heart of the Christian faith, and that consequently both those extrinsicists who view Scripture as a collection of propositions to be developed and promulgated by the church and those historicists who see the

117. Ibid., 244–64. Blondel's distinction between the "historic Christ" and the "real Christ" is aimed at showing that when historical event and spiritual reality are separated, the result is always a truncating of Christian faith.

118. Ibid., 237–38. Blondel claims further that when secular history replaces real history, "The historical facts will be given the role of reality itself; and an ontology, purely phenomenological in character, will be extracted from a methodology and a phenomenology" (240).

119. Ibid., 233.

Scriptures as a historical record of a religious community fail to grasp the lived reality of Christian faith. Since the spirit of the Christian faith, the Holy Spirit, must be understood to be infinitely greater than the spirit that characterizes the lived reality of a particular society, the Spirit's work in the lived reality of the Christian community must be described in articulating the Christian community's relationship to its foundational texts.[120] In the Christian community, tradition is the lived reality of the Spirit's transcendence over history and presence in Scripture and the church, and theological attention must be given to the role of tradition in mediating the lived reality (i.e., the "real history") of the Christian faith.

Blondel identifies the Spirit's work through tradition as that "principle distinct from" the past texts of Scripture and the collected facts of the historian which can "relate, harmonize and organize them" into the lived reality of the church.[121] Blondel emphasizes that although the mystery was *revealed* completely in Christ, the mystery cannot be comprehensively *manifested* in a particular historical event (the event of Christ) or in Scripture's witness to that event. Consequently, the church is required to continually *manifest* the reality of the living Christ.[122] This is not new *revelation*, but a continual *manifestation* of the lived reality of Christ in this community. Hence Blondel claims,

> Only a progressive and synthetic movement can lead us from the effects produced to their cause, can trace all the rays of light in the Christian consciousness over the centuries to their source, and through its unending progress imitate the infinite riches of God, revealed and always hidden, hidden and always revealed. In that profound sense, when it is a question of finding the supernatural in Sacred History and in dogma, the Gospel is nothing without the Church, the teaching of Scripture is nothing without the Christian life, exegesis is nothing without Tradition.[123]

Blondel suggests, then, that tradition "extends further than Scripture. Even in regard to what Scripture tells us, it possesses a special virtue and a distinct competence; and it does not rely only on oral transmission to lead us deeper and deeper into the reality revealed, and to the revealer

---

120. D'Ambrosio, *Traditional Hermeneutic*, 57.
121. Blondel, "History and Dogma," 237.
122. Ibid., 268.
123. Ibid., 276.

himself who constitutes it in its entirety."[124] As a result, a reciprocal relationship exists between Scripture and tradition, so that each deepens the understanding of the other.

Since access to mystery, as revelation, is necessarily a gift, and since intellectual apprehension of the mystery can only come through a series of paradoxical truths, appropriation of the mystery is never mere intellectual assent and it is never passive, but always requires participation.[125] The truth of Christian faith is one which must be lived to be understood. As a result, faith grows as it is practiced, since "perfection is in the act."[126] Since, for de Lubac, the *telos* of scriptural interpretation is incorporation into the mystery, scriptural study is better characterized by terms like encounter, participation, conversion and action than by the employment of historical scientific methods or philosophical deduction (though both scientific and philosophical inquiry are quite valuable). As a result, de Lubac understands that Christ's self-mediation through Scripture always takes place in history and finds its normative expressions in the tradition of the church.

De Lubac's project of *ressourcement* implies a going back to the sources of Christian faith to bring out theological insights and resources forgotten or overlooked in the church at present.[127] The extrinsicist reduction of Scripture to a collection of propositions ready-made for apologetic proofs and logical deductions for the development of doctrine, as well as the historicist reduction of Scripture to a historical record that can be verified by the secular historian, both failed to appreciate the infinite Christian mystery or Christ's use of these texts to mediate the mystery. De Lubac's return to the sources of the Christian faith seeks to recover both the transcendence of the Christian mystery, as well as

---

124. Ibid., 270.

125. Blondel's dissertation, *Action*, emphasizes that active participation is a prerequisite for the real understanding of lived history, and hence of Christian mystery. Blondel ("History and Dogma," 371) claims faith requires action because, "Truth does not live in the abstract and universal form of thought. . . . It is a gift, but a gift we acquire as if it were an earning."

126. Ibid., 377. Blondel argues that the "thought that follows the act is richer by an infinite degree than that which precedes it" (371). Blondel claims, "It is through action that the divine takes hold in man, hides its presence there, insinuates into him a new thought and a new life" (380).

127. D'Ambrosio (*Traditional Hermeneutic*, 3) describes the *Ressourcement* movement as a "creative hermeneutical exercise in which the 'sources' of Christian faith were 'reinterrogated' with new questions," rooted in the needs of the modern church.

the participatory manner in which individuals encounter this mystery through sacramental realities. The very "sources" recovered by the *Ressourcement* theologians were viewed by them as much more than ancient texts; they were "wellsprings of dynamic spiritual life."[128] As D'Ambrosio shows, "The events and words of Scripture, the doctrine of the Fathers, the Creeds and decrees of the councils, the rites of the liturgy—all of these are, for them, vehicles and, in an analogous sense, sacraments of the dynamic and living Mystery of Christ."[129]

Divine Action as Sacramental Mediation: Incarnation and Incorporations of the Logos

De Lubac's sacramental ontology is grounded in an understanding of Christ as the sacrament of the triune God. For de Lubac, revelation of the mystery occurred in the event of Christ, who now stands as both subject and object of Scripture. In *History and Spirit*, de Lubac follows Origen in distinguishing between Christ, the incarnation of the Logos, and Eucharist, Scripture and church as the three incorporations of the Logos and seeks to distinguish the sacramental role of each in mediating the one mystery in the divine economy.[130] The distinction between incarnation and incorporations of the Logos is decisive, since it was the historical event of the incarnation that grounds the Christian faith. Christ alone (not Scripture, church, or Eucharist) is revelation.[131] Incorporations are the creaturely mediums through which Christ presents himself to

---

128. Ibid., 9.

129. Ibid.

130. In a section of *History and Spirit* entitled "The Incorporations of the Logos" (385–426), de Lubac speaks directly to the relationship between sacramental realities in the divine economy in which dwells the eternal Logos: Christ, Scripture, Eucharist, and church.

131. De Lubac (*Medieval Exegesis*, 1:25) claims that Scripture "contains all of revelation" although revelation and Scripture are not identical. Voderholzer ("Dogma and History," 658) claims, "Revelation is achieved in the incarnate Word, which unifies and fulfills the many words of the Old Covenant, and which is then unfolded in the New Testament's witness to revelation as the word of God in the word of men." Voderholzer notes that *Dei Verbum* emphasizes that by naming Christ himself as Revelation, the council "defuse[d] a long-standing dispute about the sources of revelation; neither Scripture nor Tradition may be regarded as sources of revelation in the strict, properly dogmatic sense of the word. Rather, Christ himself is the one source of revelation" (664).

believers in the economy of redemption. De Lubac, then, subjects both Scripture and church to the event of Christ and shows that their authority and their intrinsic relationship are grounded in Christ.[132] While each incorporation has a unique role in the economy, all three mediate the same mystery. Furthermore, all three incorporations exist in a mutually causal relationship to one another, and thus each plays a constitutive and ongoing role in the economy of redemption. Consequently, de Lubac envisions the economy of redemption as structured by the reciprocal causality of Scripture, Eucharist, and church in the mediation of Christ. This section will examine this reciprocally causal structure.

The Eucharist makes the church: De Lubac's *Corpus Mysticum* (1944), focused on the causal relationship between the Eucharist and the church. There de Lubac claims that "the Eucharist corresponds to the Church as cause to effect, as means to end, as sign to reality."[133] De Lubac argues in the book that throughout the early church and up to the twelfth century, the church had been able to hold together Eucharist, church, and Christ by understanding that the Eucharist was the *corpus mysticum*, which had as its goal the unity of the church with Christ its head. During the Middle Ages, de Lubac feels, an inversion took place in the terminology between *corpus mysticum*, which had been applied to the Eucharist and now was applied to the church, and *verum corpus*, which had been applied to the church but was now applied to the Eucharist to emphasize Real Presence.[134] This inversion resulted in the loss of focus on the causal relationship between Eucharist and church, placing apologetic emphasis only on the real presence of Christ in the Eucharist. De Lubac argues that the "final result was that the first two of the 'three' bodies, that is, the historical and sacramental bodies, were identified with each other while the third, the ecclesial body, was detached from the historical and the

---

132. De Lubac (*La révélation divine*, 164–65) claims that Christ, "The revealed object 'is transmitted to us whole and entire by Scripture, and whole and entire by Tradition, both of which are intimately connected.'"

133. De Lubac, *Corpus Mysticum*.

134. De Lubac (*Catholicism*, 100, n. 68) claims "At first and for quite a long time, '*Corpus mysticum*' meant the Eucharistic body, as opposed to the '*corpus Christi quod est Ecclesia*,' which was the '*verum corpus*' par excellence. Was it not in fact quite natural to designate as 'mystical' that body whose hidden presence was due to 'mystical prayer' and which was received in a 'mystical banquet'? That body offered in forms which 'mystically' signified the Church? It is possible to trace the slow inversion of the two expressions."

sacramental."[135] The importance here is that when the church understood her existence in terms of the fourfold Christian understanding, it understood that the visible sacrament of the Eucharist constitutes the church and moves it toward its eschatological reality as the *totus Christus*. Hence an intrinsic relationship exists between sacrament and church, wherein the sacrament has a causal effect on the *Corpus Mysticum*, the body of Christ, anticipating its anagogical union as *totus Christus*.

Scripture makes the church: In *History and Spirit*, the efficacy of the Eucharist is equated with the efficacy of Scripture.[136] Like the Eucharist, Scripture constitutes the church as Scripture makes present the mystery of Christ.[137] De Lubac claims, "Scripture is . . . already like the coming of the Son of Man, for it has within itself the radiance of truth. Now the Church, in accepting it, takes in this radiance . . . Scripture is thus like the voice of Christ speaking to the Church and in the Church; it is his efficacious sign; it thus assures the luminous presence of Christ to the Church."[138] Thus Scripture, by being incorporated by the Logos, has a causal role in the divine economy in forming the church's members into the one body of Christ. Boersma claims that de Lubac "emphasized the 'efficacious sign' character of Scripture and Eucharist, both of them transforming the recipients into Christ himself: 'Scripture and Eucharist are thereby joined once again. Both never ceased to "build up" the Church.'"[139] Both Scripture and Eucharist render Christ present to the church, and thus both constitute the church and impel the church toward its eschatological reality.[140]

---

135. Wood (*Spiritual Exegesis and the Church*, 65) noting de Lubac, *Corpus Mysticum*, 184.

136. Boersma (*Nouvelle Theologie*, 163) claims, "In de Lubac's portrayal, Origen had regarded Scripture as one element in a 'triology' of 'incorporations' of the Word. Scripture and Eucharist had both functioned as 'body of Christ' sacramentally pointing to the Church and, through the Church, to the completed body of Christ, the eternal Logos."

137. De Lubac (*History and Spirit*, 418) claims "The life of the Church has its source in Scripture. It has it no less in the Eucharist." De Lubac notes that Origen gives Scripture a certain causal priority over the Eucharist because "the 'Word' is, in its pure essence, that very reality: for the Son of God, God himself, is 'Word.'" This does not mean that Scripture is above the Eucharist, but that while both "express and reveal the Logos. . . . Scripture does so, in the final analysis, with a superiority that allows one to consider it . . . as the 'truth' of which the Eucharist would be the symbol" (ibid., 419).

138. Ibid., 418.

139. Boersma, *Nouvelle Theologie*, 163, citing de Lubac, *History and Spirit*, 418.

140. See de Lubac *History and Spirit*, 422–23. Susan Wood (*Spiritual Exegesis and*

The church makes the Scripture and Eucharist: Though both Scripture and Eucharist make the church, mediation of the mystery is not one-directional, since both Scripture and Eucharist depend on the church for their existence and efficacy. With regard to Scripture, de Lubac emphasizes that "it is only in the Church, through the effect of the Church's preaching, that this Scripture ceases to be a simple mass of letters in order to become a living language."[141] The church has produced the Scriptures and has the ability to interpret Scripture, and without such interpretation, the individual could never understand the Logos within it.[142] With regard to the Eucharist, de Lubac emphasizes that the hierarchy makes the Eucharist as part of its sacramental structure. Balthasar notes this reciprocal relationship claiming, "There lies at the heart of the Church an ineradicable complementarity: the Church (through her hierarchical office) 'makes the Eucharist', and the 'Eucharist makes the Church' as incorporation into Christ's body."[143] De Lubac concludes that "we must be careful not to make the smallest break between the Mystical Body and the Eucharist. . . . The two mysteries must be understood by one another and their point of unity grasped at depth."[144] Hence there exists a reciprocal causality between Eucharist, Scripture, and church, so that all become constitutive signs that lead to the others yet are ultimately unified in the divine economy.

Of course, to note the reciprocal causality between these three parts of the economy of redemption does not mean that they are interchangeable. As de Lubac has made clear in *Corpus Mysticum*, the Eucharist is the *signum* which plays an instrumental role in building up the *res*, the church, and when the importance of these two sacramental realities is inverted, the structure of the economy becomes disordered.[145] Scripture, likewise, plays a causal yet instrumental role in the building up

the Church, 55-56) notes the necessity of anagogy for both the Eucharist/church relationship with the literal/spiritual senses of Scripture; as in both Eucharistic ecclesiology and spiritual exegesis, sign and reality can only be held together by looking forward to a full future union between the two (an anagogical sense) in the *totus Christus*.

141. De Lubac, *History and Spirit*, 422.

142. De Lubac (ibid., 420) claims that the church "dispenses" the Word, because the "Church is for each of us the place of the Logos. In the church . . . we hear the Word, and it is the hearing of the Word that builds up the Church for all eternity."

143. von Balthasar, *The Theology of Henri De Lubac*, 108.

144. De Lubac, *The Splendor of the Church*, 156-57.

145. See Boersma (*Heavenly Participation*, 112-19) for a good discussion of this reversal of *signum* and *res*.

of the church—it is the means to the end, rather than the end in itself. Furthermore, Scripture and Eucharist certainly do not mediate Christ in exactly the same way, although Christ actively presents himself through both. Each incorporation of the Logos has a unique and indispensable role in the mediation of Christ. The crucial point here is the recognition of a qualitative distinction between the incarnation of the Logos in Christ and the creaturely mediums used by Christ as incorporations of the Logos. Christ is the revelation of the mystery, and these sacramental structures mediate the revelation of Christ to readers.

Implications of a Sacramental Ontology

De Lubac's sacramental structuring of realities in the economy of redemption, as well as his use of Blondel's "living synthesis" to avoid extrinsicism and historicism, impacts his interpretation of Scripture in several key ways. First, de Lubac argues that Christian reality has an essentially sacramental structure, as God uses creaturely institutions, words, traditions, etc. to invite human beings to participate in infinite mystery. With regard to God's sacramental use of Scripture, a spiritual sense necessarily transcends the literal sense. As Hans Urs von Balthasar puts it, for de Lubac, the basis for all scriptural interpretation is the transcendence of the spirit over the letter which "forms the central event of Christianity that remains continuously present at every moment."[146] Since the scientific disciplines are structured to solve enigmas but are not able to apprehend mystery, the various scientific disciplines which inform the interpretation of Scripture can never finally determine the meaning of the text, nor will they bring encounter with the mystery. A spiritual sense of Scripture, the spiritual reality to which the text points, always transcends that which is accessible to any scientific investigation.

Second, because the mystery is intrinsically unified, de Lubac shows that a reciprocal causality exists between Scripture and church so that each constitutes and vitalizes the other, while both mediate the singular mystery. Since both Scripture and church have the same sacramental structure and mediate the same mystery, de Lubac insists that the church possesses an implicit and unique understanding of the meaning of history and has a unique ability to interpret Scripture according to its own

---

146. von Balthasar, *The Theology of Henri De Lubac*, 38.

self-understanding.¹⁴⁷ Scripture, church, and Eucharist must be understood as creaturely realities used by God for self-mediation (hence de Lubac's categories of letter and spirit). Each reality is given a particular role in the divine economy, and each leads toward the eschatological reality of the *totus Christus*.

Third, since the Christian mystery is always beyond comprehension, preservation of the mystery in Scripture depends upon keeping it open to multiple interpretations, so long as they do not marginalize or contradict the revelation of the mystery in Jesus Christ. For de Lubac, intellectual apprehension of the mystery can be pursued by separating it into various aspects, knowledge of the mystery can only be attained partially through a series of paradoxical truths, and understanding of the mystery can only occur through participation in it. As a result, scriptural interpretation (in the spiritual sense) will be open to an "infinite forest of meanings" within Scripture's christological boundaries.¹⁴⁸ As Boersma puts it, because de Lubac understands scriptural interpretation to be a "sacramental entry into the infinity of the spiritual realm, he maintains that the sacramental reality (res) of the biblical text cannot possibly be captured by one particular allegorical rendering of the text." As a result, "plurality of meaning is something to be expected, precisely because exegesis is the Spirit-guided means that enables human participation in heavenly realities."¹⁴⁹ As de Lubac feels that the human tendency is to reduce the mystery to what seems logical, thus too quickly dismissing the necessary paradoxes of faith, de Lubac articulates much more opposition to the reductive censuring of interpretation than he expresses concern for too broad a range of interpretations. As D'Ambrosio notes, de Lubac "never ceases to exhibit a passion for totality, wholeness, and the widest possible horizon in contradistinction to every kind of partiality."¹⁵⁰

---

147. For a detailed discussion of this understanding of the church, see Wood, *Spiritual Exegesis and the Church*, 71–128.

148. De Lubac, *Medieval Exegesis*, 1:75.

149. Boersma, *Heavenly Participation*, 149.

150. D'Ambrosio, *Traditional Hermeneutic*, 63.

CONVERGENCE: TRANS-FIGURAL READING AND THE SPIRITUAL SENSE OF SCRIPTURE

In the first section of this chapter, we saw that Vanhoozer moves quickly from a communicative ontology (a general claim that God all God's actions in the economy of redemption can be categorized as communication) to a covenantal ontology which gives priority to *sola Scriptura* as God's specific speech-act in the economy of redemption. Vanhoozer's insistence on a plain, canonical sense, along with his emphasis that present speaking does not change the original meaning of Scripture, cause him to emphasize Scripture's disclosure of determinate meaning over infinite mystery. In the second section, we saw that de Lubac develops a sacramental ontology which arises from his understanding of the relationship between nature and the supernatural. De Lubac's insistence on the infinite Christian mystery revealed in Jesus Christ and mediated sacramentally through Scripture, church, and Eucharist, causes him to emphasize Christ's active mediation of infinite mystery more than Scripture's determinate, plain-sense meaning. In this final section, I would like give an example of how these two ontological frameworks affect exegesis. I will suggest that the respective ontologies of Vanhoozer and de Lubac cause them to develop two distinct conceptions of meaning. Practically, Vanhoozer thinks of Scripture's meaning as the "particular referent" of the text and de Lubac thinks of Scripture's meaning as "infinite mystery." Since Vanhoozer and de Lubac both agree that figural reading is the *sine qua non* practice of the church (since it reads all Scripture in light of Christ and extends the world of Scripture, by means of Christ, to the present reader), I will examine how each describes the process of figural reading in order to specify how their prior decisions about ontology leads to different exegetical conclusions.

In light of his covenantal ontology, it is significant that Kevin Vanhoozer, in dialogue with the aims of the *Ressourcement* theologians, has recently proposed a "trans-figural" reading of Scripture.[151] This proposal attempts to appreciate the *Ressourcement* insistence on a participatory ontology of scriptural reading while rejecting their emphasis on a spiritual sense of Scripture.[152] Vanhoozer's trans-figural reading includes two

---

151. Vanhoozer, "Ascending the Mountain." In this article, Vanhoozer is in dialogue with Hans Boersma, an avid proponent of de Lubac's sacramental ontology.

152. Vanhoozer's understanding of the *Nouvelle* theologians has come through the lens of Hans Boersma's books, *Nouvelle Theologie* and *Heavenly Participation*. See

emphases, as the name indicates: A figural reading that would recover the central pre-critical practice of reading all Scripture in light of Christ while safeguarding the literal sense of Scripture as the only legitimate sense, and a trans-figural reading that would highlight the Spirit's authorial intention in Scripture to transfigure the present reader into the image of Christ, hence incorporating the reader into the meaning of Scripture. Vanhoozer believes that figural reading will preserve Scripture's determinate meaning in the literal sense while trans-figural reading will articulate the incorporation of the reader into the infinite meaning of Christ.

It is precisely this twofold conception of scriptural meaning that is at stake in the dialogue between Vanhoozer and de Lubac. *Figural* reading assumes that the meaning of the whole Scriptures is ultimately located in a particular individual, Jesus Christ, and that all other events in the scriptural narrative ultimately derive their meaning from him. In figural reading, then, meaning is found in a particular historical referent, the antitype to which all types ultimately refer. However, in *trans-figural* reading, the meaning of that referent is extended to the whole economy of redemption, and, indeed, to the whole triune mystery. In trans-figural reading, then, meaning is broadened from a particular textual referent to embrace an infinite mystery. I will refer to these two distinct kinds of conceptions of meaning as "meaning as particular referent" and "meaning as infinite Mystery." Within his model, Vanhoozer is able to convincingly demonstrate the first, while he struggles to persuasively articulate the second. De Lubac, on the other hand, often emphasizes the second to the possible neglect of the first.

Vanhoozer: Figural Reading and Meaning as Particular Referent

As we saw in the first chapter, Vanhoozer's proposal for a return to figural reading is developed largely from Hans Frei, whose central goal in recovering figural reading was to safeguard the unsubstitutable identity of Jesus Christ and show him to be the central character of the whole canonical narrative. In Frei's figural model, the literal sense can be extended to the whole scriptural canon, so that, "Without loss to its own literal meaning or specific temporal reference, an earlier story (or occurrence)

especially Boersma's treatment of de Lubac's sacramental interpretation of Scripture (*Nouvelle Theologie*, 149–89).

was a figure of a later one."[153] This means that the whole biblical canon is to be read as a unified "world of one temporal sequence" in which "there must in principle be one cumulative story to depict it."[154] Frei believes that figural reading preserves the historical reality of both type and antitype, as an Old Testament figure has a real and new meaning added by means of being incorporated into a broader story so that they are "not only preserved but enhanced."[155] As Christ is the climax of this unified story, the extension of the literal sense to the whole scriptural narrative allows all historical events to find their ultimate meaning in him as God providentially orders history toward this unique individual.[156]

Vanhoozer adopts Frei's project of figural reading and advances it in two important ways: First, Vanhoozer adds his now familiar theory of divine authorship to figural reading. Consequently, Vanhoozer argues that figural reading is a function of special hermeneutics (a method to be applied to the Bible only), since it depends on the theological presuppositions of divine authorship as well as God's providential ordering of history.[157] Second, Vanhoozer uses speech-act theory to articulate how meaning in Scripture remains determinate in figural reading, even as revelation progresses. Vanhoozer argues that the real debate in figural reading is not about the semantic content of a text (the "what" or *meaning* of a text, which Vanhoozer sees as clear and relatively determinate in most cases), but about the ultimate referent of the text (what Vanhoozer

---

153. Frei, *The Eclipse of Biblical Narrative*, 2. Frei strongly distinguishes figural reading from allegory, seeing the former as intratextual reading and the latter as extratextual reading. Allegory, for Frei, is a universal meaning not grounded in a historical event (and therefore abstract), which can be placed as a guiding structure to unify a story. For a good description of the relationship between figural reading and allegory, see also Hans Frei, "Karl Barth," 168–69.

154. Frei, *Eclipse*, 2.

155. Dawson, *Christian Figural Reading*, 143.

156. Figural reading, as Frei (*Eclipse*, 2) understands it, is "literalism at the level of the whole biblical story and thus of the depiction of the whole historical reality."

157. Vanhoozer, "Ascending the Mountain," 788. Vanhoozer claims, "I take typology [i.e. figural reading] to be a form of theological interpretation that responds to something unique to the biblical text, a special rather than general hermeneutic that is particularly attentive to the divine authorial discourse and its organic unity." This sets Vanhoozer apart from Frei, who saw typology as a function of any literary story, and as a function of the biblical text in a concentrated way. Frei does not ever posit a theory of dual authorship, although Frei (*Types of Christian Theology*, 14) realizes that the decision to read figuratively is not an inherent quality of the text itself, but is grounded in a theological presupposition of God's providential action in history.

calls the "'about what' of meaning").[158] For Vanhoozer, the meaning of an individual OT text is relatively clear in itself, yet the text is intended (by Scripture's divine author) to find its ultimate meaning in relation to Christ. Vanhoozer specifies his position in terms of speech-act theory, claiming, "The human locutions and their semantic content do not change, but the divine illocutions and their historical referents . . . do."[159] Hence the original meaning of a text does not change, but is intended by God to find further specification in the revelation of Christ.[160]

It becomes apparent, then, that Vanhoozer understands Scripture's ultimate referent to be *the scripturally narrated event of Jesus Christ*. This allows Vanhoozer to insist that textual meaning remains determinate, even while further revelation is added. In figural reading, Vanhoozer argues, "It is not that new meaning has been added, but rather that the original meaning has finally achieved its Christological *telos*."[161] Consequently, "[T]he typological meaning *is* the literal meaning of the discourse when viewed in canonical, which is to say redemptive-historical context."[162] Vanhoozer's position is both clear and orthodox: The ultimate referent of all Scripture is the event of Jesus Christ, and all the individual events of salvation history, while keeping their own particular qualities as events (semantic content), were intended to find ultimate their referent (their "'about what' of meaning") in Christ.

However, in dialogue with Boersma, Vanhoozer realizes that there has always been more to figural reading than the specification of Christ as Scripture's ultimate referent. Figural reading was traditionally used to incorporate the present reader into the story of Scripture, and hence to expand the meaning of Scripture to the whole of salvation history.[163] Vanhoozer likewise insists that evangelicals must recover a

---

158. Vanhoozer, "Ascending the Mountain," 784. Vanhoozer (ibid., 785) uses the example of the Song of Songs to show that the semantic content of the text is quite clear in most cases—what sparks disagreement is the ultimate reference of the text (the celebration of human conjugal love, the relationship between God and Israel, or the relationship between Christ and the church).

159. Ibid., 792. Locutions refer to the words themselves (in this case, the human words); illocutions refer to the stance of the author in saying words (here God's supervening of the human words); and historical referents refer to the intended object about which the Spirit communicates.

160. See ibid. and Vanhoozer, *Is There a Meaning in this Text*, 423.

161. Vanhoozer, "Ascending the Mountain," 792.

162. Ibid. Typology and figural reading are the same practice for Vanhoozer.

163. Both Vanhoozer (ibid.) and Frei (*Eclipse*, 2) agree that figural reading

participatory model of scriptural reading in which they understand that the "redemptive-historical context" of Scripture includes "both text and contemporary readers."[164] He thus argues, "We too 'figure' in the story.... We have been transferred into the story of Jesus Christ, emplotted into his narrative, drafted into the drama of redemption."[165] Figural reading, then, for Vanhoozer, extends scriptural meaning to include the present reader.

It is here, however, that Vanhoozer's figural reading reaches its limits. While figural reading may emplot readers into Scripture's story and may show how readers are related to Christ, it does not show how readers are transformed into the image of Christ. It is precisely in its inability to show how readers participate in Christ that Frei's project has been sharply criticized. Frei has always argued that figural reading allowed readers to figure into the story, yet Frei never quite clarifies how this figuring incorporates the reader into Christ.[166] Frei places emphasis on the unsubstitutable identity of Christ to such an extent that he never sufficiently examines the implications of that unsubstitutable identity on the life of the reader.[167] John David Dawson writes that for Frei,

> [A]ll the emphasis is now on preserving a conception of the text that makes sure disciples do not confuse Jesus' identity with

expanded the story of Scripture to "the whole of historical reality." For Frei (*Eclipse*, 3) figural reading extends the biblical narrative, as the "one and only real world," to "embrace the experience of any present age and reader."

164. Vanhoozer, "Ascending the Mountain," 793. Vanhoozer (ibid., 788) also suggests that using figural reading is a matter of enlarging "our notions of historical context, recognizing that later readers also figure among the divine addressees."

165. Ibid., 797.

166. It is not that Frei does not try to articulate this incorporation, but that Frei's emphasis on the particularity of Christ prevents him from adequately articulating the believer's participation in Christ. According to Frei, ("Theological Reflections," 86) readers must "identify themselves with the identity, not of a universal hero or savior figure, but of the particular person, Jesus of Nazareth, the manifest presence of God in their midst, who has identified himself with them." Frei also suggests that Christ's "identity as this singular, continuing individual, Jesus of Nazareth, includes humankind in its singularity.... To be 'the first born among many brethren' (and sisters) is his vocation and his very being" (see Frei, "On the Resurrection of Christ," 204–05).

167. Dawson (*Christian Figural Reading*, 213) worries that "the reader ... begins to drop out of sight, as all attention is directed to the way the gospel text renders the identity of Jesus." Dawson suggests further, "The literal reader of the text's realistic, narrative sense gets to encounter Jesus as only Jesus alone is, but the action of Jesus or God impinging upon the embodied, historical life of the reader is a matter left to take care of itself without much comment."

their own, rather than one that brings the reader into more direct self-awareness of his or her own place within an ongoing process of historical and personal transformation. The literal reader of the text's realistic, narrative sense gets to encounter Jesus as only Jesus alone is, but the action of Jesus or God impinging upon the embodied, historical life of the reader is a matter left to take care of itself without much comment.[168]

Bryan Hollon likewise criticizes Frei for "not approach[ing] Jesus, the hermeneutical key to all Scripture, as an absorbing character but rather as a spectacle to behold extrinsically."[169] Hollon claims, "It is not enough to suggest that we can know Jesus as we might know a character in a story, extrinsically. Rather, Christians claim to be reconciled to God through incorporation into Christ's body. . . . God's identification in Jesus can only be grasped meaningfully (soteriologically) through ontological participation in His body, the Church."[170] Although Frei claims that reading the plain sense should lead to the recognition of the Christ who is living and present, his desire to safeguard the particular identity of Christ prevents him from adequately articulating the reader's participation in mystery. Consequently, scriptural reading for Frei becomes more of a honing a set of skills based on observation of the text than a transformative encounter with the triune God through the text.[171] Vanhoozer appears to incorporate these difficulties into his own project of figural interpretation as well.

De Lubac: Meaning as Infinite Mystery

This limitation of Vanhoozer's figural reading is seen more clearly when Vanhoozer's model is compared with de Lubac's allegory. De Lubac insists on preserving a spiritual sense of Scripture (the spiritual reality to

---

168. Ibid.

169. See Hollon, *Everything is Sacred*, 151.

170. Ibid., 154.

171. This criticism of Frei is common. Dawson (*Christian Figural Reading*, 212–14) concludes literal reading and employment of interpretive skill are necessary to "make sure disciples do not confuse Jesus' identity with their own" (213). See also O'Regan, ("De Doctrina Christiana") who claims, "Understanding the biblical text . . . is according to Frei more like a skill, a species of know-how," so that the focus is on "competence or incompetence in the practice of interpretation."

which the text points), which goes beyond mere figural reading.[172] De Lubac claims that in reading Scripture, "To stop at the objective datum of the mystery would be to mutilate it, to betray it."[173] This spiritual sense, as we have seen, is essentially the process of conversion, and always transcends that which is accessible to scientific investigation.[174] De Lubac's form of figural reading (which, he claims, necessitates a spiritual sense of Scripture), incorporates the present reader into the meaning of Scripture both by referring his/her identity to the particular identity of Jesus Christ and by enveloping the reader in the infinite mystery of the triune God. It is important to clarify that de Lubac also wants to preserving the unsubstitutable identity of Christ as the intended referent of the whole canonical Scriptures. De Lubac makes it clear that the spiritual sense is not arbitrary, but is based on the particular revelation of Jesus Christ. The spiritual sense of Scripture exists, de Lubac claims, because, "At the summit of history, the Fact of Christ supposed history, and its radiance transfigured history."[175] Christian allegory was always a unification of history in an actual historical event, as opposed to pagan allegory which sought to reconcile fictitious stories and myths with "timeless philosophical truths."[176] In other words, de Lubac would say that the spiritual sense of

---

172. De Lubac (*Medieval Exegesis*, 2:98–99) insists that in this movement from locating the referent of Scripture and entering into the process of conversion an "infinite qualitative difference" exists, which, if diminished, would "make out of the allegorical sense, which is a *spiritual* sense, a new literal sense; and this would practically negate the interiority of the Christian mystery."

173. Ibid., 2:134.

174. De Lubac (ibid., 2:117) writes, "To pass from history to allegory or from the letter to the mystery or from the shadow to the truth, is without a doubt always to pass to spiritual understanding: but it is also, thereby, 'to be converted to the faith.'" De Lubac (*Medieval Exegesis*, 1:34) argues that for the premoderns, scriptural interpretation "was an undefined understanding, precisely because it was an approach to the depths of God. It was not a matter merely of a text being explicated, but of mysteries being explored."

175. De Lubac, *Medieval Exegesis*, 2:105. Hence allegory, de Lubac (2:107), claims, was a very useful and necessary tool to "construct . . . the edifice of the faith" and show "how all of biblical history bears witness to Christ."

176. D'Ambrosio, *Traditional Hermeneutic*, 99. De Lubac never tires of stressing the unique historical character of Christian allegory ("*allegoria facti*") as opposed to the allegory used by classical writers ("*allegoria verbi*"). De Lubac argues that the Christian use of allegory was developed from the Apostle Paul, who saw his own allegory grounded in real historical events. For Paul's establishment of a distinct Christian practice grounded in history and not in words, see especially de Lubac, "Hellenistic Allegory and Christian Allegory," 165–96.

Scripture exists to safeguard the full *meaning* of the particular individual, Jesus Christ.[177]

But does de Lubac really safeguard the particular identity of Christ as the ultimate referent of Scripture in his proposal for a spiritual sense? Vanhoozer would wonder if de Lubac actually conflates Christ and the church in this proposal of a spiritual sense. One possible example of this conflation can be seen in de Lubac's claim that the meaning of Scripture is the *totus Christus,* the whole Christ, head and members.[178] De Lubac argues that the mystery of Christ and the church (together) is the meaning of the "whole content of the Bible," and that because "Christ and the Church are just one great mystery," one cannot really consider one reality without the other, without risking abstraction.[179] De Lubac even suggests that in the scope of salvation history, "This ecclesial body [head and members] . . . must thus be said . . . to be 'truer' than the [incarnate body], because it constitutes a more perfect, fuller realization of the divine design."[180] Vanhoozer would worry that meaning as mystery is now overrunning the particular identity of Christ in himself, thus undermining the plain communicative nature of the literal sense of Scripture. If Vanhoozer's attempt to safeguard the unique identity of Jesus Christ has been accused of failing to show how present readers participate in Christ, so de Lubac's attempt to emphasize the infinite mystery as Christ

177. Far from undermining the historical importance of Scripture, de Lubac (*Medieval Exegesis*, 2:72) argues that allegory was actually "providing the foundation for the objective sense of history and by that very fact *giving history its proper value.*" For de Lubac (ibid., 2:71), "This is why, if any not merely partial and relative but total, comprehensive, and absolutely valid explication of history is truly possible, this explication can only be theological. Only faith anticipates the future with security. Only an explication founded upon faith can invoke a definitive principle and appeal to ultimate causes."

178. Ibid., 2:93.

179. Ibid., 2:90. One of de Lubac's most frequent uses of "mystery" is the usage taken from Paul about the relationship of Christ and the church in Ephesians 5: "[A]s Saint Paul said, Christ and the Church are just one great mystery: this is the mystery of their union. Now the whole mystery of Scripture, the whole object of *allegoria*, resides in this. This enables one to discover everywhere the 'deeper mysteries about Christ and his body.'"

180. Ibid., 2:92. De Lubac shows that at times premodern exegetes understood the object of allegory to be Christ, yet at other times they speak of the object as the church, and at times they do not distinguish between them. De Lubac (*History and Spirit*, 412) claims further, "The assumption of individual flesh has a unique importance, of course, because it constitutes the point where God inserts himself into our humanity. But it is not an end in itself. Its goal is to allow the assumption of the Church."

united with readers could be accused of conflation between Christ and the church.

Convergence

At this point, the precise nature of the problem comes into view. Regarding meaning as particular referent (Jesus Christ), there is agreement; both authors are committed to understanding the whole meaning of Scripture as unified in the person of Jesus Christ. The pressing issue that remains is how this "meaning as particular referent" (the singular identity of Jesus Christ) may be related to "meaning as infinite Mystery" (the infinite reality of the triune God acting salvation history) without either severing the two or absorbing one into the other. Vanhoozer would continue to worry that readers will depreciate the particularity of Christianity if they do not safeguard the unsubstitutable identity of Christ, while de Lubac would continue to worry that readers will depreciate the Christian mystery if Christ remains simply a historically identifiable individual.

The question that emerges from the previous discussion seems to be this: What is the true referent of Scripture—Christ as an individual person, or Christ and the church? Is Scripture's meaning located in Christ as a particular referent, or in the infinite mystery revealed in Christ? Vanhoozer seems to sense that this proposed either/or question creates a false dilemma and must be transcended. Vanhoozer's very proposal for "trans-figural" reading is a bold attempt to move beyond the limiting of scriptural meaning to a particular historical referent, and to articulate the Spirit's intention in Scripture to incorporate readers into the body of Christ. Hence Vanhoozer insists, "We too, the divine addresses of Scripture, are being transfigured, transcending history not in the sense of leaving it behind but of participating in the mystery—the glorious theodrama—in its midst."[181] In this trans-figural model, Christian scriptural reading "is ultimately a matter of reading for the Spirit's intended trans-figural meaning, *an intention that includes the reader's transfiguration.*"[182] Hence by means of trans-figural reading, "the Holy Spirit leads readers through earthly shadows to the incarnate heavenly reality of Jesus Christ."[183] Consequently, the "effective history of God's Word and Spirit is

---

181. Vanhoozer, "Ascending the Mountain," 797.
182. Ibid.
183. Ibid., 793.

a matter of transforming meaning and readers alike from one degree of glory to another by making explicit the eschatologically new at the heart of the redemptive-historical."[184]

It is clear that Vanhoozer's trans-figural conception of meaning has been stretched beyond a particular historical referent (an "unsubstitutable identity" to use Frei's claim), to embracing an infinite mystery (the participation of human beings in the very life of the triune God). Vanhoozer is now articulating scriptural meaning as an infinite, participatory mystery and this requires some new terminology. Here we would expect Vanhoozer to develop some categories to express this meaning as mystery in which we participate.

Unfortunately, at this point Vanhoozer simply returns to his familiar argument that meaning is not changed but "further specified" in new referents.[185] This "further specification" argument worked well as it referred all scriptural events to their ultimate textual referent, Jesus Christ. Yet the argument does little to articulate the "infinite qualitative difference" brought about in Christ, the Christian mystery.[186] In fact, the "further specification" argument seems to miss entirely engagement with this issue. Remember Vanhoozer's claim that the debate about scriptural meaning is not a debate about determining the semantic content of a text ("what" the text is saying), but about determining the ultimate referent

184. Ibid., 799.

185. Vanhoozer (ibid., 792) claims, "I am not inclined myself to say that meaning changes.... The new referent... is a different and higher (i.e., Christological) *realization* of the same semantic content."

186. It is nearly impossible to articulate adequately the radical newness of Christ while calling the event of Christ simply a specification of the textual indeterminacy of the Old Testament! For example, consider Vanhoozer's claim (*Is There a Meaning in this Text*, 423) that the "meaning" of the Old Testament is not changed in the New, but that God has "rather rendered its referent—God's gracious provision for Israel and the world—more specific" in Christ. Vanhoozer claims further, "What is of continuing relevance across the two Testaments is God's promise to create a people for himself and the divine action that fulfills that promise." In an even bolder claim (yet quite consistent with Vanhoozer's distinction between meaning and significance), Vanhoozer claims, "Significance just is 'recontextualized meaning.' Just as Jesus Christ recontextualizes the meaning of the Old Testament, so the church is called to recontextualize the meaning of Jesus Christ." This "further specification" argument does not appear to have changed much now in this new trans-figural model, as Vanhoozer still insists that meaning does not change. Of course, I consider Vanhoozer's under-emphasis on the radical newness of Christ to be only a symptom of the problem of focusing only on meaning as particular referent. Yet, this would be exactly de Lubac's point: the radical newness of Christ ought to be the basis for our hermeneutical rules.

of the semantic content (the "about what" of the text).[187] In light of the dialogue here, we can now see that the debate about scriptural meaning goes beyond specification of the referent. The bigger question is, how does meaning as the Spirit's intended referent, *Jesus Christ*, (a particular referent), relate to meaning as the Spirit's intended referent, *the infinite triune mystery in relationship with human beings* (infinite mystery)? Both are referents intended by the Spirit, and each could make claim to being *the* ultimate referent of Scripture. The question is now about "which" referent is being specified. If the question is a false one, and if the answer is that both are the intended referent of Scripture, both Vanhoozer and de Lubac must develop terminology to account for both without severing or conflating them.

It does not yet seem that Vanhoozer's trans-figural proposal has provided a satisfying alternative to de Lubac's proposal to account for meaning as mystery by means of a spiritual sense of Scripture. At the root of the problem, it seems, is Vanhoozer's desire to preserve a clear, christological reading of Scripture, combined with inadequate tools for describing meaning as infinite mystery. Yet Vanhoozer does appear to have resources which could strengthen his model of trans-figural reading. Utilizing the authors we have already considered, let me suggest one possible way forward.

I would suggest that Vanhoozer's trans-figural project could be advanced by adopting the language of *Jesus Christ as sacrament of the triune mystery* to account for both a concentration of meaning in a particular referent and as this referent opening meaning to infinite mystery.[188] The term sacrament is particularly fitting theologically, as brings together both kinds of meaning in the particular individual, Jesus Christ. All the content of Scripture leads to Christ, and thus all scriptural meaning is thus concentrated in Christ. Yet, the moment the reader encounters the living, present Jesus Christ revealed in Scripture, he/she is opened to infinite mystery, a reality into which the individual lives but never fully grasps. In the above discussion between Vanhoozer and de Lubac, we can see that Vanhoozer has focused almost completely on showing that all

---

187. Vanhoozer, "Ascending the Mountain," 784. Vanhoozer (785) uses the example of the Song of Songs to show that the semantic content of the text is quite clear in most cases—what sparks disagreement is the ultimate reference of the text (the celebration of human conjugal love, the relationship between God and Israel, or the relationship between Christ and the church).

188. De Lubac *Medieval Exegesis*, 2:20.

Vanhoozer's covenantal ontology and de Lubac's sacramental ontology 101

scriptural events find meaning as they are oriented toward a particular referent, Jesus Christ. We can also see that de Lubac has primarily focused on showing that the meaning of Christ opens to the whole triune mystery in which human beings participate. In describing Christ as sacrament of this mystery, both kinds of meaning are inextricably bound up in him.

Understanding of *Jesus Christ as sacrament of the triune mystery* should be agreeable to Vanhoozer's theological system, and it would yield a number of happy consequences for him.[189] First, Christ, and not Scripture, is the sacrament in this model. Consequently, Vanhoozer could avoid referring to the literal sense of Scripture as the sacrament of the spiritual sense, as de Lubac tends to describe it.[190] Scripture would still be understood as God's communicative action which leads readers to Christ. It is Christ, in turn, who acts as sacrament by opening readers to infinite mystery.

Second, the language of sacrament would enable Vanhoozer to make a clearer qualitative distinction between reading the literal, canonical sense of Scripture on the one hand, and transformation into Christ through Scripture on the other. Vanhoozer realizes that persons may *understand* the canonical sense of Scripture without themselves *participating* in the infinite Christian mystery, yet he lacks terminology to distinguish participatory reading from scholarly reading. Using the language of sacrament, Vanhoozer could show that the secular reader could understand the canonical sense (Jesus Christ as the ultimate referent of Scripture) without necessarily being incorporated into him (understanding Jesus Christ as infinite mystery). Yet for the believer, understanding the particular identity of Jesus Christ opens the reader to meaning as infinite mystery.

Third, Vanhoozer could keep his arguments about the determinate meaning in Scripture in tact and yet show that Christ infinitely transcends

189. Throughout his career, Vanhoozer has always avoided using the term "sacrament" to refer to parts of the mystery (namely Scripture or the church) for two central reasons: First, Vanhoozer wants to avoid the notion of a sacrament conferring grace (see here Vanhoozer, *The Drama of Doctrine*, 408–09, where he argues the church is not a sacrament, but is a *mimesis* of the body of Christ). Second, Vanhoozer worries that using the term to describe Scripture would depreciate Scripture as communication (this second reason, it seems, is the chief reason why Vanhoozer sees it necessary to provide an *alternative* to the *Nouvelle* sacramental theology in his article, "Ascending the Mountain"). Yet, in describing Christ as sacrament, I am attempting to avoid both of these difficulties for Vanhoozer.

190. More precisely, de Lubac understands the literal sense of Scripture as "history," and this history leads one sacramentally to Christ, the meaning of history (i.e., allegory).

this determinate meaning. Consequently, Vanhoozer could continue to insist that figural reading be governed by careful hermeneutical and theological rules, even while showing that the referent of Scripture, Jesus Christ, opens readers to a mystery infinitely greater than any scientific discipline can capture. This would allow Vanhoozer to articulate the "infinite qualitative difference" revealed in Christ in a way that could satisfy de Lubac.[191]

On the other hand, de Lubac's project could be strengthened by attending to Vanhoozer's cautions about the determinate meaning in the literal sense without greatly amending his sacramental ontology. Vanhoozer's emphasis on meaning as particular referent could chasten de Lubac's understanding of Scripture's infinite mystery by emphasizing that all meaning is revealed in the particular individual, Jesus Christ, *as communicated in the plain sense of the canonical Scriptures*. Greater attention to God's action in the formation of the scriptural texts would specify that the Christ who reveals the infinite triune mystery is precisely Christ as he is revealed in Scripture. Thus Vanhoozer's project could lead de Lubac to a greater appreciation for God's structuring and use of the literal sense to mediate the spiritual sense of Scripture.

---

191. Remember that de Lubac (*Medieval Exegesis*, 2:98–99) has insisted that in entering into the process of conversion an "infinite qualitative difference" exists, which, if diminished, would "make out of the allegorical sense, which is a *spiritual* sense, a new literal sense; and this would practically negate the interiority of the Christian mystery."

CHAPTER 3

God's Use of Scripture and Church in the Economy of Redemption

INTRODUCTION: VANHOOZER'S COVENANT ECCLESIOLOGY AND DE LUBAC'S SACRAMENTAL ECCLESIOLOGY

In the last chapter we saw that Vanhoozer envisions God's communicative action taking covenantal form in the Scriptures which mediate Christ to the church. We also saw that de Lubac envisions Christ's self-communication taking sacramental form in Scripture, church, and Eucharist, so that each builds the other sacramental realities. Without leaving the discussion of ontology aside, this chapter will focus specifically on the relationship between Scripture and church in the economy of redemption. The relationship between Scripture and church has been a significant issue in Catholic and Protestant interpretations of Scripture, and it remains the area of greatest disagreement between de Lubac and Vanhoozer. Vanhoozer develops his covenant ontology, in large part, because he wants to safeguard the Scriptures from the church and keep the Scriptures authoritative over the church. De Lubac, on the other hand, has developed his sacramental ontology, in large part, because he wants to highlight the mystical union between Christ and church and thereby to show Christ's active self-mediation to the church in Scripture, Sacrament, and church alike.

Significantly, both Vanhoozer and de Lubac developed their ecclesiologies in response to theological trajectories which tend to grant authority to the church over the Scriptures. The postliberals against whom Vanhoozer writes have often tended to make ecclesiology into First Theology, thereby reducing the role of Scripture as an external norm.[1] The neo-Thomists against whom de Lubac writes have often tended to give Tradition an ultimate authority, thereby reducing Scripture to a set of proof-texts which could be used to support what was derived from tradition.[2] As a result, both Vanhoozer and de Lubac are both acutely aware of the need to safeguard Scripture's normative status as the authoritative locus of God's self-mediation to readers. A close examination of the two projects reveals some key similarities in the way each understands the purpose of Scripture and the manner in which the Scriptures exercise authority over the church. The following seven points illustrate the fundamental similarity between the two projects. First, both Vanhoozer and de Lubac specifically speak of Scripture and the church as creaturely realities that have been drawn into the economy of redemption to share in the missions of the triune God.[3] Second, both agree that the Scriptures conduct an active, initiatory mission of confronting and renewing the church.[4] Third, both see Scripture playing a causal role over the church in

---

1. Vanhoozer (*The Drama of Doctrine*, 163) claims "Ecclesiology cannot be first theology because the church enjoys only the first fruits of its salvation." Consequently, God's use of Scripture will be First Theology.

2. De Lubac opposes neo-Thomism since it relied on propositionalism and foundationalist apologetics and granted authority to tradition to support this propositionalist understanding of truth (see, for example, "Apologetics and Theology," 94).

3. Vanhoozer (*The Drama of Doctrine*, 177) claims "To be sure, the biblical texts have a 'natural history'; they have human authors. Yet these human testimonies are caught up in the triune economy of word-acts and so ultimately become divine testimonies." De Lubac (*Medieval Exegesis*, 1:81) claims "The sacred books themselves are and remain inspired.... 'God did not create them and then depart from the scene. They come from him and exist in him.'"

4. Vanhoozer (*The Drama of Doctrine*, 210) claims "Word, Spirit, tradition, and church belong together; all have a vital role to play. Only the Word serves as magisterial norm, however, for only the written word is the commissioned testimony of the church's Lord and Master." De Lubac (*History and Spirit*, 418) claims "Scripture ... never cease[s] to 'build up' the Church."

the divine economy by mediating the present, risen Christ to the church.[5] Fourth, both ultimately locate the authority of Scripture in the action of the triune God who uses it to address the church.[6] Fifth, both agree that Scripture, since its purpose is to incorporate readers into the church, is incomplete until it accomplishes its eschatological mission.[7] Sixth, both suggest that the plain sense of Scripture has an authoritative role over the church because the church is incomplete and still sinful.[8] Seventh, both agree that a bare literal reading of the scriptural texts is insufficient for readers to participate in the realm of grace rather than nature.[9] Together, these similarities show that the real difference between Vanhoozer and

---

5. Vanhoozer (*The Drama of Doctrine*, 71) argues, "In the final analysis, the mission of Scripture is to minister Christ and to build up the body of Christ. This is what God is doing with his written words: in diverse ways and at diverse times speaking his Son into the world, giving thick (canonical) descriptions of what he is saying and doing in Jesus Christ." De Lubac (*Medieval Exegesis*, 1:237–39) presents Christ as subject and object of Scripture, using it for self-mediation to the church.

6. Vanhoozer (*Remythologizing Theology*, 264) claims that "Scripture is a means of ongoing triune communication by which the church follows her master's voice." De Lubac (*History and Spirit*, 418) claims, "Scripture is thus like the voice of Christ speaking to the Church and in the Church; it is his efficacious sign; it thus assures the luminous presence of Christ to the Church."

7. Vanhoozer (*The Drama of Doctrine*, 165) claims "The holy script . . . is both complete and incomplete. On the one hand, the story of God's word-acts in the history of Israel and in Jesus Christ is finished: the climax of the drama of redemption (cross and resurrection) has been accomplished, its conclusion (eternal life with God) is sure. On the other hand, without a people to embody it, the script lacks something essential, for the canon 'delivers its meaning only as it is "played out" in patterns of human action in Church and society.'" De Lubac (*Medieval Exegesis*, 1:227) similarly writes, "All that Scripture recounts has indeed happened in history, but the account that is given does not contain the whole purpose of Scripture in itself. This purpose still needs to be accomplished and is actually accomplished in us each day, by the mystery of this spiritual understanding. Only then . . . will Scripture bear us its fruit in its fullness."

8. Vanhoozer (*The Drama of Doctrine*, 163) claims that "Ecclesiology cannot be first theology because the church enjoys only the first fruits of its salvation. As an eschatological reality, it is indeed already in union with Christ, but not yet completely so." De Lubac (*The Church*, 24) would likely agree, saying that "this very same Church, is often unfaithful and unsubmissive. In her members she is a sinner . . . the Church is also a symbol of perpetual decline and mortality."

9. Vanhoozer ("Ascending the Mountain," 792) insists that the Spirit's ongoing role is to "transfigure" readers, "transcending history not in the sense of leaving it behind but of participating in the mystery." De Lubac (*Medieval Exegesis*, 2:98–99) insists that in this movement from locating the referent of Scripture and entering into the process of conversion an "infinite qualitative difference" exists, which is governed by Christ.

de Lubac lies not in their understanding of God's use of Scripture, but in their understanding of God's use of the church.

Vanhoozer and de Lubac move in decidedly different directions as they describe God's use of the church in the economy of redemption, and it is this difference that accounts for most of their disagreement regarding God's use of Scripture. Vanhoozer stresses the responsive nature of the church, and consequently always stresses the authority of Scripture over the church. De Lubac emphasizes that because Christ mediates himself through Scripture, Eucharist and church, there can be no competition for authority between Christ and church. It is this difference which will be examined in this chapter.

VANHOOZER'S COVENANT ECCLESIOLOGY

Vanhoozer's covenantal ontology leads to a covenantal ecclesiology, in which Scripture plays an active, initiatory role in the economy of redemption while the church plays a responsive role in the economy. Scripture is the external norm used by God to confront the church, while the church is a "creature of the Word," elected by Christ and characterized by its listening to Scripture. Vanhoozer develops a distinctly non-sacramental description of the church as a "mimesis" of the gospel, a "parable" of the kingdom, and a "commissioned" community in the economy of redemption, in order to show the church's responsive role in the economy.

The Church as Creature of the Word and Mimesis of the Gospel

The church as creature of the Word: Vanhoozer describes the church as "a 'creature of the word'—brought into being and shaped by the Spirit's ministry of the word."[10] Following Gerhard Ebeling, Vanhoozer equates tradition with the history of biblical interpretation, so that "church tradition" is defined as "the embodied social practice of biblical interpretation" and hence always "stands under the canon viewed as a dominical and spiritual practice of administering the covenant."[11] The church is consti-

---

10. Vanhoozer, *The Drama of Doctrine*, 230. Vanhoozer claims, "The church in the power of the Spirit is nothing less than the efficacy of the canonical word, rightly understood and rightly appropriated" (208).

11. Ibid., 114. Vanhoozer claims that "the history of the church is the history of

tuted by Scripture, and the church becomes the church to the extent that responds obediently to Scripture. Vanhoozer summarizes that, "As a work of the Spirit, tradition plays the role of moon to Scripture's sun: what light, and authority, tradition bears, it does so by virtue of reflecting the light of the Son that shines forth from the canon."[12] In Vanhoozer's structuring of the economy, Scripture is always given authority over the church and the church derives its authority from its faithful response to Scripture.

Vanhoozer bases his argument that God normatively speaks in Scripture rather than in tradition on the present incompleteness of the church.[13] The Scriptures are authoritative because they are God's complete speech-act, while the visible church, because it is still being led toward its eschatological fullness, cannot be authoritative in the same way. Vanhoozer claims that, "Ecclesiology cannot be first theology because the church enjoys only the first fruits of its salvation. As an eschatological reality, it is indeed already in union with Christ, but not yet completely so."[14] The only authority the church can claim for itself is its responsive participation in the economy of redemption, and this must continually be checked by the authority of Scripture.[15] Vanhoozer's emphasis on the authority of Scripture over the church is intended to be a manifesto for articulating the authority of God over the church, and thereby for chastening readers to attend submissively to God's authoritative speech. Since Scripture is the normative means by which Christ confronts the church, any elevation of the authority of the church, Vanhoozer worries, would put it in competition with God's authoritative voice in Scripture.

The church as non-sacramental mimesis: Vanhoozer specifically rejects calling the church a sacrament, and he rejects any ecclesiology in

---

biblical interpretation" (ibid., 235, 418). Vanhoozer ("The Spirit of Understanding," 222) uses Ebeling's definition in order to clearly distinguish "text" and "interpretation." In fact, *sola Scriptura* is needed to preserve just this distinction. Vanhoozer (*The Drama of Doctrine*, 418) will enhance Ebeling's claim, so that, "The history of the church is essentially the story of how the church interprets Scripture 'bodily,' through the shape of its community life. Church history is thus the history of biblical *performance*."

12. Vanhoozer, *The Drama of Doctrine*, 210.

13. Ibid., 121.

14. Ibid., 163.

15. Vanhoozer (ibid., 121) argues "The idea that cultures are closed systems, insular and internally consistent wholes that preserve a stable deposit of values and knowledge, is a distinctly modern fiction. . . . Cultures . . . are as susceptible to deconstruction as are texts." Only Scripture, because of its unique role in the divine economy, can avoid deconstruction and stand as a check to corporate pride.

which the church is considered a "sign/presence of the triune God," where "ecclesial words and actions mediate the grace of God."[16] This, he thinks, would give the church an initiatory mission analogous to the mission of Scripture. Instead, Vanhoozer suggests that "the church is less a sacrament than a means of signifying the divine grace poured out in Christ through the Spirit."[17] Vanhoozer then describes the church as a mimesis of the gospel, intending this term to provide a *tertium quid* between a sacramental description of the church as mediation of grace and a bare description of the church's action as a memorial of Christ.[18] Sacramental language of mediation of grace is intentionally replaced by language of "imitation" and "signification" of grace to stress the church's responsive role, yet language of memorial is also replaced in order to provide a more robust account of the Spirit's presence and work in the church. Imitating is distinctly a mission of response, and consequently has less authority than mediation in the economy of redemption. Using mimesis as a controlling metaphor, Vanhoozer feels, will provide the church a participatory role in redemption ("an imitation of Paul, of God, of Christ"), yet will keep that action from being confused with God's prior initiatory action.[19] The church's task is that of "performing the word in the power of the Spirit," and "present[ing] the body of Christ" as a "theater" of Christ.[20] Drama, then, provides a helpful paradigm for showing the church's responsive mimesis of God's canonical script.[21]

Vanhoozer's description of the church as mimesis leads to a new working definition of the church as "the company of the gospel, whose nature and task alike pertain to performing the word in the power of the

---

16. Ibid., 400.

17. Ibid., 401.

18. Ibid., 412. Vanhoozer sees "imitation" as a middle ground between claiming the church is a simple (almost passive) remembrance of Christ, and a channel of mediation of Christ. In fact, Vanhoozer's model of drama attempts to incorporate "imitating" as an alternative to the traditional divide between memorial and sacrament in sacramental theology. Hence Vanhoozer (ibid., 409) claims "As celebration, the church is not a literal repetition of the body of Christ, nor a sacrament, nor an empty memorial, but an active mimesis." Vanhoozer's treatment of sacraments covers only three pages in *The Drama of Doctrine* and does not focus not on the role sacraments play in God's self-communicative action. Vanhoozer has opportunity to take this up in *Remythologizing Theology*, yet he does not do so in a significant way.

19. Ibid., 401.

20. Ibid., 401 and 407, respectively.

21. Ibid., 412.

Spirit."²² Vanhoozer intends the phrase "company of the gospel" to replace the sacramental description of the church as "presence of the triune God," and the phrase "performing the word" to replace "mediating grace sacramentally."²³ Vanhoozer does claim that, "Any sufficiently thick description of the church must include something about the church being not only the people of God but the *presence* of God in the world."²⁴ The performance of the Gospel simultaneously "inserts its members into the drama of redemption" and makes Christ "*really present* in the life of the church" so that "*the reality of the already/not yet presence of Jesus Christ is in our midst.*"²⁵ Such an understanding suggests that Christ is present in the church, yet rejects the church's role in *mediating* Christ's presence. Christ is present in the church, yet normatively uses only Scripture as a means of self-mediation.

The Active Role of Scripture and the Passive Role of the Church in the Economy

On Vanhoozer's account, both Scripture and church share in mission because they are extensions of the economic missions of the triune God. Yet in his schema, Scripture is given an active, initiatory mission and the church is given a responsive commission. This structuring of the economy allows Vanhoozer to advance his argument for the authority of Scripture over the church while at the same time showing the indispensable role that the church plays in the economy of redemption.

The active mission of Scripture in the economy: Scripture's active, initiatory mission must be understood in the context of Vanhoozer's "economy of missions."²⁶ Vanhoozer describes God's existence as self-communicative Act, eternally communicating among the Persons of the immanent Trinity. Yet, Vanhoozer claims, "When directed *ad extra*, the communicative action of God is perhaps better termed mission. Hence the economy of communication is ultimately missional: divine communicative action involves the 'sendings' (missio) of Son and Spirit."²⁷

22. Ibid., 401.
23. See ibid., 400–401.
24. Ibid., 400.
25. Ibid., 410 (emphasis his).
26. Ibid., 60–75.
27. Ibid., 261.

Vanhoozer proposes that Scripture is given a mission for redemption analogous to the missions of the triune Persons, and that "Scripture's mission is tied up with the Trinitarian missions of the Son and Spirit."[28] Just as Son and Spirit were sent by the Father, so also is Scripture sent to the church in the economy of redemption. Vanhoozer argues that the missions of Word, Spirit, and Scripture must be closely connected, because "Word without Spirit is powerless; Spirit without Word is directionless" and "[t]he canon is the Spirit's chosen means to mediate the covenant and foster the communion that obtains between Christ and the church."[29] As a result, "Scripture does not simply recount action; it is part of the action . . . it contributes to the realization of God's purposes for the world . . . Scripture is thus a collection of statements—and promises, commands, warnings, and so on—all on their respective missions."[30] All of the individual speech-acts of Scripture, as they contribute to the canonical whole, have been given an authority to establish and sustain the church.

Ultimately, Scripture must be understood as God's communication rather than human communication about God.[31] Vanhoozer explains,

> The crucial point is that Scripture is holy (set apart) and authoritative because it is ingredient in the economy of communication, that is, in the way in which the triune God ministers the Word of God in the power of the Spirit. . . . Scripture is a creaturely medium taken up as an "extension of Christ's active, communicative presence in the Spirit's power through the commissioned apostolic testimony." As such, Scripture is a means of ongoing triune communication by which the church follows her master's voice.[32]

While Scripture is a "creaturely medium," it is ultimately more a species of the economic triune communicative action than a product of

---

28. Ibid., 60.

29. Ibid., 199.

30. Ibid., 70. Vanhoozer draws an "*analogia missio*" between "incarnation" and "inscripturation," based on three analogies: "(1) both are species of triune communicative action—embodied in the case of Jesus, verbalized in the case of Scripture; (2) both aim to draw communicants into the new covenant community; (3) both are accompanied by the Spirit and require the Spirit in order to complete their respective missions."

31. Ibid., 11–12. Vanhoozer (ibid., 177) argues "What becomes paramount is God's use of the biblical texts. . . . God, in and through the human authors, has an ongoing speaking part."

32. Vanhoozer, *Remythologizing Theology*, 264.

God's use of scripture and church in the economy of redemption 111

human discourse. Vanhoozer insists that, "In attending closely to Scripture we not only read about God but confront God in one mode of his self-presentation."[33] The Scriptures are revelation because they are God's definitive self-witness to "what God has done and is doing in Christ."[34] For Vanhoozer, "The human statements about God's action and passion are not accommodations of a rich reality to poor words, but rather an elevation of human words to divine discourse: these human texts have been set apart as sanctified servants of divine revelation."[35] Encounter with God's unique mode of self-presentation in Scripture places emphasis on God's complete, determinate speech acts as a canonical whole, and it equates this canonical whole with revelation itself.

It is Scripture's active mission in the economy that grounds the principle of *sola Scriptura* in Vanhoozer's later work. Vanhoozer argues that while both revisionists and postliberals want to reestablish the role of Scripture in the church, both go wrong precisely by seeing Scripture more as a privileged response to revelation than as God's communicative act.[36] To move beyond this impasse, Vanhoozer suggests that both groups must shift focus from discussions about how the uniqueness of Scripture's subject matter inverts general hermeneutical rules, to an explanation of how just these texts are caught up in God's self-communication and used in the economy of redemption.[37] Scriptural language is not a human projection about God, but is rather God's true and real self-revelation. A return to *sola Scriptura*, Vanhoozer believes, will ward off both revisionist attempts to impose some general strategy of correlation beginning with

---

33. Ibid., 189.

34. Vanhoozer, *The Drama of Doctrine*, 418.

35. Vanhoozer, *Remythologizing Theology*, 80, noting John Webster, *Holy Scripture*, 26.

36. On the one hand, Vanhoozer (*Remythologizing Theology*, 12) suggests that Ricoeur (who is associated through David Tracy to the revisionists) was correct to propose a "Copernican revolution" in biblical interpretation that would render the reader a submissive learner of the unique subject matter of Scripture. However, Vanhoozer feels that Ricoeur was unable to accomplish this project because Ricoeur could not precisely articulate how the biblical text is "of God." On the other hand, Vanhoozer (ibid., 216) claims that postliberals have not attended well enough to the way in which God establishes covenant forms of life tn hrough the various genres of Scripture.

37. Vanhoozer (ibid., 11) uses Ricoeur's emphasis on "naming God" as his point of departure, but "[G]oing beyond Ricoeur, we can say that God also speaks and acts in and through all these discourses differently as well. Consequently, this work derives a doctrine of God's being from an analysis of God's speaking, something Ricoeur never attempted."

human experience and postliberal attempts to make ecclesiology into First Theology. Thus a return to *sola Scriptura* will resolve the crisis of authority in the church, as it will allow God to use Scripture against the church.[38] *Sola Scriptura*, then, when combined with a First Theology of God's authorship, operates as a principle of authority which will conform the church's concrete practices toward Christ.[39] Thus the "canon is ... the divinely approved means by which God exercises his authority in, and over, the church."[40]

The passive mission of the church in the economy: Since the "whole theodrama is essentially missional," the church too has an essential mission in the economy of redemption.[41] Yet, while the respective missions of Scripture and church are both essential, each does not have equal authority. In order to differentiate authority between the missions of Scripture and church, Vanhoozer distinguishes between initiative "mission" and responsive "commission." Initiating mission (God's initial act) always has authority over commissioned responsive mission (the effect that God's initial act produces). Those to whom Son, Spirit, and Scripture are sent also participate in mission, but this is a commissioned mission, a mission of response. Vanhoozer emphasizes, "The church does not send itself; it is rather appointed, *commissioned*. Its mission derives from its prior commission."[42] This mission "is to participate in and continue the

38. Vanhoozer (ibid., 17) claims "The supreme *norm* for church practice is Scripture itself: not Scripture as used by the church but Scripture as used by God, even, or perhaps especially, when such use is *over against* the church."

39. *Sola Scriptura* appears to be used by Vanhoozer as a theoretical construct to locate authority in Scripture rather than the church. Vanhoozer (ibid.) claims that *sola Scriptura* does not mean Scripture alone (*solo Scriptura*), but is "a responsive, directional practice of the Church.... Namely, the practice of corresponding in one's speech and action to the word of God." It is difficult, on this account, to distinguish *sola Scriptura* from First Theology. And, for Vanhoozer, this appears to be precisely the function of *sola Scriptura*. Vanhoozer ("Scripture and Tradition," 166) claims that *sola Scriptura* means that "Scripture ... should enjoy epistemic and existential primacy in the life of the Church."

40. Vanhoozer, *The Drama of Doctrine*, 124.

41. Ibid., 69.

42. Vanhoozer (ibid., 71) emphasizes church doctrine, a construction of the church's practice, is caught up in the divine drama and has its own mission, but this mission is one of response to Scripture. Vanhoozer (ibid., 60) keeps the direction clear: "The mission of theology is to enable the people of God to participate in the mission and ministry of the gospel.... Scripture's role in the economy of the gospel ... is that of the gospel's normative specification." The church's responsive mission depends on the Scriptures' initiative mission.

joint mission of Word and Spirit."⁴³ Vanhoozer clarifies this relationship between Scripture and church by claiming,

> The human readers of Scripture are indeed active, but in a peculiarly passive way. The Spirit catches readers up into the theodramatic action not by inspiring but illumining them, enabling them to read the Bible in order to hear and do the Word. . . . The church is ultimately not the author but the passive recipient of the canonical Scriptures.⁴⁴

The church's "active" role as "passive recipient" emphasizes the authority of Scripture over the church as well as the indispensable role of the church in the economy of redemption. What is important to notice is that Vanhoozer only presents two options: the church is either "passive recipient" or "author." Since the church is not author of Scripture, the church must only have a mission of response to Scripture's author. In recent dialogue with Catholic theologians, Vanhoozer reemphasizes this either/or structure of authority by suggesting that the theologian "needs to appeal *either to the church or divine authorship*" to explain the canonical unity of Scripture.⁴⁵ Not so surprisingly, Vanhoozer chooses divine authorship over the church as the principle of authority, and contrasts his view with the position of Pope Benedict XVI. In response to Benedict's claim that, "Without faith, Scripture itself is not Scripture, but rather an ill-assorted ensemble of bits of literature that cannot claim any normative significance," Vanhoozer responds, "For Benedict, then, the faith of the church alone [*sola ecclesia!*] makes the disparate texts into a single Bible. Protestants demur, claiming that God's inspired word is prior to human faith."⁴⁶ Vanhoozer's response is telling, because it shows that for Vanhoozer, the authority of Scripture is grounded *either* in the all too human action of the church, *or* in God's speaking action. Consequently, to locate authority in the faith of the church is necessarily to diminish the authority of God speaking through Scripture.

Vanhoozer, then, insists upon the *necessity* of the church for scriptural interpretation while denying the *authority* of the church in scriptural interpretation. Since the very mission of Scripture is to "form a new people," this mission cannot be fulfilled without the incorporation of the

---

43. Ibid., 71.
44. Ibid., 230.
45. Vanhoozer, "Interpreting Scripture," 215.
46. Ibid., citing Thornton and Varenne, *The Essential Pope Benedict*, 146.

church into a commissioned mission.[47] Scripture is "complete" insofar as "the story of God's word-acts in the history of Israel and in Jesus Christ is finished," yet "incomplete . . . without a people to embody it . . . for the canon "delivers its meaning only as it is 'played out' in patterns of human action in Church and society."[48] As a result, Vanhoozer suggests that "script and performance are equally necessary, though not equally authoritative. Biblical script without ecclesial performance is empty; ecclesial performance without biblical script is blind."[49] With Gadamer, Vanhoozer suggests that "only the performance brings out everything that is in the play. . . . To be occasional is essential to it: the occasion of the performance makes it speak and brings out what is in it."[50] The church, then, is called the "theater of the gospel," the location where the gospel drama is played out, while those incorporated into the church are "the company of performers" who can "function as a 'hermeneutic of the gospel'" as they "perform . . . texts."[51] The church's responsive role is indeed quite active, even if it lacks the authority given to Scripture.

Implications of a Covenantal Ecclesiology

Since Vanhoozer's ecclesiology is developed almost entirely as a response to postliberals, the problematic of authority governs his entire discussion of the church. This ecclesiology leads to particular emphases in scriptural reading. First, Vanhoozer's non-sacramental description of the church as mimesis places much more emphasis on the mission of the church than on the ontological reality of the church.[52] For Vanhoozer, all realities in the economy of redemption are structured by their respective missions:

47. Ibid., 182.

48. Ibid., 165. See also Vanhoozer's claim that the "canon as script comes into its own only when it is realized in understanding and responsive action" (235).

49. Ibid., 362.

50. See Gadamer, *Truth and Method*, 147, cited in Vanhoozer, *The Drama of Doctrine*, 235.

51. Vanhoozer, *The Drama of Doctrine*, 413 and 179.

52. For example, Vanhoozer claims that "The full measure of the gospel and of saving faith—'Christ in us' and 'we in Christ'—can ultimately be *exhibited* only in and by community" (ibid., 402). This ought to be contrasted with de Lubac's emphasis on the primacy of the church as an ontological reality (the body of Christ) into which individuals are incorporated. Vanhoozer does often speak of the whole church as the "larger catholic whole," yet the whole tends to be understood as the whole collection of the smaller parts (see ibid., 454).

"Mission impels the theo-dramatic action forward," first in the mission of the Son who revealed the Father, then in the Spirit, whose "unique mission is to minister the word, a ministry of revelation and reconciliation alike," then in Scripture, which "like the Son, is sent on a mission," and finally the church, which is "actually and actively *participating* in the missions of Son and Spirit" in a vital but supporting role, as the "church is the very form that the *mission Dei* currently takes."[53] Described as a "theo-dramatic mimesis," the church *is* as the church responds to the covenantal document of Scripture and thereby extends the redemptive missions of the triune Persons. As a result, the "life of the church just *is* its theological interpretation of Scripture," and the church's practice is the "history of biblical interpretation."[54] Consequently, for Vanhoozer, the church is viewed more as a community of individuals who perform the gospel by practicing the covenant form of life structured in Scripture than as a corporate humanity ontologically united with Christ. While Vanhoozer's bibliology is one of presence, his ecclesiology is decidedly one of absence, stressing that until the eschaton, the church "must rest content with announcing—and, more important, with *rehearsing*" the kingdom.[55]

Second, Vanhoozer's continual emphasis on Christ's use of Scripture to confront the church leads to a cumulative argument which tends to suggest that Christ uses Scripture *rather than* the church for self-mediation. While Vanhoozer intends to show that the authority of Scripture and church alike derive from Christ's use of them, Scripture is associated so much more closely with Christ's communicative action than is the church that a dismissal of the church's authority often seems to be a prerequisite to accepting Scripture's authority.[56] Vanhoozer's close asso-

---

53. Ibid., 69, 70, and 72, respectively.

54. Ibid., 418.

55. Ibid., 443. The church is a parable of the kingdom, which missions a "glimpse, and taste, of truth." The term "rehearse" is carefully chosen to emphasize the not-yet dimension of the church, thus stressing the mission of the church over the ontological reality of the church.

56. Vanhoozer's emphasis on Christ's self-mediation in Scripture and absence of Christ's self-mediation in the church closely associates Christ with Scripture *rather than* the church. For example, when Vanhoozer (ibid., 208, citing Webster, *Word and Church*, 39) claims that "the authority of the church 'is nothing other than its acknowledgement of the norm under which it stands,'" he intends to show that the church stands under the authority of Christ. However, in the immediate context, Vanhoozer (*The Drama of Doctrine*, 208) speaks of Scripture as "Christ's scepter, the means by

ciation between the Word (Christ) and the written word (Scripture), with little discussion of the Word's (Christ's) presence in the church, is fairly common throughout his work, and it serves to leave the "Word's" (i.e., Christ's) presence in the church underdeveloped.[57][58] Vanhoozer tellingly calls the church the "'Body' of the Text," thus closely associating Scripture with Christ.[59] When such an association of Word (Christ) and word (Scripture) becomes the basis for Scripture alone as a final authority, this discourages reflection on Christ's use of the church for self-mediation.

DE LUBAC'S SACRAMENTAL ECCLESIOLOGY

De Lubac's ecclesiology is characterized by a sacramental ontology in which Christ is mediated through Scripture, Eucharist, and church. In this sacramental ecclesiology, Scripture, Eucharist, and visible church (in which the Magisterium have a special role in embodying the sacramental structure of the church), are all temporary *signum* that lead to the *res,* the eschatological fulfillment of the *totus Christus.* As de Lubac understands the Scripture/church relationship in terms of reciprocal sacramental causality, he employs the Blondelian synthesis to show how Christ uses tradition as the living link between Scripture and church. De Lubac's ecclesiology and his spiritual interpretation of Scripture are only intelligible together, as the church interprets Scripture in terms of its own

---

which Christ rules his church," thus closely associating Christ with Scripture while bypassing discussion of Christ's "rule" by means of the church.

57. For example, Vanhoozer (*The Drama of Doctrine*, 209) claims "Only the Word serves as magisterial norm, however, for only the written word is the commissioned testimony of the church's Lord and Master." Notice that Christ is directly associated with the written word (Scripture) as opposed to the church. Vanhoozer ("Triune Discourse," 76) suggests "To claim that the Trinity is our Scripture Principle is to confess that the supreme authority in the church is the triune God speaking in the Scriptures." Notice once again how God's communicative action is located in Scripture *instead of* in the church.

58. Vanhoozer, "Triune Discourse," 76.

59. Ibid., 418. Vanhoozer describes the church as a "corporate rendering of the Word of God in the power of the Spirit" where Word of God refers distinctly to the mission of Christ extended *in Scripture*. Vanhoozer then claims, "While the core of the theo-drama consists in what God has done and is doing in Christ, the Scriptures, as testimony to this act, are themselves caught up in it and become a means for God for building up his church in Christ through the power of the Spirit."

participation in the mystery as it incorporates individuals and yearns for its eschatological fullness as the *totus Christus*.[60]

The Church as Mystery and Sacrament

The church as mystery: As we have seen in de Lubac's treatment of allegory, de Lubac insists that the church, in an incomplete but real way, is the mystery. De Lubac claims, "The Church is a mysterious extension in time of the Trinity, not only preparing us for the life of unity but bringing about even now our participation in it. She comes from and is full of the Trinity."[61] The church really is mystery because it is the emerging reality of the *totus Christus*: the body of Christ incorporated into its head (allegory), incorporating individuals into itself (tropology), and yearning for its eschatological completion as the *totus Christus* (anagogy). The church is in the process of becoming what it already is. De Lubac insists, "The Church on earth is not merely the vestibule of the Church in heaven . . . for she stands to our heavenly home in a relation of mystical analogy in which we should perceive the reflection of a profound identity. It is indeed the same city which is built on earth and yet has its foundations in heaven."[62] The church is not the cause of the mystery, nor can it claim any role in mediating the mystery other than what it has received as a gift from its union with Christ. Rather, "The Church is a mystery because, coming from God and entirely at the service of his plan, she is an organism of salvation, precisely because she relates wholly to Christ and apart from him has no existence, value or efficacity."[63] The church is mystery because the church is the organism ordained by God and united with Christ in which

---

60. See Wood, *Spiritual Exegesis and the Church*, 152–54. The structure of his ecclesiology depends on his understanding of the fourfold sense of Scripture, and the church exhibits this same fourfold structure of Christian reality in its own self-identity.

61. De Lubac, *The Church*, 24.

62. De Lubac, *Catholicism*, 72. De Lubac (*The Splendor of the Church*, 119) suggests that the difficulty in seeing the eternal nature of the church is "because we don't yet see her from a viewpoint wide-embracing enough. We are thinking of the Church only as the Church Militant, not as the perfect and glorious Bride." A theological understanding of the church must include the church militant, purgatory, and the church triumphant.

63. De Lubac, *The Church*, 15. De Lubac (*The Splendor of the Church*, 106) notes that the church is both "holy" and "the Church of the holy," not because there are no sinners in the church, but because it is the church that sanctifies and the church that is purified by the Holy Spirit.

salvation history receives its meaning. Anagogy thus unites the church as it exists today with the fulfillment of the *totus Christus*.

De Lubac insists on accepting the implications of understanding the church as mystery. While the church is sinful and its visible structures are not eternal, these present features of the church are not its primary identity. De Lubac claims that the church should not understand "herself ... so much from her structures or her history as from her predestination in Jesus Christ and her orientation towards the parousia."[64] Even in the present state of the church, "there is between her and Him a certain relation of mystical identity," so that, "Practically speaking, for each one of us Christ is thus His Church."[65] De Lubac will even occasionally claim that the church is the incarnation continued, the ongoing "presence of Christ on earth."[66] So intrinsic is this relationship between the church in its "transitory, imperfect state" and its "complete, spiritual, definitive state" that a certain "exchange of idioms" should be allowed between Christ and the church, because "between the means and the end there is not merely an extrinsic relationship."[67] Refocusing attention on the divine reality of the church and its anagogical completion as mystery is, of course, an act of faith. Hence de Lubac claims that "no one can believe in the Church, except in the Holy Spirit."[68] To grasp the intrinsic relationship between visible church and divine reality is to enter the very mystery, which is intelligible but not comprehensible.

Though de Lubac insists on understanding the church in terms of its divine reality, he nonetheless demonstrates a very realistic picture of the sinfulness of the church, admitting that the visible church will often

64. De Lubac, *The Church*, 16.

65. De Lubac, *The Splendor of the Church*, 210–11.

66. De Lubac, *The Church*, 24; Wood ("The Ecclesial Meaning," 112) clarifies that the church as "continued Incarnation" is only an eschatological reality, "Since the *totus Christus*, the whole Christ, represents the church in its eschatological dimension, it is only in this sense that we can say that the church is a continuation of the Incarnation. We can only affirm this of the church as the body of Christ, not as an organization. The Eucharist signs and makes sacramentally real this fullness of Christ, which will be definitively achieved only eschatologically. We anticipate a fullness and wholeness under sacramental sign even while our present experience of the body is one of brokenness and alienation through sin."

67. De Lubac, *Catholicism*, 68. De Lubac claims that because "The Church, without being exactly co-extensive with the Mystical Body, is not adequately distinct from it ... there should arise a kind of exchange of idioms: *Corpus Christi quod est ecclesia*" (ibid., 72–73).

68. Ibid., 74.

hide rather than disclose this divine reality. De Lubac claims that "this very same Church, is often unfaithful and unsubmissive. In her members she is a sinner ... the Church is also a symbol of perpetual decline and mortality."[69] On account of the communication of idioms between the church and Christ, the visible church is often the same kind of stumbling block that the humanity of Christ posed to understanding his divinity. Yet the ability of the body of Christ to hide Christ is much greater in the church than in Christ's human body, because the behavior of the church is often sinful.[70] De Lubac realizes that the church has a responsibility to continually be a fitting sign. The actions of the church serve to either hide or disclose the divine reality of the church. The behavior of those within the church has a real effect on whether the sign hides or discloses the reality.[71] Yet de Lubac claims that the ability to see the divine reality of the church is part of the gift of faith itself and stands despite the witness of its members.[72] In fact, faith that the church will truly be eschatologically transformed is one of the tests of Christian faith.[73]

69. De Lubac, *The Church*, 24.

70. De Lubac (*The Splendor of the Church*, 48–49) claims, "[T]here is something yet more 'scandalous' and 'foolish' about belief in a Church where the divine is not only united with the human, but presents itself to us by way of the all-too-human, and that without any alternative.... Truth to tell, the Church is even more compact of contrast and paradox than Christ. We can say of the Church, as of Christ, 'a great mystery and wonderful sacrament,' but we are driven to say of her even more than of Christ.... 'A stone of stumbling and a rock of offence.' . . . If a purification and transformation of vision is necessary to look on Christ without being scandalized, how much more is it necessary when we are looking at the Church!"

71. De Lubac (ibid., 228–35) spends much of his chapter on the church as sacrament exhorting the church to realize its sacramental position and not mute the sacramental value of the sign (see esp. 228–35). The behavior of the church has a real effect on its value as sacramental sign.

72. De Lubac (ibid., 46) claims, "But the dark side of the mystery is there too, and just as surely.... For the unbeliever whom the Father has not begun to draw to Him, the Church remains a stumbling-block. And she can be a testing-round for the believer too, which is a good thing; perhaps the test is all the more strenuous in proportion as his faith is purer and more vital."

73. De Lubac (ibid., 49) claims "Let us within the Church, who speak of ourselves as being 'of the Church', manage to grasp the fact as sharply as it is sensed by those who are afraid of her and those who run away from her." However, this sense of faith will result in optimism for the church rooted in faith. De Lubac (ibid., 78) claims "We should ... be on our guard against cramping within concepts that are inadequate to it God's power to transfigure His Bride. Far from struggling against belief in something which our imagination cannot picture, we ought to let the daring of faith sweep us off our feet."

Because human beings exist in relation to the supernatural, since Christ is mediated through the church, and since the church participates in the mystery already while moving toward its completion in the mystery, the church is the locus where the "human being becomes a person."[74] For de Lubac, it is in union with Christ that human beings find personhood, as they become part of the *totus Christus*.[75] Furthermore, since personhood is associated with communion with others and with Christ, human beings await their becoming fully persons until the final realization of the *totus Christus*. De Lubac never makes a strict identification between the visible church and the *totus Christus*, but neither is he willing to separate the present visible church from the emerging *totus Christus*. De Lubac uses the threefold spiritual senses of allegory, tropology, and anagogy to show that the *totus Christus* is an eschatological reality that already participates in the mystery (allegory), presently incorporates individuals into the corporate mystery (tropology), and is not yet fully achieved (anagogy). Throughout his work, de Lubac's insistence is that the Christian life is a life within the church in which readers become what they are and yearn toward the full eschatological union of Christ and the church.

The church as sacrament: De Lubac has been a leading figure in developing the sacramental nature of the church, resulting in the Second Vatican council stating that "the Church is in Christ like a sacrament."[76] In *The Splendor of the Church*, de Lubac describes the church as "the great

---

74. De Lubac, *The Christian Faith*, 277. In this work, de Lubac describes the response to revelation as that which enables the human being to become a person: "On the part of man, who responds to God's call, faith is the discovery and recognition of the divinity as a personal Absolute. It is precisely in this discovery and this recognition that, as a result, the human being becomes a person."

75. De Lubac (*Catholicism*, 279) claims that "the Church is nothing else than humanity itself, enlivened, unified by the Spirit of Christ." This certainly does not mean that de Lubac is arguing for universalism; only that the human being is really a person only when in union with Christ. Joseph Mangina (*Karl Barth*, 167–68) also emphasizes that "the anti-Nazi and anti-communist de Lubac" is quite concerned not to simply subsume all humanity into one collective reality, nor is he interested in erasing the distinction between Head and body. Yet because the 'event of Christ' stands as the center-point for all history, all human beings are oriented toward a common yearning for participation in Christ. See also O'Sullivan, *Christ and Creation*, 371.

76. See Dogmatic Constitution on the Church, *Lumen gentium* 1:1. This is the first time the church is called a sacrament in an ecumenical council. See also *Lumen gentium* 2:9, where the church is called "the visible sacrament of this saving unity," and *Lumen gentium*, 7:48, which calls the church the "universal sacrament of salvation."

God's use of scripture and church in the economy of redemption

sacrament which contains and vitalizes all the others."[77] The church is the great sacrament precisely as it operates in a sacramental chain from triune God to Christ to church to Eucharist. De Lubac writes in Catholicism,

> If Christ is the sacrament of God, the Church is for us the sacrament of Christ; she represents him . . . she really makes him present . . . she is his very continuation . . . the . . . exterior organization . . . is but an expression . . . of the interior unity of a living entity, so that the Catholic is not only subject to a power but is a member of a body as well, and his legal dependence on this power is to the end that he might have part in the life of that body.[78]

This description of the church as sacrament will form the background for all de Lubac's discussion of the church. On account of its sacramental nature, de Lubac feels that the church can only be understood in terms of a series of paradoxes. The visible is the indispensable means to the invisible, as is the human to the divine and the temporal to the eternal.[79] Since de Lubac's ecclesiology has the same fundamental fourfold structure as his understanding of Scripture, it can be assumed that the sacramental relationships which exist in the church can illumine de Lubac's understanding of the movement from letter to spirit in his theology of Scripture.

Due to the intrinsic relationship between the human and divine aspects of the church, De Lubac emphatically rejects any division between the invisible church and the visible church which would reduce the visible to merely a human institution.[80] On the one hand, because the visible church is "the sign of something else, it must be passed through, and this not in part but wholly . . . it is not something intermediate, but something mediatory."[81] On the other hand, however, a sacramental sign cannot simply "be changed at will" because it is "essentially related to our present condition." Hence, de Lubac claims, "We never come to the end of passing through this translucent medium, which we must, nevertheless, always pass through and that completely. It is always through it that we reach what it signifies; it can never be superseded, and its bounds cannot

---

77. De Lubac, *The Splendor of the Church*, 203. De Lubac's chapter, "The Sacrament of Christ" (203–35) forms the climax of his first concentrated work on ecclesiology.

78. De Lubac, *Catholicism*, 76.

79. See especially de Lubac, *The Church*, 23–29.

80. De Lubac, *The Splendor of the Church*, 85–87.

81. Ibid., 203.

be broken."⁸² If viewed from the perspective of the sacramental structure of the church, the visible church is inferior to the spiritual reality it signifies. And yet it is impossible to discover that spiritual reality without the historical, institutional, visible church.⁸³ The individual believer will never be able to discover Christianity without the church nor go beyond the church to a purely spiritual faith.⁸⁴

Since much of the function of the visible church is to mediate sacramentally the mystery, however, those aspects which exist for this purpose (e.g., hierarchical organization, sacramental system, etc.) will disappear with the return of Christ. De Lubac claims, "The sacramental element in the Church, being adapted to our temporal condition, is destined to disappear in the face of the definitive reality which it effectively signifies; but this should not be thought of as one thing's effacing of another. It will be the manifestation of sacramentality's own proper truth; a glorious epiphany and a consummation."⁸⁵ Thus de Lubac emphasizes, "We ought, indeed, to love that very element in the Church which is transitory—but we ought to love it as the one and only means, the indispensable organ, the providential instrument, and at the same time as 'the pledge, the passing image, the promise of the communion to come.'"⁸⁶ The church, then, has a sacramental structure that is destined to pass away, yet which at present has an essential role in mediating the mystery. Certainly the Magisterium, as well as the Eucharist and the Scriptures (though de Lubac does not speculate on the role of the Scriptures in the eschaton), are present realities which are used by Christ to build the *totus Christus*, but which will cease to be used in this way when anagogy becomes reality. Yet

---

82. Ibid., 204.

83. De Lubac (ibid., 147) claims "Recognition of authority in the Church is the first and indispensable condition without which we cannot have any part in her vitalizing work." De Lubac (*The Motherhood of the Church*, 68) emphasizes that the three functions of "Word, worship, and government" cannot be "dissociated," and thus the visible structure could never be considered optional.

84. De Lubac (*The Splendor of the Church*, 205–09) recounts the many enthusiastic proposals by Enlightenment philosophers and theologians to move to a purely spiritual faith, a "Church of the Holy Spirit" (the new era prophesied by Joachim of Fiore). De Lubac emphasizes that the age of the Spirit has already occurred simultaneously with the age of Christ, and that the Spirit is the Spirit of Christ. As a result, it is impossible to move beyond the church Christ formed to a less institutional faith.

85. Ibid., 68.

86. Ibid., 83. Wood (*Spiritual Exegesis and the Church*, 107) summarizes the relationship in this way: "the human element in the Church makes the divine element present by making Christ present."

God's use of scripture and church in the economy of redemption

this does not mean that the visible church will give way to the invisible church, but that the two will be seen clearly as one reality.

De Lubac resists two extremes, then, one a Roman Catholic tendency to "reduce the mystical body of Christ to equivalence with the forms of the Roman Church," and the other a Protestant tendency to "water down the Church until it becomes a 'body' conceived in an entirely 'mystical' fashion." Instead, the visible and invisible must be held in tension so that "What we shall affirm is that the Church mysteriously transcends the limits of her visibility, that by her very essence she carries herself, as it were, above herself."[87] Protestant theology, de Lubac feels, has lost the intrinsic relationship between visible and invisible by focusing only on the invisible church.[88] This disregard for the visible church causes Protestantism to implicitly deny the structure of the Christian mystery.[89] By denying the sacramental necessity of the visible, they also disregard the radical newness of the invisible. De Lubac argues that such Protestant understandings of the church are "more inspired by the Old than the New Testament or, in other words, does not fully enter into the logic of the Mystery of the Incarnation."[90] In their stress on the invisible church, they have lost the uniqueness of the entry of God into human history and the formation of the church as a visible reality.

De Lubac's criticism is not limited to Protestants, but even includes the Vatican II drafters of *Lumen Gentium*, for their choice to describe the church as the people of God instead of other New Testament images such as bride or body of Christ. De Lubac fears that the designation of the church as people of God threatens the sacramental structure of the

---

87. De Lubac, *The Church*, 27.

88. De Lubac (*Catholicism*, 75–76) claims that "the experience of Protestantism should serve us as sufficient warning. Having stripped it of all its mystical attributes, it acknowledged in the visible Church a mere secular institution; as a matter of course it abandoned it to the patronage of the state and sought a refuge for the spiritual life in an invisible Church, its concept of which had evaporated into an abstract ideal." One could suspect that de Lubac is primarily lamenting the current state of German Lutheranism.

89. De Lubac, *The Church*, 25.

90. Ibid. De Lubac dislikes the Protestant argument to liken the visible church to rebellious Israel, in which a remnant (the invisible church) will be saved. To appreciate the Christian mystery, one must realize that the church really consists of something that the OT people of God did not. Christ really is joined to this body in a way that the OT people of God did not have access to. The church is really the reality that the OT people of God pointed toward as a sign.

church in two ways.⁹¹ First, this phrase stresses continuity over transformation, thus straining the sacramental nature of the church.⁹² Instead, de Lubac emphasizes, as always, the radical transformation brought about by the event of Christ, in which "the infusion of the Holy Spirit placed the people of God in an essentially new position . . . the Spirit of Christ has renewed, transfigured, and 'spiritualized' everything."⁹³ Second, de Lubac feels that the phrase people of God, undervalues the eschatological reality in which the church already participates.⁹⁴ For de Lubac, the eschaton has already broken in to the natural order, and because of its union with Christ, the church is the eschatological reality, the kingdom, already, even if it still awaits its full union.⁹⁵ Consequently, de Lubac will always insist on a sacramental description of the church in order to preserve the tension between the church's present and eschatological participation in Christ.

The Mutually Causal Roles of Scripture and Church in the Economy

As we saw in the last chapter, both Scripture and church are fellow mediators of the mystery of Christ, and the intrinsic relationship between them is grounded in the incarnate Christ. Eucharist, Scripture, and church are the three incorporations of the Logos and each has been given a distinct

---

91. While de Lubac (*The Church*, 55) appreciates the council's desire "to emphasize the human traits of the Church," he laments that the image of church as bride of Christ is "subordinated to that of the people of God," since it is well-represented in both Scripture and in the Fathers. Thus, says de Lubac, "readers must be careful not to take this expression in isolation" (ibid., 23).

92. Ibid., 39–44.

93. Ibid., 43.

94. Ibid., 49–50. See *Lumen Gentium*, 2:9–17. De Lubac (*The Church*, 50) sees the problem mostly as a matter of emphasis, claiming that the council did not "suppress the consideration of collective eschatology, showing the people of God being guided, generation after generation, towards, and already mystically united to, the heavenly Jerusalem" (50). The problem of immanentism, then, is largely a problem of the subsequent application of the council.

95. De Lubac (*The Church*, 51) criticizes the council for "a certain narrowing of the patristic horizons," which neglects the "already" aspect of the eschatological understanding of the church. De Lubac claims, "In one way, for the people of God envisaged as still on pilgrimage through the obscurity of this world, it is altogether a matter of the 'not-yet'. But in another way—and one that cannot be disassociated from the first—for which the Church considered as a gift from above and the habitation of Christ and his Spirit, we are faced with the 'already-present'" (52).

sacramental role in mediating the one mystery in the divine economy.[96] This section will show how Scripture and church exercise sacramental causality upon each other so that each is an instrument of Christ's self-mediation.

The causal role of Scripture in the economy: De Lubac would agree with Vanhoozer that the Scriptures exercise a causal role over the church. In *History and Spirit*, de Lubac equates the efficacy of the Eucharist with the efficacy of Scripture, so that "Scripture is thus like the voice of Christ speaking to the Church and in the Church; it is his efficacious sign; it thus assures the luminous presence of Christ to the Church."[97] De Lubac insists that Scripture constitutes the church as Scripture makes present the mystery of Christ.[98] Yet how exactly does Scripture's causality operate? In his treatment of tropology, de Lubac provides an important discussion of how Christ uses the texts of Scripture to structure understanding and incorporate readers into the *totus Christus*.[99] De Lubac suggests that Christ confronts and converts individuals precisely by causing them to see their own experience in the scriptural account of salvation history. De Lubac speaks of Scripture as a mirror in which the individual readers read their own history in the narration of history in Scripture. De Lubac claims,

> In this mirror we learn to know our nature and our destiny; in it we also see the different stages through which we have passed since creation, the beautiful and the ugly features of our internal face. It shows us the truth of our being by pointing it out in

---

96. See de Lubac, *History and Spirit*, 385–426. Once again, the distinction between *"Incarnation"* and *"Incorporations"* is decisive, since it was the historical event of the Incarnation which grounds the Christian faith. Incorporations are ways of making the mystery made present in the historical event present today.

97. Ibid., 418.

98. De Lubac (ibid.) claims, "The life of the Church has its source in Scripture. It has it no less in the Eucharist." De Lubac notes that Origen gives Scripture a certain causal priority over the Eucharist because "the 'Word' is, in its pure essence, that very reality: for the Son of God, God himself, is 'Word.'" This does not mean that Scripture is above the Eucharist, but that while both "express and reveal the Logos . . . Scripture does so, in the final analysis, with a superiority that allows one to consider it . . . as the 'truth' of which the Eucharist would be the symbol" (419).

99. Tropology, as discussed in chapter 2, refers to the ongoing process of conversion, the incorporation of the individual into the eschatological body of Christ through the interiorization of the Christian mystery. As interiorization, de Lubac (*Medieval Exegesis*, 2:141) can claim that "whatever page I meditate upon, I find in it a means that God offers me, right now, to restore the divine image within me." It is the mystery interiorized that transforms the reader, not the moral instruction of the text.

its relation to the Creator. It is a living mirror, a living and efficacious Word, a sword penetrating at the juncture of soul and spirit, which makes our secret thoughts appear and reveals to us our heart. It teaches us to read in the book of experience, and makes us, so to speak, our own exegesis.[100]

Scripture can be described as a mirror because for de Lubac, all human beings have been created with the imprint of the Logos upon their souls since they have been created in the image of God.[101] De Lubac suggests that interiorization takes effect through a double movement of, on the one hand, sustained contemplative reflection on the relationship between history and allegory, and on the other hand, repentance and conversion.[102] As this takes place, "Interior experience and meditation on Scripture accordingly tend to merge in a unique 'experience of the Word,'" in which each deepens and furthers the other.[103] Consequently, de Lubac claims that through Scripture, "By taking possession of man, by seizing hold of him and by penetrating to the very depths of his being Christ makes man go down deep within himself, there to discover in a flash regions hitherto unsuspected. It is through Christ that the person . . . becomes conscious of his own being."[104] Spiritual reorientation takes place as Christ confronts the reader while the reader reads her own history in light of God's action in history culminating in Christ.[105] Though

---

100. Ibid., 142.

101. Ayres ("The Soul and the Reading of Scripture," 176) has shown that tropology depends on a doctrine of the soul as a spiritual meeting place between God and human beings, where the mystery may take effect and elicit the return response. Ayres claims that for De Lubac the soul "is the existence of an inner spiritual core to the human person that is both the source of moral action and the location of Christ's restoring grace which draws together the various senses of Scripture." This discussion of the soul "enables De Lubac's account of Christ's restorative action and it provides a site for exploring the mystery of human action and the presence of Christ and Spirit" (ibid).

102. De Lubac (*History and Spirit*, 421) claims that "the essential work of the Christian will be meditation on Scripture, in order to achieve an understanding of it. But, on the other hand, since this understanding of Scripture is identically the act of listening to what the Word makes heard interiorly, it necessarily presupposes purification of the soul."

103. De Lubac, *Medieval Exegesis*, 2:142. De Lubac claims, "When the Word comes to the soul, it is to instruct her in wisdom, and this understanding of the soul with the Word" is not "imaginary;" rather, "the mystery interiorizes itself within the heart, where it becomes experience" (2:174).

104. De Lubac, *Catholicism*, 338–39.

105. De Lubac, *Medieval Exegesis*, 2:140–41.

de Lubac wrote before the popularity of narrative theology, he would probably say that the very narrative construction of the individual is one which yearns toward the Logos. Because the Logos is inscribed on the human heart, the narrative structure of the Bible reflects the narrative structure of the individual.

From this discussion of tropology, it is quite clear that de Lubac emphatically insists upon reading one's own experience in light of Scripture rather than reading Scripture in light of one's own experience, and he shows how Christ's self-mediation in Scripture makes this possible. De Lubac is certainly no supporter of revisionist or correlational theologies, as Scripture is always the standard which judges the experience of the reader. Because Christ uses precisely the narrative of Scripture to transform the reader, the scriptural narrative must govern and describe individual experience. Spiritual reorientation takes place as Christ confronts the reader while the reader reads her own history in light of God's action in history culminating in Christ.[106] In this way "Christ reveals man to himself."[107]

The causal role of the church in the economy: Scripture, Eucharist, and hierarchical structure of the church all act as various *signum* that lead to the *res*, the eschatological union between Christ and the perfected church. Consequently, is through scriptural interpretation that the church becomes what it is—the *totus Christus*.[108] Yet the church exercises a reciprocal sacramental causality on Scripture. De Lubac claims, "In the Church . . . we hear the Word, and it is the hearing of the Word that builds up the Church for all eternity."[109] Though the Scriptures make the church, the Scriptures depend on the church for their existence and efficacy. It is only "in the Church," and "through the effect of the Church's preaching," that "Scripture ceases to be a simple mass of letters" and instead becomes a "living language."[110] The church exercises this causal role by bringing forth the Scriptures (apostolic preaching led to the writing of New Testament texts and their acceptance by the church), and by establishing

---

106. Ibid.

107. "Gaudium Et Spes" §22.

108. Moulins-Beaufort ("Henri De Lubac," 680) claims, "The reading of the holy Scriptures grants us communion with the faith of these concrete men who were seized by God and opened to the mystery of Christ by the Holy Spirit; Christ unites us with them."

109. De Lubac, *History and Spirit*, 420.

110. Ibid., 422.

the doctrinal and participatory framework in which Christ can be recognized in the Scriptures.

Ultimately only the church could have authority to safeguard the authority of Scripture, since only the church participates in the mystery.[111] De Lubac insists that "it is in the Spirit that the Church . . . receives her heritage and understands this heritage in truth. The 'true' meaning of Scripture, its full and definitive meaning, cannot be other than the one 'that the Spirit gives to the Church.'"[112] Only the church can engage Scripture with the correct theological presuppositions, since only the church has the instinct to read Scripture in this way.[113] The Catholic insistence on interpreting Scripture within the church has long been viewed suspiciously by Protestants, who are concerned that emphasizing the necessity of the church for interpretation will cause human beings to place themselves above of the word of God. Yet while de Lubac admits that the church is incomplete in its union with Christ and is often sinful, he is unwilling to remove final interpretive authority from the church, simply to grant it instead to either the individual reader or the trained secular exegete. Since the authority and efficacy of Scripture is grounded in Christ's use of Scripture for self-mediation, the creaturely reality which can best interpret Scripture is that which is joined in union to Christ.[114]

Yet how does the church exercise this causality? Two principles guide de Lubac's thought. First, the church both brought forth the Scriptures and continues to interpret the Scriptures by focusing on the event of Christ as revealing the meaning of all history. De Lubac suggests that the

---

111. De Lubac, *Medieval Exegesis*, 1:27.

112. Ibid., 1:242, and *The Sources of Revelation*, 114.

113. De Lubac (*The Sources of Revelation*, 114) claims that the church always knows by instinct the relationship between the two Testaments: "In subtle balance, ordered by an extremely sure instinct, the Church affirms from the time of her birth and will maintain during the whole course of her history 'the precise and indissoluble interdependence of the Old and New Testaments.'"

114. De Lubac (*The Church*, 25) accuses those Protestants who deny the unique role of the church in mediating interpretation of Scripture of "not fully enter[ing] into the logic of the mystery of the Incarnation," of being "more inspired by the Old than the New Testament," and of failing to adequately appreciating the mystery of the church. De Lubac dislikes the Protestant argument to liken the visible church to rebellious Israel, in which a remnant (the invisible church) will be saved. To appreciate the Christian mystery, one must realize that the church really consists of something that the OT people of God did not. Christ really is joined to this body in a way that the OT people of God did not have access to. The church is really the reality that the OT people of God pointed toward as a sign.

very writing of the New Testament documents, as well as their acceptance by the church, was based on the church's belief that these documents were a correct allegorical interpretation of the Old Testament. De Lubac then calls upon the successors of the apostles to continue the same interpretive movement of allegory in explaining Christ as the meaning of history. For de Lubac, all "Christian preaching is an exegesis, and indeed an 'allegorical' exegesis," and the chief duty of preaching is to "proclaim the whole Christian faith as revealed in Scripture."[115] De Lubac suggests that little difference exists between the method of the apostles and the method of their successors in interpreting the Scriptures christologically since,

> Up until the end of the second century, the writings later referred to as the New Testament were considered not as "Scripture," but as the spiritual or allegorical interpretation of Scripture. The apostles and evangelists were then considered exegetes. Hence, the apostolic writings, in their literal sense, are already *allegoria*.[116]

De Lubac notices a fundamental continuity in interpretive method between the apostles and their successors in reading of the whole Scriptures in light of Christ. The New Testament serves as the prototypical allegorical document, as it provides the foundation for continuing allegorical interpretation of Scripture. All successive Christian expositors are called to the task of allegory, since what "was true of the first Christian preaching, that of the apostles . . . is equally true of the preaching of those who succeed them in the Church: the Fathers, the Doctors, and our present-day pastors."[117] The "great miracle of Pentecost" in which "the disciples there were filled with the Spirit" and read Scripture allegorically "is being perpetuated from generation to generation" as those entrusted with preaching continue "always in unfolding the Scripture, as Jesus did, by relating it all to Jesus."[118] Even after these New Testament writings were unified in a canonical whole, the fundamental task of allegorical interpretation continued in the same way. It is the role of successors to go beyond the apostles in tracing lines of allegory between Old and New, as successors reproduce the same spiritual movement of the first

---

115. Ibid., 222 and 217–18, respectively.

116. D'Ambrosio, *Traditional Hermeneutic*, 194. See this discussion of allegory in *Medieval Exegesis*, 2:216–26, where de Lubac shows this awareness on the part of the successors to the apostles, who typically write literal expositions on the works of the apostles, not allegorical commentaries on the apostolic writings.

117. De Lubac, *Medieval Exegesis*, 2:218.

118. Ibid., 2:219.

apostles. This emphasis on the continuation of interpretation as apostolic preaching seems to suggest that all generations of successors are called to contemplate the event of Christ in qualitatively the same way as the first apostles. Furthermore, it necessarily places all scriptural interpretation within the church, since only the church can understand the mystery of Christ. Consequently, the church produces the Scriptures as the successors have been invested with a unique capacity to understand allegory and advance the original interpretations of the first apostles which have been codified in Scripture.

Second, the primary responsibility of the church is to keep scriptural reading open to the mystery, and hence to a certain interpretive maximalism that is always guided by reflection on Christ. Hence, de Lubac claims,

> The Magisterium merely guarantees that the development of the mysteries of the faith in the minds of believers remains within the complete and definitive "figure" of this mystery. It guarantees that the communion of these believers remains open to an Object that is "incomprehensible" in the etymological sense of the word, because it is he who "embraces me beyond my capacity to embrace him—and this embrace is that of a living Person."[119]

The role of the Magisterium is to keep the interpretation of the text oriented toward the singular mystery, and to proscribe those interpretations that prohibit such Christian readings. Here de Lubac's focus is on the chastening of readers rather than the muting of the text. The reading of Scripture within the church is meant to eliminate those readings of Scripture that are incompatible with the identity of the church and to illumine the mystery that only the church can sense. De Lubac is always wary of the tendency to reduce the mystery to propositions, thereby eliminating the necessary paradoxes theology reducing the mystery. He insists that, "No mystery is a simple truth, and if we become attached with too narrow an attention to one of its aspects in order to establish the main part of it, we risk ending in many an absurdity or many a heresy."[120] The church's temptation to too tightly define the boundaries the truth is as pernicious to the Christian mystery as no doctrinal boundaries at all.[121] The very pres-

---

119. De Lubac, *La révélation divine*, 158–59, cited by Moulins-Beaufort, "Henri De Lubac," 692.

120. De Lubac, "The Problem of the Development of Dogma," 265.

121. De Lubac, of course, spent a good deal of his life under suspicion from the church, and knew first-hand the dangers of "too narrow" an official focus. For a good

ence of the mystery in the church impels the church to interpret Scripture according to her nature, and this means both placing those boundaries around Scripture and engaging in that doctrinal development which will best facilitate Christ's ongoing self-mediation in Scripture.

Implications of a Sacramental Ecclesiology

While the topic of authority has dominated Vanhoozer's covenantal structuring of Christ's use of Scripture and church, the unique capacity of the church to understand the Scriptures according to its own participation in Christ dominates de Lubac's sacramental structuring of Scripture and church. De Lubac's focus on this unique capacity leads to particular emphases for scriptural reading. First, de Lubac envisions the causal role of the church primarily as keeping scriptural interpretation open to the mystery until the completion of the *totus Christus*, at which time the sacramental roles of Scripture, Eucharist, and the hierarchical structure of the church will be completed. This means that de Lubac's focus will remain on the distinct sacramental role which Magisterium of the church must play in order to keep the mystery open to Christ. Since the church, which participates in the mystery, is the only organization which has a sense of this mystery, the church's primary responsibility is to keep scriptural readings open to the widest possible range of christological interpretations possible without reducing the mystery.[122] De Lubac suspects that attempts to grant all authority to the plain sense of Scripture actually serves to grant authority to the secular scholar rather than to the church. By describing the church's authority as its responsibility to enable and safeguard interpretive maximalism, de Lubac may provide resources for Vanhoozer to acknowledge Christ's authoritative use of the church while resisting the tendency to make ecclesiology into First Theology.

Second, de Lubac's argument for the authority of the church depends on a particular understanding of the realized union between Christ and the church as the *totus Christus*. De Lubac emphasizes that Christ is *already* joined to his body in a way that he was not joined to the OT people of God and thus the church is *already* the reality that the OT people of

---

summary of de Lubac's relationship with neo-Thomist Catholicism, see David Grumett, *De Lubac*, 47–74.

122. De Lubac, *Medieval Exegesis*, 1:27.

God pointed toward as a sign.[123] As a result, Christ uses the church for self-mediation in a way that God did not use the people of Israel. De Lubac would likely claim that Vanhoozer's understanding of Scripture as a covenant document is much "more inspired by the Old than the New Testament," and therefore "does not fully enter into the logic of the Mystery of the Incarnation."[124] Since the New Testament documents are essentially an allegory of the Old Testament, de Lubac understands the canon of Scripture arising from reflection on the event of Christ from the standpoint of the church's participation in Christ. It is this present union with Christ that makes the New Covenant different from the Old Covenant, and any hesitance to describe Christ's self-mediation through the church is viewed by de Lubac as a failure to show what is qualitatively different about the church from Israel in the economy of redemption.

Yet caution must be exercised with de Lubac's emphasis on the realized union between Christ and the church, as this model may serve de-emphasize the role that the completed canon now plays in regulating a Christian understanding about God. As de Lubac envisions the Scriptures as developing organically within the life and practice of the church, he practically shows priority for the church over Scripture, as the model makes it difficult to show how God uses Scripture to confront the church. Furthermore, the more de Lubac endorses a continuity of allegorical method between the apostles and the successors of the apostles, the more Scripture begins to appear as a paradigmatic moment of allegorical interpretation to be repeated by the apostles' successors than as a covenant document used by God to structure boundaries around a Christian understanding of Christ. Vanhoozer's emphasis on Scripture as the normative means by which God confronts the church may allow de Lubac to place more emphasis on the plain sense as structuring a Christian understanding of the mystery.

---

123. De Lubac (*The Church*, 51 and 43 respectively) claims that the "infusion of the Holy Spirit placed the people of God in an essentially new position" as "the Spirit of Christ has renewed, transfigured, and 'spiritualized' everything."

124. De Lubac (ibid., 25) dislikes the Protestant argument to liken the visible church to rebellious Israel, in which a remnant (the invisible church) will be saved. To appreciate the Christian mystery, one must realize that the church really consists of something that the OT people of God did not. Christ really is joined to this body in a way that the OT people of God did not have access to. The church is really the reality that the OT people of God pointed toward as a sign.

CONVERGENCE: DEVELOPMENT OF DOCTRINE AS EXTENDING CANONICAL MEANING POTENTIAL OR READING AS THE TOTUS CHRISTUS?

Hans Boersma has recently claimed that significant evangelical and Catholic rapprochement could be made on the topic of doctrinal development by recognizing that "Catholics accept the evangelical point that all doctrine is a matter of biblical interpretation," and that "Evangelicals . . . accept the Catholic point that all doctrine is a matter of development."[125] So long as both sides recognize their position as grounded in the authority of Scripture, Boersma believes, the discussions will have a common foundation. Yet although Boersma may be correct that post-Vatican II Catholics tend to understand doctrinal development as a "matter of biblical interpretation," I wish to suggest this principle alone will do little to resolve disagreements in doctrinal development. Because Catholics and evangelicals understand the relationship between Scripture and church quite differently, they continue to differ substantially about how Scripture contributes to doctrinal development.

Perhaps this difference may be most clearly seen in the way each approaches Marian dogmas. Employing his allegorical approach, de Lubac assumes the Marian dogmas are a legitimate examination of the church's conscience, and then moves quickly to an understanding of Mary as a type of the church, the mother of all humankind, and even identifies her with "created Wisdom."[126] As a result, Mary is understood to be a "concrete universal," the "effective figure of the Church" as she contains, or embodies, the mystery of the church in an analogous manner to the way in which the literal sense contains the mystery of the spiritual sense.[127] Both Mary and Christ are "eschatological figure[s]" who "in their person[s] they realize individually what will only be complete eschatologically."[128] While a complete discussion de Lubac's Mariology is beyond the scope of this book, what is important to notice is how de Lubac's christological logic governs his understanding of Scriptural interpretation and consequently of the development of this doctrine. De Lubac's emphasis on the radical transposition from Old to New Covenant, seen in a

---

125. Boersma, *Heavenly Participation*, 135–36.

126. See Wood, *Spiritual Exegesis and the Church*, 98–103; and de Lubac, *The Eternal Feminine*, 95.

127. Ibid., 102.

128. Ibid., 103.

sacramental ontology and exemplified in the relationship between the literal sense and spiritual senses of Scripture, encourages this Mariology through the use of the rule of faith and the employment of spiritual exegesis of Scripture.[129]

Employing his theo-dramatic approach, on the other hand, Vanhoozer suggests that readers work out an understanding of Mary that corresponds to both "canon sense" (i.e., "fittingness to the Script") and "catholic sensibility" (i.e., "fittingness to the situation").[130] Vanhoozer agrees that the Council of Ephesus used both correct "canon sense" and "catholic sensibility" in declaring Mary to be the *theotokos*, and Vanhoozer even seems to favor (in principle) Duns Scotus's rule that "'it seems preferable to attribute greater rather than lesser excellence to Mary" as long as one does not contradict the authority of Scripture."[131] Yet Vanhoozer quite predictably argues that the 1854 papal pronouncement of the Immaculate Conception is "unfitting" to the "canon sense" as it contradicts 1 Timothy 4:10, which declares Christ to be the savior of all.[132] Here Vanhoozer quite clearly shows his priority of "canon sense" over "catholic sensibility," and would likely suggest that de Lubac's "catholic sensibility" (his christological logic and understanding of the rule of faith) leads to an unfitting performance of the theodrama in which "canon sense" is not accepted. While some may conclude that Vanhoozer is merely proof-texting, we should see Vanhoozer's "canon sense" principle operating here at a much deeper level than as a mere proscription of doctrines based on certain prooftexts. Even if Vanhoozer were to grant the Roman Catholic explanation that 1 Timothy 4:10 does indeed apply to Mary (as Mary is saved through Christ's merit and thereby uniquely *spared* of original sin), Vanhoozer would still suggest that de Lubac's explanation is an unfitting performance of the theodrama. This is because Vanhoozer would feel that such a Mariology shifts attention from the central focus of the canonical speech-acts toward a doctrine that lies at the periphery of Scripture's canonical witness. For Vanhoozer, since the trajectory of canonical witnesses places Mariology at the periphery of New Testament teaching, so also ought the church. Vanhoozer's project of developing canonical meaning potential, then, seeks to illumine which doctrines lie at the center God's speaking

---

129. Wood (ibid., 99n83) notes that "Such an identification, of course, is only accomplished within the practice of spiritual exegesis."

130. Vanhoozer, *The Drama of Doctrine*, 179 and 181, respectively.

131. Vanhoozer, "A Drama-of-Redemption Model," 196.

132. Vanhoozer, *The Drama of Doctrine*, 190.

action in Scripture (those which the plurality of human speech-acts affirm as central), and consequently which doctrines ought to lie at the center of the church's faith. Doctrines which lie at the periphery of the scriptural witness (those which *could* be exegetically allowed but are not central in the plurality of authorial speech-acts), conversely, ought to be kept at the periphery of the church's faith.

The real issue at stake, then, is how Scripture and church operate in the economy of redemption, and discussions in Mariology will be advanced less by determining what Scripture says than by reassessing the respective roles of Scripture and church in God's economy. The key difference is that Vanhoozer bases doctrinal development on the meaning potential inherent in the plain sense of the canonical Scriptures and works to "make explicit what was already implicit in Scripture," while de Lubac bases doctrinal development on the infinite meaning of the Person of Christ and works to "interrogat[e] its conscience" to provide explicit definition of what it already possesses fully, yet knows implicitly.[133] As a result, this disagreement could never be solved merely through the exegesis of Scripture. In this section, I will specify why significant differences remain on the topic of doctrinal development, and will show how key insights by each author may serve as correctives to the other and may help advance dialogue between Evangelicals and Catholics.

Vanhoozer: Doctrinal Development as Extending Canonical Meaning Potential: Vanhoozer follows Ricoeur in explaining the development of doctrine as the *"realization of canonical* [meaning] *potential."*[134] The surplus of meaning in the canonical texts allows for doctrine to develop in agreement with the "judgments" of Scripture yet beyond what is explicitly inscribed in the plurality of canonical genres.[135] Vanhoozer declares that doctrine develops when the meaning potential is further specified without changing the *ipse*-identity of revelation (i.e., without changing the meaning of Scripture).[136] The Spirit guides interpretation so

---

133. See Ibid, 209 and de Lubac, "Problem of the Development of Dogma," 263, respectively.

134. Vanhoozer, *The Drama of Doctrine*, 352.

135. See Vanhoozer's thesis (ibid., 348) that "what ought to govern the play of theology in other times and places are the cultural-linguistic patterns of Scripture itself, *not* because those ancient cultures are authoritative but because the judgments that come to specific cultural-linguistic expression in them are."

136. Vanhoozer ("Ascending the Mountain," 792) suggests that the scriptural texts

that in "different contexts" the improvisations "render the same canonical judgments."[137] The goal of doctrinal development is to recreate the "pattern of judgments that were intrinsic" to Scripture in new situations.[138] Thus "*ipse*-identity is improvisatory in the best sense: it is a creative means of rendering for a new situation the same judgment made in an earlier situation, thus insuring *both the identity and the relevance* of the claim being made."[139] Vanhoozer claims that, "The canonical-linguistic embodiment of authoritative theological judgments constrains but does not exhaustively determine how we participate in the theo-drama today."[140] As a result, the church is "tied to the canonical texts, but not to the past. The Spirit continues to lead the church into all truth."[141] Thus "God may do new things with the canonical script. The church continues to translate and interpret—improvise on—Scripture in order to find the right conceptual terms and social forms for new cultural-linguistic situations."[142] This allows Vanhoozer to maintain that while "Christian doctrine is the realization of canonical potential," yet "[a]uthority ultimately remains with the canonical text."[143] God's speaking action, on

contain a surplus of meaning that can be "further specified" without changing the meaning of Scripture.

137. Vanhoozer, *The Drama of Doctrine*, 354.

138. Vanhoozer's use of the council of Nicaea (ibid., 344), is helpful here: "Nicaea neither imposed *homoousios* onto Philippians nor deduced it from Paul's text; instead, it discerned a pattern of judgments that were intrinsic to the text—canonical judgments—and articulated them in terms of the language and conceptuality of the day."

139. Ibid.

140. Ibid., 348.

141. Ibid., 349. Consequently, Vanhoozer (ibid., 351) claims the "canon is the norm of theology, but it need not follow that theological understanding be confined to the past."

142. Ibid., 344. In extending the message of Scripture to new contexts, Vanhoozer is careful not to simply revert back to propositionalism in which a certain principle is found to be the meaning of Scripture and then is applied to a new situation. On the other hand, Vanhoozer is also careful to not simply repeat the scriptural narrative in a new context and expect that it will be effective. Vanhoozer, then, tries to find a middle ground between repetition and correlation.

143. Ibid., 352. Vanhoozer rejects Gadamer's "fusion of horizons" on the ground that such a fusion is "actually *monologic*," absorbing both dialogue partners into one another. Instead, Vanhoozer insists that each dialogue partner ought to be "mutually enriched" by dialogue while "retaining" his own identity. This preservation of identity is necessary to stress in Vanhoozer's covenant model, as Scripture and church are qualitatively different realities and the church must be kept submissive to Scripture.

this account, emerges precisely as it is directly discerned from the plain meaning of the scriptural texts in new contexts or in new situations.

Consistent with his covenant ontology, Vanhoozer suggests that doctrinal development is based on the attempt to conform to the covenant life offered in the Scriptures through a plurality of genres.[144] Development of doctrine arises from the need to conceptualize the plurality of scriptural truth in new contexts. The canonical Scriptures present "the judgment that God has spoken and acted in Israel and supremely in Christ to save the world—in a variety of literary and conceptual forms."[145] The canon structures a covenant form of life through many genres, and the plurality of truth expressed in all of them ought to be preserved and developed in just the ways that God and the human authors intended. This means that Vanhoozer, like de Lubac, will reject propositionalist explanations of revelation and the development of doctrine. Yet while de Lubac rejects propositionalist (extrinsicist) theologies because he understands revelation as a unified mystery, of which propositions are abstractions, Vanhoozer rejects propositionalist theologies because he worries that reducing Scripture to a set of propositions would reduce the plurality of genres which together establish a covenant form of life.[146] Corresponding to this plurality of genres in Scripture, Vanhoozer suggests that there ought to be "an equivalent plurality on the level of interpretative traditions."[147] Consequently, the overall trajectory of Vanhoozer's project seems to indicate that a certain interpretive maximalism should exist and that the development of doctrine should be kept as broad as possible so long as the doctrines which emerge can be logically justified through the plain canonical sense of Scripture.[148]

---

144. Vanhoozer's very project of "dramaturgy" (the "working of drama") suggests a strong conceptual priority on the texts of Scripture as the focal point of Christian faith (see ibid., 244).

145. Ibid., 353.

146. Ibid., 273.

147. Ibid., 275.

148. It should be noted that Vanhoozer expresses a strong desire for ecumenism while emphasizing the benefit of doctrinal plurality. Vanhoozer insists that "Church unity is more than a pragmatic goal; it is a doctrinal imperative." He also emphasizes that doctrinal diversity is a healthy sign of the church living out the gospel. Vanhoozer (ibid., 422) claims that "the canon is properly realized only by a plurality of interpretative traditions, by a plurality of church performances." Vanhoozer's "catholic principle" (455) encourages local churches to remain "radically committed to the doctrines that lie at the center of the theo-drama, all the while remaining charitable with regard to

Vanhoozer's insistence that doctrinal development emerges from canonical meaning potential leads him to suggest that even the church's rule of faith (that essential Gospel content that guided the formation of the canon and continues to guide scriptural interpretation), is authoritative only insofar as it emerges from the canonical sense alone. In fact, Vanhoozer goes so far as to say that "canonical scripture alone is the rule of faith."[149] Vanhoozer's concern is that many contemporary theologians appeal to the rule of faith in order to suggest that the canonical Scriptures are "insufficient" and in need of a "hermeneutical key" which has been "developed by the Ante-Nicene church fathers."[150] Vanhoozer suspects that many theologians who appeal to the rule of faith do so in order to reduce Scripture's "hermeneutical norm" to community consensus, thus allowing the community to ignore parts of Scripture that it finds difficult or inconvenient.[151] To counter this tendency, Vanhoozer asks whether the rule is "extratextual" to Scripture (i.e., derived from the performance of the church) or "intratextual" to Scripture (i.e. derived from the Scriptures themselves), and concludes that it is intratextual.[152] The rule is not simply "an extratextual control," a "result of a community decision to read Scripture in a particular way," or "an arbitrary *communal* rule, but is rather a "summary of Scripture's own story line," and a "servant of intratextuality" which "allows Scripture to interpret itself."[153] Consequently, Vanhoozer emphasizes that final authority cannot be placed in "ecclesiastical magisterium," "unchanging communal tradition," "private interpretation," or even in the "gospel," itself, since it would remain unclear what the gospel

doctrines that lie at the periphery."

149. Ibid., 206, citing Hutter, *Suffering Divine Things*, 275n138.

150. Vanhoozer, *The Drama of Doctrine*, 203. Vanhoozer is concerned about the claim that "that only the so-called Rule of Faith, an early summary of apostolic teaching, shows us how to interpret Scripture correctly," choosing instead to say that the Rule is grounded in the plain sense of Scripture. Vanhoozer summarizes the rule of faith as emphasizing "reading the Old Testament in relation to the New (e.g., christocentrically, eschatologically) and holding together God the Creator with God the Father of Jesus Christ. The Rule states that the creator God and covenant Lord of Israel is also the Father of Jesus Christ; the one who brought Israel out of Egypt is also the one who raised Jesus from the dead" (204).

151. Ibid., 205. Vanhoozer then relishes pointing out that many who opt for community consensus conveniently overlook a number of elements within the rule they find inconvenient today.

152. Ibid., 203.

153. Ibid., 205–6.

is unless the gospel is defined in canonical form.¹⁵⁴ The rule is "responsive, not constructive," as it emerged from Scripture and is an "implication of the perspicuity of Scripture."¹⁵⁵ As a result, Vanhoozer suggests that the rule of faith is subject to the canonical Scriptures, rather than suggesting that the Scriptures are shaped and read by the rule of faith.¹⁵⁶

In his discussion of the development of doctrine, then, Vanhoozer consistently develops his active/responsive ordering of Scripture and church in the economy of redemption. The development of doctrine will always be an activity practiced by the church in response to the plain canonical sense of Scripture, the church's authority will always be dependent upon the authority of Scripture, and all conclusions will be granted their provisional authority based on their ability to be justified by Scripture. Even the rule of faith derives its authority from Scripture, and its employment must be directly dependent upon Scripture.

De Lubac: Doctrinal development as recognizing Christ: Whereas Vanhoozer has provided a short-hand definition for the development of doctrine as the church "improvising with a canonical script,"¹⁵⁷ de Lubac provides a short-hand definition as the church "interrogat[ing] her own conscience."¹⁵⁸ For de Lubac, the starting-point for all doctrinal development is the presupposition that in Christ, "all has been both given and revealed to us at one stroke," so that "in consequence, all the explanations to come, whatever might be their tenor and whatever might be their mode, will never be anything but coins in more distinct parts of a treasure already possessed in its entirety."¹⁵⁹ Hans Boersma claims that since, "[A]t

---

154. Ibid., 122 (citing Lindbeck, "Postcritical Canonical Interpretation," 39). Vanhoozer (*The Drama of Doctrine*, 124) furthermore rejects the possibility that "the Spirit-directed *use* of Scripture in the church" as being authoritative, suggesting that tradition has unanimously affirmed that the Spirit speaks in Scripture.

155. Ibid., 207 and 206, respectively.

156. Ibid., 207. Vanhoozer's claim is that *"the Rule rules but is itself ruled (by the canon); the canonical script rules but is not itself ruled."*

157. Ibid., 353.

158. Ibid., 263.

159. De Lubac, "Problem of the Development of Dogma," 275. De Lubac follows the logic of Pierre Rousselot, who says, "Since the self-revelation of God, found in the deposit of faith, must be absolutely one, that deposit cannot be conceived as 'a sum-total of distinct truths, limited in number, presented under the form of logical propositions like the Augsburg Confession or even the Apostles' Creed'" (see Nichols, *From Newman to Congar,*" 23, 359).

no point in time could anyone grasp the fullness of the mystery of Christ," the development of doctrine for de Lubac could be described simply as "cashing in Jesus."[160] Revelation, although at once complete in Christ and therefore "unsurpassable," is approached with ever more specification through the continual participatory life of the church.[161] As Blondel puts it, while Tradition does not "innovate because it possesses" Christ completely, it "has always to teach something new because it transforms what is implicit and 'enjoyed' into something explicit and known."[162] What tradition "discovers," it merely "recovers," since it has possessed Christ in his fullness from the beginning.[163] Notice, then, that while Vanhoozer's discussion of plurality of meaning and hence on doctrinal development is based on textual theory, de Lubac's discussion is based on a particular christological logic.

Consistent with his sacramental ontology, de Lubac suggests that doctrinal development is never the product of mere logical development, but is the church's attempt to understand what it already implicitly possesses. De Lubac strongly objects to the neo-Thomists attempt to describe the development of doctrine largely as the process of drawing a primary premise from Scripture or tradition, then drawing a secondary premise from philosophy or some scientific discipline, and then drawing out the logical conclusions. Yet where Vanhoozer would object to the neo-Thomist approach on the grounds that it reduces Scripture to one kind of genre (that of propositions), de Lubac objects to this approach on the grounds that just as the unified mystery transcends our logical comprehension,

---

160. Boersma, *Nouvelle Theologie*, 222 and 219. For de Lubac, see "Problem of the Development of Dogma," 275. Blondel (*History and Dogma*, 267) claims that tradition "discovers and formulates truths on which the past lived, though unable as yet to evaluate or define them explicitly . . . it enriches our intellectual patrimony by putting the total deposit little by little into currency and making it bear fruit."

161. De Lubac, "Problem of the Development of Dogma," 274. Nichols (*From Newman to Congar* 210) claims that Revelation is the "divine redemptive *action* which is summed up in God's gift of his Son. . . . The mystery of Christ is 'le Tout du dogme' dogma in its unified entirety." All doctrinal development is explication of what the church has already been given and knows implicitly.

162. Blondel, *History and Dogma*, 268. Blondel claims that "whoever lives and thinks as a Christian really works for this, whether it be the saint who perpetuates Jesus among us, the scholar who goes back to the pure sources of Revelation, or the philosopher who strives to open the way to the future, and to prepare for the unending birth of the Spirit of newness."

163. Ibid., 267.

so do all conclusions which are deduced from the unified mystery.[164] Although rational reflection is used, development of doctrine cannot simply assume revelation as its first principle and then employ a straightforward process of scientific reason. For de Lubac, neither revelation nor the development of doctrine can ever be reduced to purely logical development, as all developments are expressions of the unified mystery and can never be explicated through a scientific process.[165] De Lubac certainly does not mean to exclude propositional truth from revelation; rather, he wants to show that all propositional truths are (necessary) abstractions of the unified mystery. The church, then, must always be aware that all developments are abstractions of the unified mystery and that these abstractions should not be confused with the entirety of the mystery. While the church must "interrogate her conscience" and explicate the mystery, yet this cashing in of the infinite mystery (always understood through abstraction) is better described as participation in mystery than purely logical development.

Since doctrinal development is neither new revelation nor simple logical deduction from Scripture, de Lubac insists that it must rely on the church's employment of the rule of faith. Yet where Vanhoozer understands the rule of faith as derived from the plain sense of Scripture, de Lubac understands the rule of faith as that self-awareness of the gospel by the church (which derives from its union with Christ), which keeps the church oriented toward the singular mystery. Because the development of doctrine always remains mystery, the church must read Scripture in light of the rule of faith. De Lubac claims that when the church defines dogma, "What she seeks to find is not if such a proposition is or is not correctly deduced but if such an assertion is or is not contained

---

164. De Lubac, "Problem of the Development of Dogma," 265.

165. De Lubac (*The Sources of Revelation*, 222) has emphasized that the mystery is one. Consequently, any understanding of the mystery must come through abstraction. In fact, several layers of abstraction can be identified in de Lubac's analysis of revelation. Christ, the sacrament of the Triune God, the revelation of the mystery, is the first layer of abstraction. Second, human response to mystery is a "lived knowledge," a participation in the event of revelation, which is stabilized over time in tradition. Third, this lived knowledge was normatively codified in Scripture that materially "contains all revelation." Fourth, this lived knowledge is further structured by propositions, models, and doctrinal categories about revelation. Each of these layers of abstraction is necessary for understanding the mystery, and de Lubac is never comfortable with pitting the authority of one against another.

in her faith."¹⁶⁶ Normative Christian decisions, such as the christological definitions pronounced at the council of Nicaea, were indeed attempts to make explicit what was implicit in Scripture (as Vanhoozer claims), yet de Lubac insists that the council's conclusions were not guaranteed by merely employing a skillful reading of Scripture.¹⁶⁷ Rather, those conclusions were guaranteed through Christ's use of the church, and can be identified in the special competence the church possesses in virtue of its union with Christ. What de Lubac believes is at stake in his account of the development of doctrine is not the sufficiency of Scripture (de Lubac insists that Scripture "contains all revelation" and is thus materially sufficient for the whole Christian faith), but an adequate description of the *reasoning* by which the church makes certain implicit truths in Scripture explicit.¹⁶⁸ For de Lubac, it is clear that the church must be guided by some principle other than simply the plain sense of Scripture, since the secular scholar could only observe a continuity in the development of doctrine in hindsight, and the church's decision may often appear unpersuasive to the outside observer. While recognizing that the church can err, de Lubac would still insist that the same hermeneutic of trust be accorded to Christ's use of the church in establishing boundaries for interpretation as is accorded to Christ's use of Scripture for establishing the structure of Christian faith.

In his discussion of the development of doctrine, then, de Lubac consistently develops his mutually causal ordering of Scripture and church in the economy of redemption. De Lubac, with Blondel, suggests that the church could not "rest entirely on the Scriptures," since "the History in which Catholicism obliges us to believe" will necessarily be different from "the history which the historian can establish," and will transcend even the historical account recorded by the first apostles.¹⁶⁹

---

166. De Lubac, "Problem of Development of Dogma," 262. It seems that de Lubac would say it is possible for a proposition to be "correctly deduced" from the mystery according to certain principles of logic, yet that very logical proposition may diminish the mystery and hence should not be considered normative. De Lubac consistently desires to keep the mystery as broad as possible, full of paradox, and encouraging of interpretive maximalism.

167. See Vanhoozer, *The Drama of Doctrine*, 354.

168. De Lubac, *Medieval Exegesis*, 1:25.

169. Blondel, *History and Dogma*, 264. Blondel lays out the problem in the following way: "[W]hile it is true that historical fact are the foundations of the Catholic faith, they do not of themselves engender it, nor do they suffice to justify it entirely; and, reciprocally, the Catholic faith and the authority of the Church which it implies

Tradition, then, is needed to "relate, harmonize and organize" the texts of Scripture into a correctly ordered whole that orients readers toward the mystery.[170] Because the church "possesses another means of knowing her author, of participating in his life, [and] linking facts to dogma," tradition "extends further than Scripture" and "[e]ven in regard to what Scripture tells us, it possesses a special virtue and a distinct competence."[171] The development of doctrine, then, must be guided by the Church's unique sense of the presence and direction of its head, Jesus Christ. While Scripture is materially sufficient for the development of all doctrine, it is formally insufficient, as the church alone has been entrusted with the responsibility of keeping its reading oriented to the mystery of Christ so that Christ may use Scripture to build the church into the eschatological reality of the *totus Christus*.[172]

Convergence: A Necessary Tension?

Overall, then, the central focus of each author is quite different. Vanhoozer's chief aim is to keep the church's activity of doctrinal development *responsive* to God's speaking action in Scripture, while de Lubac's chief aim is to show why the church is the only human institution which can understand Scripture as Scripture, and therefore is the only institution which is able to participate in the process of doctrinal development. Instead of attempting to resolve the disagreement between Vanhoozer and de Lubac, I wish to suggest that maintaining a tension which affirms

---

guarantee the facts and draw from them a doctrinal interpretation which convinces the believer as would a historical reality itself, but on other grounds than those which the historian is able to verify. In order that that circle should not be a vicious one ... there must be an explanatory principle ... which accounts for ... the movement from faith to really objective affirmations and to realities which constitute Sacred History inserted into the heart of ordinary, everyday history, and incarnating the ideas in the facts" (223).

170. Ibid.

171. Ibid., 268–69 and 270, respectively. Hence Blondel claims, "Only a progressive and synthetic movement can lead us from the effects produced to their cause, can trace all the rays of light in the Christian consciousness over the centuries to their source, and through its unending progress imitate the infinite riches of God, revealed and always hidden, hidden and always revealed. In that profound sense, when it is a question of finding the supernatural in Sacred History and in dogma, the Gospel is nothing without the Church, the teaching of Scripture is nothing without the Christian life, exegesis is nothing without Tradition" (276).

172. See Moulins-Beaufort, "Henri De Lubac," 692.

both God's use of Scripture to confront and change the church (Vanhoozer's emphasis) and God's use of the church to understand, interpret and safeguard Scripture (de Lubac's emphasis) may lead to more faithful engagement of Scripture in the economy of redemption. In what follows, I will present a central insight of each author which ought to be preserved.

De Lubac's insight: from authority to capacity: De Lubac recognizes with clarity that the church's unique ability to read Scripture to hear God cannot be grounded in an inherent quality in the text, nor a mere (notional) theological presupposition for reading, nor in community consensus, but in the church's participation in Christ. Contrary to Vanhoozer's suggestion that the potential to hear God in Scripture be located *either* in God's use of the texts *or* in the faith of the church, de Lubac shows that both are complementary and necessary components which must be present in order for encounter with God to occur.[173] In fact, I suspect that a good deal of the apparent incompatibility between Vanhoozer and de Lubac about the relationship between Scripture and church could be resolved by recognizing that God's use of Scripture and God's equipping of the church to hear God's voice in Scripture are complementary aspects of the same interpretive process. While Vanhoozer insists on the primacy of the plain, canonical sense in order to encourage the church to safeguard a normative *method* which will keep Christ's speaking action in Scripture from being muted, this *method* is itself grounded in a deeper reality, which is the *capacity* of the church to recognize Christ's presence in Scripture. De Lubac's project shows that describing Christ's use of the church to develop and safeguard doctrine does not detract from a description of Christ's use of Scripture, but rather provides the reason why the church is able to hear God's speaking in Scripture instead of merely the collection of human authors.

Vanhoozer's very distinction between Scripture as initiatory (missioned) and the church as responsive (commissioned) is quite difficult to maintain consistently, since both Scripture and church could be viewed as either active or passive depending on how one views Christ's use of each for self-mediation. On the one hand, both Scripture and church could be said to have active/initiatory roles. Certainly God has given Scripture an active role in confronting the church, yet at the same time, it also seems that Christ has given the church an active role in writing, adopting, safeguarding, and interpreting the Scriptures as authoritative documents.

---

173. See Vanhoozer, "Interpreting Scripture," 215.

On the other hand, however, both Scripture and church could be viewed as having responsive roles in the economy of redemption. Certainly the church must respond to God's speech in Scripture. Yet in Christian self-understanding, much of the very writing of Scripture took place as the New Testament writers saw themselves responding to the revelation of Christ. In this sense, both Scripture and church can be viewed as responsive mediators of revelation. Stressing the responsive role of each, Catholic theologian Gavin D'Costa suggests that instead of looking for an active/passive relationship, a better ordering would highlight that "both scripture and tradition belong to the process of history and are 'responsive' to God's action of the Spirit, in different modalities, but are still *intrinsically* and *necessarily* related."[174] De Lubac rejects Vanhoozer's either/or scenario, stressing instead that both Christ's use of Scripture (divine authorship) and Christ's use of the church (the reason the church recognizes Scripture's canonical unity and reads christologically) are complementary aspects of Christ's building of the *totus Christus*.

It would seem that Vanhoozer could more effectively employ his own covenantal ecclesiology if he embraced de Lubac's emphasis on the church's unique capacity to understand Scripture and develop doctrine. Vanhoozer's own theory of God's speaking action in Scripture seems to depend on a theory of the church's unique capacity to understand God's illocutionary action instead of simply the human speech-acts. Vanhoozer has based his project on the claim that "it is the divine illocutions—God's use—that constitute biblical authority."[175] Yet if scriptural authority is located in God's supervening of a unifying illocutionary stance upon the scriptural texts in such a way that God's speaking action can be perceived only through the eyes of faith, it seems that deeper theological description of Christ's active presence in the church is needed to show how the church is uniquely equipped to recognize God's speaking action and to establish normative boundaries around this interpretation. When Van-

---

174. D'Costa, "Revelation, Scripture And Tradition," 341. D'Costa (ibid., 344) goes on to argue that "The genius of [*Dei verbum*] was . . . to show that both scripture and tradition (which included the Magisterium) were . . . creaturely realities that are sanctified by the Holy Spirit so as to communicate God's presence in the world."

175. Vanhoozer, *The Drama of Doctrine*, 179. It is clear that Vanhoozer does not want to say that the church is simply a responsive human community. For example, Vanhoozer ("Interpreting Scripture," 214), explains, "The church is not just another interpretive community . . . but the divinely appointed context wherein God ministers new life via his word and Spirit." The problem is that his active/passive schema prevents him from saying more about God's use of the church.

hoozer claims that the church's "canonical judgments" recognize God's ability to "do new things with the canonical script," readers need to know how the church can insure that these "new things" are not merely human innovation.[176] Ironically, Vanhoozer's tendency to locate authority in Scripture *rather than* the church may actually prevent him from describing adequately the authority of Scripture, as it prevents description of the church's unique capacity to recognize Christ's prophetic voice in Scripture.[177] It does little good, after all, to suggest that the church has recognized the voice of God in Scripture and clarified this speaking in the development of doctrine unless the reader has a reason to believe that the church can safeguard this divine speaking by establishing normative doctrinal boundaries. As Hans Boersma suggests, it is one thing to say that the church has no authority to "define doctrine that runs counter to Scripture or to invent new truth," and quite another to say that the Church lacks authority to "preserve doctrine . . . and to pronounce doctrinal definitions of the faith" because Scripture stands as an authority over the church.[178] Vanhoozer's tendency to develop Christ's "magisterial authority" in Scripture into an active/passive schema underemphasizes the unique capacity of the church to formulate and interpret the Scriptures according to its relationship with Christ.[179] Yet de Lubac shows that while the Scriptures indeed have magisterial authority as they are used by Christ, such authority cannot be recognized without Christ's simultaneous authority in the church. This commitment to Christ's simultaneous use of Scripture and church allows de Lubac to emphasize the church's *capacity* to recognize and safeguard Christ's voice in Scripture, thereby easing the problem of authority.

Vanhoozer's central insight: Scripture's structuring of mystery: Vanhoozer recognizes with clarity that the scriptural texts are a rich and polyvalent source of divine communication used by Christ to normatively shape the church's understanding of the mystery. Vanhoozer would

---

176. Vanhoozer, *The Drama of Doctrine*, 344.

177. See D'Costa, "Revelation, Scripture And Tradition," 342.

178. See Boersma, "On Baking Pumpkin Pie," 254.

179. See Vanhoozer, *The Drama of Doctrine*, 207–10, for a discussion on the distinction between Christ's magisterial authority in Scripture and the Spirit's ministerial authority in the church. One could ask, based on Vanhoozer's model, why, if there is no competition of authority between Son and Spirit or their respective missions, is it not possible to describe God's use of Scripture and Church without reference to competition of authority?

suspect that de Lubac's emphasis on similarity in Christ's use of Scripture and church has the unintended, yet deleterious effect of devaluing this unique and normative role of Scripture in structuring a Christian understanding of Christ. As we have seen, de Lubac's argument for the mutually reciprocal sacramental relationship between Scripture and church proceeds in two ways. First, de Lubac claims that because Christ, the incarnation of the Logos, uses Scripture and church as mutual incorporations of the Logos, both have a similar role as sacramental realities in extending the self-mediation of Christ.[180] Second, de Lubac believes that since Scripture originated within the life of the church as the apostles read the Old Testament allegorically, Christ uses the successors of the apostles in qualitatively the same way as Christ used the original apostles in allegorizing the whole Scriptures in light of Christ.[181] Vanhoozer would likely suggest that both of these arguments fail to describe adequately God's use of Scripture, as both fail to show how God now uses the canon for self-mediation to confront the church and call it to repentance. Whereas de Lubac understands the Scriptures as developing organically out of the life and practice of the church, Vanhoozer envisions a rather decisive shift taking place in God's governance of the economy of redemption with the completion of the canon of Scripture, as God now normatively uses Scripture to address the church. This emphasis on the importance of the closed canon for structuring the Christian understanding of the mystery would be of particular use to de Lubac's model in several ways.

First, Vanhoozer's model shows how doctrinal development is governed by Christ's use of the plain, canonical sense of Scripture. As we have seen, de Lubac's account of the scriptural texts often accords the literal sense of Scripture a mere functionary role in leading readers to the "facts" of history so that they can then be drawn into the mystery disclosed in the spiritual sense. The result is that de Lubac tends to view the development of doctrine as church's use of the rule of faith in which the literal sense of Scripture only forms a *guide* for doctrinal development. Yet Vanhoozer's model presents a useful alternative to de Lubac's proposal, as it suggests that God's speaking action emerges out of the plurality of human speech-acts, rendering Scripture a sufficiently clear, if multifaceted tool for recognizing God's self-mediation. Vanhoozer would agree with de Lubac that Scripture must be read by employing

---

180. See de Lubac, *History and Spirit*, 385–426.
181. See de Lubac, *Medieval Exegesis*, 2:216–26.

the rule of faith, yet he rightly emphasizes that since the completion of the canon this rule of faith emerges with clarity from the plain, canonical sense of Scripture. While Vanhoozer's description of the rule of faith appears insufficient for explaining the emergence, use, and canonization of the Christian Scriptures by the early church, his description is quite useful for describing how the rule of faith is now stabilized as an "intratextual" norm of the plain sense of Scripture. The emergence of the canon does mark a decisive shift in God's ordering of the economy of redemption, as God now normatively uses Scripture to regulate understanding of the rule of faith. Thus Vanhoozer insists that "preserving *ipse*-identity in repeating canonical judgments," depends on pursuing Scripture's divine meaning in the various complex forms it is presented.[182] Consequently, Vanhoozer would argue that in all doctrinal development, the church must keep central those doctrines which emerge as central in the canonical Scriptures, and place at the periphery those doctrines which are not central to the plain, canonical sense. While both Vanhoozer and de Lubac encourage interpretive maximalism in scriptural reading, Vanhoozer rightly emphasizes that certain doctrines emerge from the plain sense of Scripture much more centrally aligned with the unified witness of Scripture, and therefore ought to function with much greater importance in the ongoing life of the church than those doctrines that are developed at the periphery of Scripture's unified witness. Greater attention to God's use of the plain sense of Scripture would not call de Lubac's whole project into question, but would simply chasten his use of the spiritual sense of Scripture to be more attentive to and governed by the plain, canonical sense of Scripture as the locus of God's communicative action.

Second, as Vanhoozer's model shows the decisive shift in God's governance of the economy of redemption which occurred with the closure of the canon, it highlights the distinctive difference between doctrinal formation in the early church before the formation of the canon and the subsequent development of doctrine grounded in canonical rule. De Lubac emphasizes a continuity between the allegorical method practiced by the apostles and the allegorical method practiced by their successors, as both apostles and their successors are seeking to understand the whole mystery of Christ in light of the Old Testament. Yet such an emphasis on continuity of allegorical method between apostles and their successors practically causes de Lubac to view the scriptural witness to the event of

---

182. Vanhoozer, *The Drama of Doctrine*, 344.

Christ more as a paradigmatic moment in the church's self-understanding of Christ which is, to some extent, to be *reproduced* and *extended* in the development of doctrine, rather than as a qualitatively unique testimony to Christ safeguarded in canonical form.

Recently David Williams has challenged de Lubac's suggestion that the successors of the apostles ought to carry out the same interpretive strategy of allegory as did the original apostles, arguing instead that a much greater distinction exists between the employment of allegory by the New Testament authors and the employment of allegory by subsequent interpreters of Scripture after the canon was formed. Williams suggests that the first apostles did not, in fact, *interpret* the Old Testament in light of the New, as much as they *applied* the Old Testament to their new experience of the reality of the risen Christ. Consequently, the early church's use of allegory was "not strictly speaking . . . interpretation . . . inasmuch as it stems from lived experience and oral communication rather than encounter with the written texts."[183] However, with the closure of the New Testament canon, Williams claims, this situation changed. After the closure of the canon, Christian spiritual interpretation became primarily an investigation of God's communicative action at the level of the canonical whole. Consequently, Williams suggests that allegory (the correlation of individual OT historical events to Christ), can now be relegated to a non-essential role in biblical interpretation today without destroying the spiritual sense of Scripture.[184] Such correlations, Williams claims, may still have great value, but they must be classified as "applications" rather than interpretation, since the "[i]nclusion of the NT in the body of authoritative Scripture provides a stable if many-sided narrative and explanatory center to God's action. Drawing what had gone before into more explicit connection with that center then becomes a matter of discerning purpose and meaning operative at the level of the canonical whole."[185] For Williams, interpretation today is primarily the process of discerning God's communicative purpose in the whole canon, and only secondarily the exploring of continual correlation of Old Testament types with New Testament antitype.

---

183. Williams, *Receiving the Bible in Faith*, 208–9.

184. Thus Williams (ibid., 210–12) suggests separating allegory (what he calls the responsibility to make connections between biblical events) from the spiritual sense (what he calls the "meaning" of the Bible).

185. Ibid.

Vanhoozer rightly insists that the New Testament is not simply a paradigmatic instance of allegorical interpretation which has developed organically out of the life and practice of the early church, but is a covenant document through which God speaks to address and confront the church.[186] John Webster's claim that the Scriptures must be considered a "properly segregated, discontinuous, intrusive" document that confronts and judges "ecclesial invention" must be maintained to show how the completed canon marks a qualitative shift both in human understanding about God and in God's self-mediation of revelation.[187] Vanhoozer's "canonical sense" helpfully brings this decisive shift of method into focus, as it insists that God's speaking action can be discerned after the closure of the canon in a way previously unavailable to the church. Scripture, as Christ's tool for self-mediation, stands as an other, and the church must always be ruled by the canonical witness to Christ, even if Christ likewise uses the church to authoritatively guide the interpretation of Scripture.

---

186. See Vanhoozer, *The Drama of Doctrine*, 140. As John Webster ("Purity and Plenitude," 412) puts it, "[S]cripture's task as prophetic and apostolic witness to the divine Word can only be accomplished if it is in some sense an alien element in the church."

187. Webster, "Purity and Plentitude," 410.

Conclusion

THE CUMULATIVE ARGUMENT OF this book has been that a much greater similarity between Vanhoozer and de Lubac (and hence between much Evangelical and Catholic theological interpretation of Scripture) can be seen when explicit focus is placed upon God's use of Scripture and church in the economy of redemption. I have argued that Vanhoozer's development of an economy of communication is very similar to de Lubac's development of a sacramental ontology, as both insist on God's ongoing self-mediation through Scripture, both develop an understanding of scriptural meaning which requires participation and which emerges in the whole economy of redemption, and both recognize the church's indispensable role in fulfilling Scripture's divinely intended purpose. In light of these agreements, I suggest that it is possible to appropriate the work of Vanhoozer and de Lubac in relation to one another. Vanhoozer has recently claimed that "Evangelicalism is best viewed as a renewal movement within confessional Protestantism, just as Protestantism is best viewed as a renewal movement within Catholicism."[1] In the same article Vanhoozer associates his covenantal ontology with Evangelicalism and a sacramental ontology with Roman Catholicism, and suggests that his model shows that "[t]here is a properly Protestant moment to *ressourcement*."[2] I wish to suggest that Vanhoozer's impulse is correct, and that Vanhoozer's covenantal ontology may be best appropriated as a specific critical moment within the larger sacramental ontology of de Lubac.

1. Vanhoozer, "Ascending the Mountain," 782.
2. Ibid., 786.

This claim in some ways resembles David Tracy's suggestion that "proclamation" theologies (such as that of Karl Barth) should be understood as a useful critical moment in the broader context of "manifestation" theologies.³ Within de Lubac's sacramental model, Vanhoozer's chastening of readers to listen to the voice of God in Scripture by attending to God's use of the plurality of speech-acts provides a useful model which specifies *how* God's uses Scripture as a sacramental reality and *how* the church participates sacramentally in the economy of redemption. Conceiving the relationship between Vanhoozer and de Lubac in this way has the potential of highlighting significant agreement between the two in each of the topics covered in this book.

Vanhoozer's communicative ontology could be better developed within the conceptual framework of de Lubac's sacramental model. As it stands, Vanhoozer's communicative ontology often provides a general theological backdrop which merely sets the stage for Vanhoozer's more specific covenantal ontology. This means that Vanhoozer's communicative ontology moves too quickly from a general claim that God's "Authoring . . . covers what God does as creator, reconciler, redeemer, and perfecter, and so serves as a metaphor for the economic Trinity," to an almost exclusive focus on God's covenantal use of Scripture.⁴ As a result, Vanhoozer does not adequately explore the various ways in which God uses other creaturely realities for self-communication. De Lubac's broader sacramental model is able to specify God's use of Scripture, church, and sacraments, as he makes a decisive distinction between Christ as the incarnation of the Logos, Scripture, Eucharist and church as incorporations of the Logos, and all creation as bearing the imprint of the Logos.⁵ Such a qualitative distinction is useful in de Lubac's model to safeguard the particularity and perfection of Christ while showing how Christ uses particular creaturely realities for self-communication in the economy of redemption. It would be interesting to see how Vanhoozer's project could be advanced if these distinctions were developed within his distinctive

---

3. See Tracy, *The Analogical Imagination*, 376–89. I would not, however, label de Lubac a "manifestation" theologian in quite the way that Tracy suggests. I think the key difference between de Lubac and Tracy is de Lubac's insistence upon the particularity of Christ and the indispensable role of Scripture and church in mediating Christ to individuals. De Lubac's sacramental model contains a christological center which is much more "proclamation"-oriented than Tracy's "manifestation" model envisions.

4. Vanhoozer, *Remythologizing Theology*, xiii and 26.

5. See de Lubac, *History and Spirit*, 385–426.

communicative model. Perhaps a greater distinction could be specified between Christ as revelation and Scripture as a unique and privileged locus of Christ's self-mediation which would ease the emphasis on God's closed, past determinate speaking action in Scripture, and would allow for greater reflection on God's ongoing speaking action in Scripture, Eucharist and church. Perhaps scriptural meaning could be viewed more as infinite Mystery in such a way that the participatory nature of meaning could be better emphasized. Vanhoozer's own dialogue with Catholic theologians has been a very recent development, and his communicative ontology already tends in this direction. Perhaps de Lubac's conceptual model could provide resources for its further development.[6]

At the same time, de Lubac's sacramental approach requires Vanhoozer's critical moment, lest the church listen more to itself than to Christ its head. Vanhoozer, much more clearly than de Lubac, develops God's use of the literal, canonical sense of Scripture for self-communication in a way that respects both the various human speech-acts and the textual record of God's self-revelation in history. It is precisely by providing a covenantal model which articulates how God uses human authors to assemble the particular history of the drama of redemption ordained by God as normative for the church, and in showing how God supervenes upon those various speech-acts to provide a unified witness to God's redemptive action, that Vanhoozer can benefit de Lubac. Vanhoozer proposes a method whereby all scientific exegesis of Scripture can be encouraged, yet must be submitted to the theological interpretation of the church before conclusions can emerge as truly Christian meaning. Vanhoozer's method also preserves Scripture's ability to break in on the theological interpretation of the church and correct it. Vanhoozer's approach encourages readers to look for determinate meaning, yet realize that participation in scriptural reading includes conversion and transformation, and is never complete until the complete union of the *totus Christus*. One may wonder if de Lubac's proposal for spiritual interpretation would have been better received among biblical scholars and theologians had he incorporated Vanhoozer's appreciation for God's communicative action in the plain sense of Scripture as well as in the spiritual sense.

Both Vanhoozer and de Lubac have moved beyond particular impasses in theological trajectories by examining God's use of creaturely

---

6. Vanhoozer's explicit dialogue with Catholic theologians is seen only in recent works such as "Ascending the Mountain" (2012) and "Interpreting Scripture" (2013).

realities in the governing of the economy of redemption. It is this commonality that has functioned as the lens to examining their respective projects in this book, and I suggest that this lens has illumined deep similarities between the two despite a number of ongoing differences. It seems both possible and beneficial to develop a theological interpretation of Scripture which attends to both the cautions and emphases of Vanhoozer and the broader ontology of de Lubac, and it may even be possible to conceive of Vanhoozer's covenantal model as a necessary critical moment in de Lubac's larger sacramental ontology. As the discussion about a theological interpretation of Scripture continues between Evangelicals and Roman Catholics, it is hoped that further reflection on God's use of creaturely realities in the economy of redemption will reveal further opportunities to appreciate God's gracious invitation to the church to participate in the life of the Triune God through reading Scripture.

Bibliography

"Aeterni Patris: Encyclical of Pope Leo XIII on the Restoration of Christian Philosophy." Vatican, August 4, 1879, accessed February 4, 2014. http://www.vatican.va/holy_father/leo_xiii/encyclicals/documents/hf_l-xiii_enc_04081879_aeterni-patris_en.html.

Alston, William. *Illocutionary Acts and Sentence Meaning*. Ithaca, NY: Cornell University Press, 2000.

Ayres, Lewis. "The Soul and the Reading of Scripture: A Note on Henri de Lubac." *Scottish Journal of Theology* 61:2 (2008) 173–90.

Balthasar, Hans Urs Von. *The Theology of Henri de Lubac: An Overview*. San Francisco: Ignatius, 1991.

Bertoldi, Francesco. "Henri de Lubac on Dei Verbum." Translated by Mandy Murphy. *Communio* 17 (1990) 6–31.

Blondel, Maurice. *Action, 1893: Essay on a Critique of Life and a Science of Practice*. Translated by Olivia Blanchette. Notre Dame, IN: University Of Notre Dame Press, 1984.

———. *The Letter on Apologetics and History and Dogma*. Translated by Alexander Dru and Illtyd Trethowan. Grand Rapids: Eerdmans, 1994.

Boersma, Hans. *Heavenly Participation: The Weaving of a Sacramental Tapestry*. Grand Rapids: Eerdmans, 2011.

———. *Nouvelle Theologie and Sacramental Ontology: A Return to Mystery*. Oxford: Oxford University Press, 2009.

———. "On Baking Pumpkin Pie: Kevin Vanhoozer and Yves Congar on Tradition." *Calvin Theological Journal* 42 (2007) 237–55.

Bowald, Mark Allen. *Rendering the Word in Theological Hermeneutics*. Burlington, VT: Ashgate, 2007.

Boyer, Charles. "Sur un article des Recherches de science religieuse." *Gregorianum* 29 (1948) 152–54.

Brown, Raymond. *The Sensus Plenior of Sacred Scripture*. Baltimore: St. Mary's University Press, 1955.

Buckley, James J. "Revisionists and Liberals." In *The Modern Theologians: An Introduction to Christian Theology Since 1918*, edited by David Ford and Rachel Muers, 213–28. Malden, MA: Blackwell, 2005.

Childs, Brevard. "Speech-act Theory and Biblical Interpretation." *Scottish Journal of Theology* 58:4 (2005) 375–92.

Clarke, William Norris. *Explorations in Metaphysics: Being, God, Person*. South Bend, IN: University of Notre Dame, 1994.

———. *The One and the Many: A Contemporary Thomistic Metaphysics*. South Bend, IN: University of Notre Dame, 2001.

Comstock, Gary. "Two Types of Narrative Theology." *Journal of the American Academy of Religion* 55:4 (1987) 687–717.

D'Ambrosio, Marcellino G. "Henri de Lubac and the Critique of Scientific Exegesis." *Communio* 19 (1992) 365–88.

———. *Henri de Lubac and the Recovery of the Traditional Hermeneutic*. Ann Arbor, MI: Umi Dissertation Services, 1991.

Davis, Joshua. "The Call of Grace: Henri de Lubac, Jean-Louis Chrétien, and the Theological Conditions of Christian Radical Phenomenology." In *Words of Life: New Theological Turns in French Phenomenology*, edited by Bruce Ellis Benson and Norman Wirzba, 181–95. New York: Fordham University Press, 2010.

Dawson, John David. *Christian Figural Reading and the Fashioning of Identity*. Berkeley, CA: University Of California Press, 2002.

D'Costa, Gavin. "Revelation, Scripture and Tradition: Some Comments on John Webster's Conception of 'Holy Scripture.'" *International Journal of Systematic Theology* 6:4 (2004) 337–50.

"Dei Verbum: Dogmatic Constitution on Divine Revelation." Vatican, November 18, 1965, accessed March 7, 2014. http://www.vatican.va/archive/hist_councils/ii_vatican_council/documents/vat-ii_const_19651118_dei-verbum_en.html.

de Lubac, Henri. *At the Service of the Church: Henri de Lubac Reflects on the Circumstances that Occasioned His Writings*. Translated by Anne Elizabeth Englund. San Francisco: Ignatius, 1993.

———. *Augustinianism and Modern Theology*. Translated by Lancelot C. Sheppard. New York: Herder, 1969.

———. *A Brief Catechesis on Nature and Grace*. Translated by Richard Arnandez. San Francisco: Ignatius, 1984.

———. *Catholicism: Christ and the Common Destiny of Man*. Translated by Lancelot C. Sheppard and Elizabeth Englund. Paris: Cerf, 1947. Reprint, San Francisco: Ignatius, 1988.

———. *The Christian Faith: An Essay on the Structure of the Apostles' Creed*. Translated by Richard Arnandez. San Francisco: Ignatius, 1986.

———. *The Church: Paradox and Mystery*. Translated by James R. Dunne. Staten Islane, NY: Alba, 1969.

———. *Corpus Mysticum: The Eucharist and the Church in the Middle Ages: A Historical Survey*. Edited by Laurence Paul Hemming and Susan Frank Parsons. Translated by Gemma Simmonds, Richard Price, and Christopher Stephens. South Bend, IN: University Of Notre Dame Press, 2007.

———. *de Lubac: The Theologian Speaks*. Translated by Stephen Maddux. Los Angeles: Twin Circle, 1985.

———. *The Discovery of God*. Translated by Alexander Dru et al. Grand Rapids: Eerdmans, 1996.

———. *The Eternal Feminine*. Translated by Rene Hagne. New York: Harper and Row, 1971.

———. "Hellenistic Allegory and Christian Allegory." In *Theological Fragments*. Translated by Rebecca Howell Balinski, 165–96. San Francisco: Ignatius, 1989.

———. *History and Spirit: The Understanding of Scripture According to Origen*. Translated by Anne Englund Nash. San Francisco: Ignatius, 2007.

———. "La Revelation Divine." In *Oeuvres Completes IV*. Edited by Eric De Moulins-beaufort and Georges Chantraine. Paris: Cerf, 2006.

———. *Medieval Exegesis: The Four Senses of Scripture*. Ressourcement Retrieval and Renewal in Catholic Thought 1. Translated by Mark Sebanc. Grand Rapids: Eerdmans, 1998.

———. *The Motherhood of the Church: Followed by Particular Churches in the Universal Church and an Interview Conducted by Gwendoline Jarczyk*. Translated by Sergia Englund. San Francisco: Ignatius, 1982.

———. *The Mystery of the Supernatural*. Translated by Rosemary Sheed. London: Chapman, 1967.

———. "On an Old Distich: The Doctrine of the 'Fourfold Sense' in Scripture." In *Theological Fragments*, translated by Rebecca Howell Balinski, 109–27. San Francisco: Ignatius, 1989.

———. *Paradoxes of Faith*. Translated by Ernest Beaumont. Vol. 1. San Francisco: Ignatius, 1986.

———. *Paradoxes of Faith*. Translated by Ernest Beaumont. Vol. 2. San Francisco: Ignatius, 1987.

———. "The Problem of the Development of Dogma." In *Theology in History*, translated by Anne Englund Nash, 248–86. San Francisco: Ignatius, 1996.

———. *The Sources of Revelation*. Translated by Luke O'Neill. New York: Herder and Herder, 1967.

———. *The Splendor of the Church*. Translated by Michael Mason. San Francisco: Ignatius, 1986.

———. *Surnaturel: Etudes historiques*. Paris: Aubier, 1946.

———. *Theological Fragments*. Translated by Rebecca Howell Balinski. San Francisco: Ignatius, 1989.

———. "Typology and Allegorization." In *Theological Fragments*, translated by Rebecca Howell Balinski, 129–64. San Francisco: Ignatius, 1989.

"Dei Filius: Dogmatic Constitution Vatican I." Interdisciplinary Encyclopedia of Religion and Science, 2003, accessed February 14, 2014. http://www.inters.org/Vatican-Council-I-Dei-Filius.

de Moulins-beaufort, Eric. "Henri de Lubac: Reader of Dei Verbum." *Communio* 28 (2001) 669–94.

———. "The Spiritual Man in the Thought of Henri de Lubac." *Communio* 25 (1998) 287–302.

English, Adam C. *The Possibility of Christian Philosophy: Maurice Blondel at the Intersection of Theology and Philosophy*. Routledge Radical Orthodoxy Series. Edited by John Milbank, Catherine Pickstock, and Graham Ward. New York: Routledge, 2007.

Fodor, James. "Postliberal Theology." In *The Modern Theologians: An Introduction to Christian Theology Since 1918*, edited by David F. Ford and Rachel Muers, 229–48. Malden, MA: Blackwell, 2005.

Frei, Hans. *The Eclipse of Biblical Narrative: A Study in Eighteenth and Nineteenth Century Hermeneutics*. New Haven: Yale University Press, 1974.

———. *The Identity of Jesus Christ: The Hermeneutical Bases of Dogmatic Theology*. Philadelphia: Fortress, 1975.

———. "Karl Barth: Theologian." In *Theology and Narrative*, edited by George Hunsinger and William Placher, 167–76. Oxford: Oxford University Press, 2003.

———. "The 'Literal Reading' of Biblical Narrative in Christian Tradition: Does it Stretch or Will it Break?" In *The Bible and the Narrative Tradition*, edited by Frank McConnell, 36–77. Oxford: Oxford University Press, 1986.

———. "On the Resurrection of Christ." In *Theology and Narrative*, edited by George Hunsinger and William Placher, 200–206. Oxford: Oxford University Press, 1993.

———. "Theological Reflections on the Accounts of Jesus' Death and Resurrection." In *Theology and Narrative*, edited by George Hunsinger, 45–93. Edited by George Hunsinger and William Placher. Oxford: Oxford University Press, 1993.

———. *Types of Christian Theology*. Edited by George Hunsinger and William Placher. New Haven: Yale University Press, 1992.

Gadamer, Hans-Georg. *Truth and Method*. 2nd rev. ed. New York: Continuum, 2002.

Garrigou-lagrange, Reginald. "La Nouvelle Theologie ou va-t-elle?" *Angelicum* 23 (1946) 126–45.

"Gaudium Et Spes: Pastoral Constitution on the Church in the Modern World." Vatican, December 7, 1965, accessed February 14, 2014. http://www.vatican.va/archive/hist_councils/ii_vatican_council/documents/vat-ii_cons_19651207_gaudium-et-spes_en.html.

Grumett, David. *de Lubac: A Guide for the Perplexed*. New York: T. and T. Clark, 2007.

Higton, Mike. "Hans Frei and David Tracy on the Ordinary and the Extraordinary in Christianity." *The Journal of Religion* 79:4 (1999) 566–91.

Hollon, Bryan C. *Everything is Sacred: Spiritual Exegesis in the Political Theology of Henri de Lubac*. Theopolitical Visions 3. Eugene, OR: Wipf and Stock, 2009.

"Humani Generis," Vatican, August 12, 1950. Accessed March 8, 2014. http://www.vatican.va/holy_father/pius_xii/encyclicals/documents/hf_p-xii_enc_12081950_humani-generis_en.html.

Hunsinger, George. "Postliberal Theology." In *The Cambridge Companion to Postmodern Theology*, edited by Kevin Vanhoozer, 42–57. Cambridge: Cambridge University Press, 2003.

Hutter, Reinhard. *Suffering Divine Things: Theology as Church Practice*. Grand Rapids: Eerdmans, 2000.

Kelsey, David H. *The Uses of Scripture in Recent Theology*. Philadelphia: Fortress, 1975.

Lindbeck, George. *The Nature of Doctrine: Religion and Theology in a Postliberal Age*. Philadelphia: Westminster, 1984.

———. "Postcritical Canonical Interpretation: Three Modes of Retrieval." In *Theological Exegesis: Essays in Honor of Brevard S. Childs*, edited by Christopher R. Seitz and Kathryn Greene-McCreight, 26–51. Grand Rapids: Eerdmans, 1999.

———. "Toward a Postliberal Theology." In *The Return to Scripture in Judaism and Christianity: Essays in Postcritical Scriptural Interpretation*, edited by Peter Ochs, 83–106. New York: Paulist, 1993.

Milbank, John. "Henri de Lubac." In *The Modern Theologians: An Introduction to Christian Theology Since 1918*, edited by David Ford and Rachel Muers, 76–91. Reprint, 3rd ed. Malden, MA: Blackwell, 2005.

———. *The Suspended Middle: Henri de Lubac and the Debate Concerning the Supernatural*. Grand Rapids: Eerdmans, 2005.

Mitchell, Basil. "Revelation Revisited." In *The Making and Remaking of Christian Doctrine: Essays in Honour of Maurice Wiles*, edited by Sarah Coakley and David A. Palin, 177–91. New York: Oxford University Press, 1993.

Moberly, R. W. L. "What is Theological Interpretation of Scripture?" *Journal of Theological Interpretation* 3 (2009) 161–78.

Murphy, William F. "Henri De Lubac's Mystical Tropology." *Communio* 27 (2000) 171–201.

Nichols, Aidan. *From Newman to Congar: The Idea of Doctrinal Development from the Victorians to the Second Vatican Council*. Edinburgh: T. and T. Clark, 1990.

O'Keefe, John J., and R. R. Reno. *Sanctified Vision: An Introduction to Early Christian Interpretation of the Bible*. Baltimore: John Hopkins University Press, 2005.

O'Regan, Cyril. "De Doctrina Christiana and Modern Hermeneutics." In *De Doctrina Christiana: A Classic Study of Western Culture* 9, edited by Duane W. H. Arnold and Pamela Bright, 217–43. South Bend, IN: University Of Notre Dame Press, 1995.

O'Sullivan, Noel. *Christ and Creation: Christology as the Key to Interpreting the Theology of Creation in the Works of Henri de Lubac*. Bern: Peter Lang, 2009.

Pelikan, Jaroslav. *Mary Through the Centuries: Her Place in the History of Culture*. New Haven: Yale University Press, 1996.

Placher, William C. "Paul Ricoeur and Postliberal Theology: A Conflict of Interpretations." *Modern Theology* 4:1 (1987) 35–52.

———. "Revisionist and Postliberal Theologies and the Public Character of Theology." *The Thomist* 49 (1985) 392–416.

Ricoeur, Paul. "Biblical Hermeneutics." *Semeia* 4 (1975) 29–148.

———. *Oneself as Another*. Translated by Kathleen Blamey. Chicago: University Of Chicago Press, 1992.

Searle, John R. *Expression and Meaning: Studies in the Theory of Speech Acts*. Cambridge: Cambridge University Press, 1979.

Spinks, D. Christopher. *The Bible and the Crisis of Meaning: Debates on the Theological Interpretation of Scripture*. New York: T. and T. Clark, 2007.

Thiselton, Anthony C. *New Horizons in Hermeneutics: The Theory and Practice of Transforming Biblical Reading*. Grand Rapids: Zondervan, 1992.

Tracy, David. *The Analogical Imagination: Christian Theology and the Culture of Pluralism*. New York: Crossroad, 1981.

———. *Dialogue with the Other, the Inter-Religious Dialogue*. Grand Rapids: Eerdmans, 1990.

———. "Lindbeck's New Program for Theology: A Reflection." *The Thomist* 49:4 (1985) 460–72.

———. "On Reading the Scriptures Theologically." In *Theology and Dialogue: Essays in Conversation with George Lindbeck*, edited by Bruce Marshall, 35–68. Notre Dame: University Of Notre Dame Press, 1990.

Treier, Daniel J. *Introducing Theological Interpretation of Scripture: Recovering a Christian Practice*. Grand Rapids: Baker Academic, 2008.

Vanhoozer, Kevin J. "The Apostolic Discourse and its Development." In *Scripture's Doctrine and Theology's Bible: How the New Testament Shapes Christian Dogmatics*, edited by Markus Bockmuehl and Alan J. Torrance, 191–207. Grand Rapids: Baker Academic, 2008.

———. "Ascending the Mountain, Singing the Rock: Biblical Interpretation Earthed, Typed, and Transfigured." *Modern Theology* 28:4 (2012) 781–803.

———. *Biblical Narrative in the Philosophy of Paul Ricoeur: A Study in Hermeneutics and Theology*. Cambridge: Cambridge University Press, 1990.

———. "Body Piercing, the Natural Sense and the Task of Theological Interpretation." In *First Theology: God, Scripture and Hermeneutics*, edited by Kevin Vanhoozer, 275–308. Downers Grove, IL: InterVarsity, 2002.

———, ed. *Dictionary for Theological Interpretation of the Bible*. Grand Rapids: Baker Academic, 2005.

———. *The Drama of Doctrine: A Canonical Linguistic Approach to Christian Theology*. Louisville: Westminster John Knox, 2005.

———. "A Drama-of-Redemption Model." In *Four Views on Moving Beyond the Bible to Theology*, edited by Stanley N. Gundry and Gary T. Meadors, 151–99. Counterpoints. Grand Rapids: Zondervan, 2009.

———. *First Theology: God, Scripture and Hermeneutics*. Downers Grove, IL: InterVarsity, 2002.

———. "First Theology: Meditations in a Postmodern Toolshed." In *First Theology: God, Scripture and Hermeneutics*, edited by Kevin Vanhoozer, 15–44. Downers Grove, IL: InterVarsity, 2002.

———. "From Speech Acts to Scripture Acts: The Covenant of Discourse and the Discourse of Covenant." In *First Theology: God, Scripture and Hermeneutics*, edited by Kevin Vanhoozer, 159–203. Downers Grove, IL: InterVarsity, 2002.

———. "Interpreting Scripture Between the Rock of Biblical Studies and the Hard Place of Systematic Theology: The State of the Evangelical (dis)union." In *Renewing the Evangelical Mission*, edited by Richard Lints, 201–25. Grand Rapids: Eerdmans, 2013.

———. *Is There a Meaning in This Text? The Bible, the Reader, and the Morality of Literary Knowledge*. Grand Rapids: Zondervan, 1998.

———. "A Person of the Book? Barth on Biblical Authority and Interpretation." In *Karl Barth and Evangelical Theology: Convergences and Divergences*, edited by Sung Wook Chung, 26–59. Grand Rapids: Baker Academic, 2006.

———. *Remythologizing Theology: Divine Action, Passion, and Authorship*. Cambridge Studies in Christian Doctrine. Edited by Daniel W. Hardy. Cambridge: Cambridge University Press, 2010.

———. "Scripture and Tradition." In *The Cambridge Companion to Postmodern Theology*, edited by Kevin Vanhoozer, 149–69. Cambridge: Cambridge University Press, 2003.

———. "The Semantics of Biblical Literature: Truth and Scripture's Diverse Literary Forms." In *Hermeneutics, Authority and Canon*, edited by D. A. Carson and John Woodbridge, 49–104. Grand Rapids: Zondervan, 1986.

———. "The Spirit Of Understanding: Special Revelation and General Hermeneutics." In *First Theology: God, Scripture and Hermeneutics*, edited by Kevin Vanhoozer, 207–35. Downers Grove, IL: InterVarsity, 2002.

———. "Triune Discourse: Theological Reflections on the Claim that God Speaks, Part 1." In *Trinitarian Theology for the Church: Scripture, Community, Worship*, edited by Daniel J. Treier and David Lauber, 25–49. Downers Grove, IL: InterVarsity, 2009.

———. "Triune Discourse: Theological Reflections on the Claim that God Speaks, Part 2." In *Trinitarian Theology for the Church: Scripture, Community, Worship*, edited by Daniel J. Treier and David Lauber, 50–78. Downers Grove, IL: InterVarsity, 2009.

Vidu, Adonis. Review of *Is There a Meaning in This Text? The Bible, the Reader, and the Morality of Literary Knowledge* by Kevin J. Vanhoozer. *Trinity Journal* 21:2 (2000) 209–13.

Volderholzer, Rudolf. "Dogma and History: Henri de Lubac and the Retrieval of Historicity as a Key to Theological Renewal." *Communio* 28 (2001) 648–68.

Watson, Francis. Review of *Is There a Meaning in This Text? The Bible, the Reader, and the Morality of Literary Knowledge* by Kevin J. Vanhoozer. *Journal of the Evangelical Theological Society* 44:4 (2001) 744–46.

Webster, John B. "Purity and Plenitude: Evangelical Reflections on Congar's Tradition and Traditions." *International Journal of Systematic Theology*. 7:4 (2005) 399–413.

———. *Word and Church: Essays in Christian Dogmatics*. New York: T. and T. Clark, 2001.

Williams, David M. *Receiving the Bible in Faith: Historical and Theological Exegesis*. Washington, DC: Catholic University of America Press, 2004.

Wimsatt, William K., and Monroe Beardsley. *The Verbal Icon: Studies in the Meaning of Poetry*. Lexington, KY: University of Kentucky Press, 1954.

Wolterstorff, Nicholas. *Divine Discourse: Philosophical Reflections on the Claim that God Speaks*. Cambridge: Cambridge University Press, 1995.

Wood, Susan K. "The Ecclesial Meaning of the Eucharist." In *Critical Issues in Ecclesiology: Essays in Honor of Carl E. Braaten*. Edited by Alberto L. Garcia and Susan K. Wood. Grand Rapids: Eerdmans, 2011.

———. *Spiritual Exegesis and the Church in the Theology of Henri de Lubac*. Grand Rapids: Eerdmans, 1998.

Work, Telford. *Living and Active*. Grand Rapids: Eerdmans, 2002.

Wright, William M. "The Literal Sense of Scripture According to Henri de Lubac: Insights from Patristic Exegesis of the Transfiguration." *Modern Theology* 28:2 (2012) 252–77.

www.ingramcontent.com/pod-product-compliance
Lightning Source LLC
Chambersburg PA
CBHW050028240426
43662CB00046B/1700